BROAD-BASED TAXES

BROAD-BASED TAXES

NEW OPTIONS AND SOURCES

Editor — *Richard A. Musgrave*

Harvey E. Brazer • Helen F. Ladd • Nancy H. Teeters • Charles J. Goetz • C. Harry Kahn • Charles E. McLure, Jr. • John F. Due • Carl S. Shoup • Richard E. Slitor • William H. Branson

A Supplementary Paper of the Committee for Economic Development

THE JOHNS HOPKINS UNIVERSITY PRESS
Baltimore and London

Copyright © 1973 by the Committee for Economic Development

All rights reserved. No part of this book may be reproduced or utilized in any form or by any means, electronic or mechanical, including photocopying, recording, or by any information storage or retrieval system, without permission in writing from the Committee for Economic Development, 477 Madison Avenue, New York, New York 10022. Manufactured in the United States of America.

The Johns Hopkins University Press, Baltimore, Maryland 21218
The Johns Hopkins University Press Ltd., London

Library of Congress Catalog Card Number 72-12361
ISBN 0-8018-1489-8 (clothbound edition)
ISBN 0-8108-1490-1 (paperback edition)

Originally published, 1973
Johns Hopkins Paperbacks edition, 1973

Library of Congress Cataloging in Publication data will be found
on the last printed page of this book.

In memory of C. Harry Kahn
1921–1972

CONTENTS

Richard A. Musgrave

INTRODUCTION

CONTROVERSY OVER TAX REFORM never ceases. The vision
of the good tax system remains a moving target that recedes as legislation advances. However, the gap between target and performance
narrows at times and widens at others. There are periods in which
major changes occur, for example, the early 1940s, when the income
tax rose to its dominant position in the federal tax structure. Since then,
there have been numerous attempts at reforming the structure. The
Eisenhower reform of 1954, the Kennedy reform of 1964, the Tax
Reform Act of 1969 were the more important measures; but they have
not been reforms of a fundamental sort. The mid-1970s, however, may
well prove to be a period of major change.

First of all, there has been a distinct change in the federal
revenue outlook. Whereas the fiscal trend of the past decade was one
of tax reduction, that of the coming decade will see expenditures out-
stripping built-in revenue growth. This change is of fundamental importance. Revenue legislation from 1962 to 1971 proceeded against the
background of built-in revenue gains well in excess of automatic increases
in the cost of existing programs. Over the decade from 1963 to 1973,
built-in revenue gains amounted to about $160 billion, while rising costs
of base-period (1963) programs amounted to only $90 billion, thus giv-
ing rise to a *net* fiscal dividend of about $70 billion. Of this, $45 billion
was used for rate reduction and other forms of tax relief. Measured at
1973 levels of GNP (and excluding social-security taxes), this amounted
to a reduction of nearly 25 per cent. The remainder of the dividend,
bolstered by draft on an initial full-employment surplus and rising
payroll-tax rates, went to finance new programs.

The prospects for the coming decade differ. The period begins with an estimated deficit of about $25 billion for fiscal 1973 and $12.7 billion for fiscal 1974. The full-employment position shows a deficit of $2 billion for 1973 and is expected to turn into a slight surplus by 1975. Based on the rule of budgetary balance at full-employment, the Budget Message concludes that no tax increase will be needed. This happy outlook rests on three assumptions. First, national defense expenditures are assumed to rise in money terms due to increased costs but to remain level in real terms. Secondly, reconstruction aid in Vietnam is not allowed for. Finally, and most important, built-in increases in other expenditures are to be offset in substantial part by sharp cutbacks in certain programs, cutbacks which by 1975 are estimated to reach $22 billion. This compares with past experience which indicates that over the same period new programs would have pushed up outlays by, say, $5 billion.

It seems highly unlikely that so drastic a change in expenditure behavior accounting for a reduction of from $25 to $30 billion will materialize. A substantial share of the proposed cutbacks is in programs such as social-service grants, Medicare, air-pollution abatement, and housing, most of which have had substantial congressional support in past years. Moreover, it is unlikely that all development of new programs will be halted. Such programs—including income maintenance, child care, federal support for education, health care, environmental improvement, urban reconstruction, housing and so forth—as discussed in recent years might have called for an eventual expenditure expansion of from $50 to $100 billion, and chances are that these pressures will reemerge in the years to come.

While it is not the purpose of this volume to evaluate the wisdom of the proposed cutbacks or of further expansion, the expenditure outlook is of strategic importance for the future of tax reform. Chances are not only that the budget will remain very tight, but that increased tax revenues will be needed as expenditures rise above the levels projected in the President's budget. This means that revenue pressures during the 1970s will render tax reform a continuous and acute issue. When the trend is toward tax reduction, it is easy to spread the benefits without taking too hard a look at the shortcomings of the existing tax structure. When it comes to increasing revenue, the situation differs. Voters' attitudes become less benevolent, and the search for additional revenue points to gaps in existing taxes. Beyond this, it calls for the exploration of new sources not covered heretofore. This should be expected to occur in the coming decade.

A second rei son for federal tax reform arises from the changing nature of fiscal federalism. While federal finances enjoyed a decade of tax reduction, state and local finances had to struggle hard to hold their own. The growth in expenditures under old and new programs exceeded the built-in revenue gain, providing a negative fiscal dividend. Notwithstanding increasing federal aid, tax increases of close to 20 per cent (1973 levels) were needed to close the gap. As a result, the state-local share in total revenue increased, and tax pressure came to be felt most heavily at the state-local level. Although complaints became most audible in connection with the property tax, the rate of increase was sharpest for income and sales taxation.

While the fiscal position of state and local governments has improved over the last two years, due largely to increased federal aid and a surplus in social-security funds, the longer view continues to point to substantial revenue shortages. Many of the most pressing expenditure needs involve functions that are traditionally and properly performed at the state-local level. Since it will hardly be feasible for state and local own-revenue sources to keep up with this advance, increased federal support will be called for. Whatever form this may take—general revenue sharing, categorical aid, or federal assumption of certain expenditure functions—the result will be to increase pressure on federal revenue requirements.

Moreover, federal finance is concerned not only with the adequacy of state-local revenue as a whole but also with securing some degree of balance between fiscal needs and capacities among lower-level jurisdictions. Lack of such balance has been of increasing concern and underlies the fiscal distress of the cities as well as of poor rural communities. Recent concern with unequal levels of educational services resulting from reliance on local school finance points to another aspect of this problem. Thus, there is an increased responsibility of central finance, whether of the states, in relation to local finance, or of the federal government, in relation to that of states and localities; and this again increases pressures on federal tax resources.

These problems, finally, will have to be faced in a setting of increased voter and congressional concern with the fairness of the tax system and with what appears to be widely considered an excessive level of tax burden. The confrontation of these attitudes with the recognition of increased revenue needs should produce a climate in which a hard look at problems of tax reform will be unavoidable and a search for new options will be called for.

All this leads to the crucial question of where the money will come from. The chapters in this volume are designed to examine the many aspects of this question. The search is for both the improved utilization of traditional sources and the exploration of alternatives, using new tax bases or new forms of taxation.

Harvey E. Brazer, in the first chapter, deals with the individual income tax. This tax has been the mainstay of the federal tax structure since the 1940s. Brazer argues that it will, and should, continue in that role; but he points to ways in which the income tax may be improved. Such improvements will be increasingly necessary as the income tax is called upon to contribute additional revenue. At the same time, the reader is warned that potential new gains from broadening of the tax base should not be exaggerated. Not all desirable changes will be feasible, and others will be linked to revenue-losing rate adjustments

Next in importance in the overall picture is the property tax Although this tax is not part of the federal tax structure, its future is closely linked to federal revenue needs through its bearing upon the required level of federal aid. Helen Ladd reexamines the role of this tax, which is not only the oldest component of the American tax structure but has also recently returned to the center of attention. Ladd considers the controversial questions of burden incidence and concludes that the tax for the most part tends to be progressive. Next, she examines whether housing is overtaxed or given preferential treatment under the present system and concludes that on balance (and considering the burden of other taxes as well as of the property tax) housing is favored rather than discriminated against. In all, the conclusion is that the property tax needs to be improved but that it plays a constructive role in the tax system. Given prospective revenue needs, Ladd feels that we can ill afford to dismantle this tax.

The chapter by Nancy H. Teeters explores the future of social security finance and the role of the payroll tax. One of the striking developments in the federal tax structure over the last decade has been the rising share of the total tax revenue derived from payroll taxation. Although this has been matched by rising social security benefits, it nevertheless involves sharply increased tax burdens at the lower end of the income scale. Teeters favors the introduction of exemptions into the payroll-tax base in order to reduce their regressive impact. She also argues that social security finance should be on a pay-as-you-go basis and supports recent moves in that direction. Nevertheless, the level of payroll taxation is apt to rise because expanded health insurance is likely to call for even further additions to payroll-tax finance.

Although user charges have long been a source of government finance, their more intensive use has been advocated in recent years. This development is examined in the chapter by Charles J. Goetz. The case for increased utilization of user charges is based on their role in securing more efficient planning of public expenditures and use of resources; but beyond this, the question arises whether such charges could also be expanded to provide a substantial amount of additional revenue. Goetz explores the situations in which increased utilization of user charges is technically possible and economically sound and surveys their role in state and local finance. He supports more extensive use of such charges to improve resource allocation but concludes that substantial increases in revenue are unlikely. Not only are the technical difficulties of implementation greater than is sometimes assumed, but public attitudes do not seem to support the pricing of public services in those areas (e.g., higher education) where substantial revenue gains might be obtained.

The discussion then turns to alternative tax bases. The merits of such alternatives, including a general consumption tax and a net-worth tax, are considered by C. Harry Kahn. He concludes that consumption as a tax base need not be inferior to income and that its use would serve to fill gaps left by the income tax. Kahn feels that the case for net-worth taxation is less strong, and he believes that a revision of estate and gift taxes is the preferable approach.

The use of a broad-based consumption tax is explored further in the chapter by Charles E. McLure, Jr. He investigates the economic implications of a value-added tax and shows that the tax would be capable of providing substantial amounts of revenue. A broad base is favored, although certain areas such as housing cannot be reached effectively. If the distribution of the burden is compared with the income tax or the corporation tax, it is found to be regressive provided the corporation tax is not shifted. However, considered as part of a package involving income-tax reform, the net result of the entire change may be adjusted to avoid regressive impact. Such is the case especially if income-tax reform includes a negative income tax at the lower end of the income scale and base broadening at the upper end. McLure thus concludes that the equity case for or against the introduction of such a tax will depend greatly on other measures of tax reform undertaken at the same time. With regard to its effects on the domestic economy, the value-added tax is credited with being able to avoid inefficiencies caused by the partial nature of the corporation tax. McLure examines its balance-of-payments effects and concludes that no major gains on current account should be expected from a substitution of the value-added tax for the corporation tax but that gains on capital account may ensue. In all these respects, McLure believes that the effects of a retail-sales tax will be essentially the same as those of a value-added tax, since both are broad-based consumption taxes differing only in administrative respects.

The chapters by Carl S. Shoup and John F. Due examine the narrower question of the choice between the retail-sales and value-added tax approaches, assuming that a broad-based federal consumption tax were to be introduced. Due finds the retail-sales tax superior in most all respects; whereas Shoup points to certain advantages of the value-added tax.

Whatever view is taken regarding the merits of consumption as a tax base, there remains another distinction between the income and the consumption (retail-sales or value-added) taxes. This is the fact that the income tax is imposed as a personal tax with exemptions, progressive rates, and certain deductions; whereas the general consumption tax would be imposed as an *in rem* tax that would not relate directly to the taxpayer's economic setting and needs. The possibility of designing a personal-type consumption tax—referred to as an expenditures tax—is explored in the chapter by Richard E. Slitor. He finds that such a tax would be feasible but that it would introduce substantial administrative difficulties in its application, especially over the upper-income ranges, where balance-sheet accounting may be called for in the tax return.

In the final chapter, William H. Branson discusses the role of tax policy in stabilization. He explores the comparative merits of income and consumption taxation for purposes of stabilizing tax-rate adjustments. He concludes that the stabilizing effects of income-tax changes are less than had been traditionally assumed but that the effects of temporary changes in consumption-tax rates, by acting upon the consumers' responses to price changes, should be more powerful. This is especially true if changes in consumption-tax rates are applied to consumer durables.

Discussions of tax-policy issues, such as those included in this volume, are necessarily controversial. The authors have been asked to speak their mind, and not everyone (including the Committee for Economic Development and the editor) will agree with all that is said. However, these chapters should provide constructive background material for those interested in tax reform.

Part One: New Revenue from Old Sources

INCOME TAX

Harvey E. Brazer

THE INCOME TAX IN THE
FEDERAL REVENUE SYSTEM

IF FEDERAL BUDGETARY RECEIPTS must be substantially increased, either to finance new programs or to permit reduction in state and local taxes, the income tax stands tall as a prospective source of additional funds. It does so partly because, irrespective of their form and no matter where their initial impact may fall, taxes can be borne only by individuals or families. The collection of tax receipts by the government brings about a reduction in private consumption or saving, or both, although in some instances, this result may come about only indirectly, and those actually affected may not even understand that it is happening. In the complex case of the corporate income tax, for example, people bear that tax in their capacities as owners or, possibly, as employees if wages respond to profit levels and if the tax reduces after-tax profits; alternatively, the corporate income tax may be distributed, at least in part, among people according to their consumption of corporate products if the tax is shifted forward through higher prices. Taxes on property and on other things, including transactions of various kinds, are similarly borne by people, through diminution of sources of income or reduction in the opportunity to consume and/or to save. Meaningful debate on tax policy, therefore, should focus mainly on the distribution of tax liabilities among people, rather than on the distribution of taxes between people and things or legal entities.

It may, nevertheless, be useful and even desirable to impose taxes on corporations or property or certain transactions, as well as directly on people, according to some index governing liability for taxes. The

3

corporation, for example, may be an appropriate conduit through which to reach profits that accrue to the benefit of stockholders. And taxing selective things or transactions may be an effective means of using taxes as quasi charges or of harnessing market forces to serve social objectives in areas such as pollution control and efforts to reduce urban congestion. But the main point remains: It is not possible to relieve individuals of tax burdens by taxing them less and corporations or other things more.

On the premise that only people pay taxes, this chapter first considers alternative bases for federal taxation and then examines deficiencies in the base of the income tax, major legislative changes in federal taxation that have been effected in the past decade, various means of raising additional revenue through the income tax, and finally, the future role of the individual income tax in the federal revenue system.

The Choice of Major Tax Base

Irrespective of the tax base, the payment of taxes reduces the ability of families and individuals to command goods and services for consumption and investment (saving). Given certain unrealistic assumptions, it indeed may be argued that it is a matter of indifference whether the major tax base is measured in terms of income, net worth, or consumption. The relationship between income and net worth is easily seen. Given perfect capital markets, the value of an asset equals the capitalized value of the expected income stream to which it gives rise. If net worth is defined to include a person's total capital assets (human as well as man-made) minus his debts, the value of his net worth equals the present value of his future income, be it from wage or from capital sources. Thus, if the appropriate discount rate to be used in arriving at present values of future yields or income flows is 5 per cent, there is no appreciable difference in principle between a 20 per cent annual tax on income and a 1 per cent tax on net worth. Net worth or income similarly may be equated with consumption, provided that lifetime consumption equals lifetime income and that comprehensive averaging is employed so that the timing of tax payments is a matter of indifference.

Given these definitions, all three bases become equivalent and lend themselves equally well to measuring economic capacity. *Horizontal equity,* the equal treatment of equals or similarly circumstanced persons, can be attained under each of the three bases. *Vertical equity,* the appropriate pattern of differences in tax liabilities among people of different capacities, may similarly be applied to each base. Under the assumptions accepted up to this point, there is no choice between the income, net worth, and consumption bases because each leads to the same distribution of tax liabilities.

But once a more realistic view is taken, this equivalence of tax bases breaks down. For one thing, the taxation of wealth or net worth is generally not understood to include in its base the capitalized value of personal earnings. Nor would such inclusion be practicable. Hence, the net-worth tax, at best, can be thought of as a general tax on all other wealth and thus equivalent to a tax on net capital income. And whereas such a tax may appeal to some as a supplement to a tax on total income, it differs from the income tax and, indeed, conflicts with the prime requirement of income taxation: the application of progressive rates to global income. Furthermore, not all income is consumed during a person's lifetime. Part is saved and transferred at death, and the consumption base falls short of income by this amount. Finally, taxes are not subject to the perfect averaging devices underlying the equivalence assumption. The period of time over which the tax base accrues and tax payments fall due does matter, as does the volatility of changes in the base. For these reasons, the three bases are not identical in practice. The net-worth and consumption bases tend to be narrower and inferior to the income base as an index of a person's economic well-being or ability to pay.

Even with averaging, both consumption and net-worth taxes are less likely to be payable in a time pattern that is as convenient to the taxpayer as the income tax. Very young and older people, for example, are likely to be dissavers and thus especially hard-pressed by a tax on consumption expenditures. A net-worth tax, on the other hand, would hit younger people with least weight but would be most difficult for older taxpayers, particularly those whose incomes are reduced because of retirement or the death of the principal breadwinner.

Neither the consumption nor the net-worth base offers any advantage over the income base for purposes of ease in compliance or administration. Accurate withholding under a consumption tax certainly would be more difficult, and it is unlikely that consumption could be estimated with adequate precision without information on income *and* savings. Determination of net worth, quite apart from the exclusion of human capital, would present even greater problems. In order to be comprehensive, it would have to include the present value of all income flows. Thus, the difficulties encountered in arriving at net income would be compounded by those involved in selection of the "correct" discount rate or rates (if allowance is to be made for differences in risk) and time spans.

Arguing strongly in favor of the use of income as the major tax base is the fact that insofar as any one measure provides an index of a person's *current* economic status and relative ability to pay taxes, that measure is income, always provided that it is properly defined. A person's income for tax purposes is defined in line with the accretion concept as the money value of his consumption (including the services of consumer durables and housing) plus his savings (equal to the increase in his net worth).[1] Defined in these terms, income merits choice over consumption expenditures or net worth. Most arguments against the use of income as the principal tax base stem from deficiencies found in practice in the definition of *taxable* income.[2]

The Individual Income Tax Base

The accretion concept of income as consumption plus net savings (including accretions to the value of owned assets) is the appropriate objective index for determining tax liabilities because it encompasses all elements of the power to command goods and services. It does not coincide closely with either the Department of Commerce concept of "national income" or personal income, nor does it equal income as currently defined in the Internal Revenue Code.[3] *Personal income* is the sum of the earnings of labor, property income, and transfer payments. It includes various forms of income in kind, such as imputed rental income on owner-occupied homes and the value of food produced for consumption on farms, but it does not include capital gains, whether

---

[1] This is based on the work of Simons. See Henry C. Simons, *Personal Income Taxation* (Chicago: University of Chicago Press, 1938), p. 50. If taxes are direct, then in a world in which taxes are paid, income must be defined as consumption plus change in net worth plus tax payments.

[2] See, for example, the criticism offered in Nicholas Kaldor, *An Expenditure Tax* (London: Allen and Unwin, 1955).

[3] For a reconciliation of personal income, adjusted gross income, and taxable income for federal individual income-tax purposes, see Joseph A. Pechman, *Federal Tax Policy*, rev. ed. (New York: Norton, 1971), pp. 272 and 275.

realized or not, or personal contributions for social insurance. Irrespective of the virtues of the personal income account as a social-accounting measure, it has no special merit as a tax base. It was not designed to provide an index of taxpaying capacity. Its exclusion of capital gains simply reflects its relationship to measures of production as a flow in the economy as a whole, rather than accretions to the economic power of individuals or households, however obtained. Thus, the inclusion or exclusion of any particular gain or receipt in income for tax purposes cannot be made to turn on the basis of its treatment by the Department of Commerce for purposes of its income and product accounts.

Income subject to federal taxation departs extensively from the accretion concept by allowing the omission or exclusion of a wide range of sources of income and by permitting the deduction of selected uses of income. To the extent that it does so, it is not adequate to the purpose of providing a base for equitable and efficient taxation.[4] Income "from whatever source derived" must be subject to tax, and all sources must be treated alike. The same rule applies with respect to the various uses or dispositions of income. Exceptions may be justified with respect either to sources or to uses, but only if they are defensible on equity grounds or serve an overriding social purpose that cannot be equally well served or better by means of direct appropriations or regulations. Under present law, the federal individual income-tax base excludes certain sources of income in whole or in part and permits some uses to reduce taxable income.

Exclusions. Although the Sixteenth Amendment to the Constitution authorizes the Congress "to lay and collect taxes on incomes, from whatever source derived," the list of sources of income excluded in whole or in part is a long one. On it are various kinds of income in kind in the form of the value of self-rendered services; services provided

---

[4] Taxation is efficient or inefficient according to whether it leads to decisions different from those that would have been made if the taxes had not been levied but if incomes were, nevertheless, lower by the amount of tax collected. By this criterion, virtually all taxes are inefficient, including even the accretion-type income tax, which affects the choice between goods and leisure and between future and present consumption. Although this inefficiency is unavoidable if the tax is to be equitable, the present statutory definition of income introduces many other distortions that not only are inefficient but also interfere with equity. Tax policy should minimize such inefficiencies, particularly those that stem from aspects of the tax law that also give rise to inequities.

to its owners by tangible personal and real property; goods produced in the home and on the farm for personal consumption; public transfer payments in such forms as social security, workmen's compensation, unemployment insurance benefits, veterans' benefits, and welfare receipts; various employee fringe benefits; $100 of dividends received for each taxpayer ($200 on joint returns); one-half of realized long-term capital gains and all of capital gains accrued on assets transferred by gift or bequest; interest accumulated on life insurance policy reserves; interest on state and local (municipal) bonds; and a number of less important exclusions such as the rental value of homes provided for clergymen and discounts provided by stores to employees. Recent estimates indicate that the 1972 total for capital gains, municipal-bond interest, dividend exclusion, imputed rental value of owner-occupied homes, transfer payments, and interest on life insurance reserves amounts to $137 billion, $80 billion of which is accounted for by transfer payments.[5] It is probably this group of exclusions that most warrants discussion and consideration for inclusion in the tax base.

Capital gains. Half of realized capital gains on assets held for more than six months are excluded from income for federal individual income-tax purposes.[6] Arguments in favor of this special treatment include the case to be made on the basis of the bunching problem that arises under progressive rates when gains accrue over a number of years and are realized in one year, the spurious nature of gains attributable to general inflation or a decline in interest rates, and the need to encourage risk taking and to avoid barriers to capital mobility.

In response, however, it may be pointed out that the bunching problem is just another excellent reason for introducing an adequate averaging scheme. Immobility of capital induced by the tax laws or the so-called lock-in problem results primarily from the fact that gains accrued until death are not subject to income tax at all. The holding of

---

[5] Joseph A. Pechman and Benjamin A. Okner, "Individual Income Tax Erosion by Income Classes," in *The Economics of Federal Subsidy Programs: A Compendium of Papers Submitted to the JEC,* U.S. Congress, Joint Economic Committee (Washington, D.C.: Government Printing Office, 1972), Table 3, p. 23.

[6] Under the Tax Reform Act of 1969 the maximum rate applicable to the taxable half of long-term capital gains is 50 per cent (25 per cent on the total actual gain) on the first $50,000 of such gains. On capital gains in excess of $50,000, the effective rates are one-half of the statutory marginal rates on other property income. Capital gains are also subject to the 10 per cent "minimum tax."

assets that appreciate in response to inflation provides one with a valuable hedge, and certainly a more fortunate position than that of the fixed-dollar claim holder or the person without assets.[7] Holding assets that appreciate in value as interest rates drop places one in the fortunate position of having net worth (defined as potential consumption value) increase without added effort or risk. Measures designed to encourage risk bearing should be of more general applicability; among them, fuller loss offsets and a properly designed investment allowance certainly deserve higher priority than exclusion of half of realized long-term capital gains.

This exclusion makes major incursions into both horizontal and vertical equity. It seems patently inequitable when people with the same income and other circumstances may pay top marginal tax rates as different as 25 and 70 per cent and correspondingly different average effective rates. Vertical equity is simply incompatible with the present treatment of capital gains. The proportion of adjusted gross income (AGI) accounted for by excluded but realized and reported capital gains in 1969 ranged from 1.9 per cent on all returns with AGI of less than $5,000 and 0.9 per cent in the $5,000-to-$10,000 bracket up to 50.2 per cent for all those with reported AGI of $200,000 and up. Within the top bracket, for those with AGI of $1 million or more, the proportion was 70 per cent.[8] Tax liability (before surcharge and credits) reported on returns with AGI of $200,000 and over amounted to 42.1 per cent of AGI and 53.0 per cent of taxable income, but these proportions drop to 28.0 and 32.5 per cent, respectively, if excluded capital gains are added to income. Even more striking is the fact that for this group of very-high-income taxpayers, if realized long-term capital gains had been treated as ordinary income in 1969, the average effective tax rates would have been equal to approximately 55 per cent of AGI (including 100 per cent of capital gains) and 64 per cent of taxable income.[9]

---

[7] Given the fact that a comprehensive accounting for real gains and losses from all assets would be infeasible.

[8] Derived from U.S. Department of the Treasury, Internal Revenue Service, *Statistics of Income, 1969, Individual Income Tax Returns* (Washington, D.C.: Government Printing Office, 1971), p. 13. The total of net gains excluded in 1969 amounted to more than $16 billion on all returns.

[9] Derived from ibid., pp. 13–15. The corresponding percentage for returns reporting over $1 million of income are in the same order as they are presented in the text: 44.4 and 53.6; 26.2 and 29.1; and 61 and 68.

The so-called step-up in basis of assets passing to heirs at death means that gains accrued while the assets were held by the decedent are simply added to the basis used in calculating gains or losses upon subsequent sale or other nongratuitous transfer by the heir. Thus, the tax rate on such accrued gains is zero even when they are ultimately realized, in contrast with a rate as high as 35 per cent[10] under present law on gains realized during life. This provision of the law is obviously both inequitable and inefficient. Its inefficiency stems from the strong inducement it offers to investors to refrain from selling assets even though nontax considerations suggest selling. In the case of major stockholders in closely held corporations, these provisions also tend to encourage statutory mergers (exchanges of stock) as a means of converting assets without incurring tax liability.

Treating accrued gains as "constructively" realized at death, when the assets are transferred to the heirs, or upon transfer by gift is indispensable to the attainment of both horizontal and vertical equity under the income tax. It is important as well as a means of substantially reducing the so-called lock-in effect of taxing only realized rather than annual accruals of capital gains. Its feasibility is being demonstrated by Canada's experience under recent legislation providing for constructive realization at death.

Municipal-bond interest. Since its inception in 1913, the federal income tax has exempted interest on state and local government bonds. Whatever the merits of the legal arguments to the effect that the Constitution requires this exemption under the dictum regarding intergovernmental immunity laid down by Chief Justice Marshall in 1819 in *McCulloch* v. *Maryland*,[11] they have not been subject to testing in the courts since passage of the Sixteenth Amendment. Nevertheless, an estimated $1.9 billion of municipal-bond interest is currently excluded from adjusted gross income.[12]

As a consequence of their privileged tax status, the interest rate on municipal bonds is about 30 per cent less than it is on corporate

---

[10] When the minimum tax applies, the rate is 45 per cent.

[11] Wheaton (U.S.) 316. Marshall was concerned, of course, with *discriminatory* taxation.

[12] Pechman and Okner, "Individual Income Tax Erosion by Income Classes," p. 23.

bonds of the same rating.[13] The interest saving to state and local governments associated with tax exemption is currently equal to about 200 to 250 basis points (2 to 2.5 percentage points). This is also the price paid by purchasers of municipal bonds for the exempt status of the interest to be received. Obviously, therefore, municipals are a poor buy for anyone subject to a federal marginal income-tax rate of less than 30 per cent.[14] But for those subject to higher rates, the gain increases as income goes up. Thus, when taxable income reaches $200,000 (married, joint return), $1 of exempt interest is worth $3.33 of taxable income in terms of after-tax income; the gain to the taxpayer is $1.90; and the cost to the federal treasury is $2.33, or $1.90 greater than the $.43 interest saving realized by the state or local issuer of the bonds.[15] This $.43 is the difference of 30 per cent between the $1 of exempt interest and the $1.43 that would have been paid had the interest been subject to tax. The interest saving to the municipal government is thus given by the marginal tax rate of the investor who only breaks even if he buys tax-exempt bonds.

It follows, therefore, that the exemption of municipal-bond interest is horizontally as well as vertically inequitable. It is inefficient viewed simply as a federal subsidy because its cost far exceeds its value to the recipient units. It is also inefficient from the point of view of rationality in the allocation of resources because projects financed with tax-exempt bonds may appear to pay their way at an interest cost far lower than the actual cost to society. In addition, debt-financed capital outlays of the states and their local subdivisions are favored relative to other kinds of expenditure.

The extent to which a state or local governmental unit incurs

---

[13] As of the week ending April 1, 1972, the yields reported on corporate bonds rated Aaa and Baa were 7.24 and 8.25 per cent, respectively, compared with 5.05 and 5.70 per cent for municipals carrying these ratings. Data from *Federal Reserve Bulletin,* April 1972, p. A36.

[14] This includes unmarried individuals with taxable income of less than $14,000, heads of households with less than $16,000, and married individuals filing joint returns with less than $20,000 of taxable income.

[15] Given the 30 per cent differential in interest rates between taxable and similarly rated nontaxable bonds, the $1 in exempt interest paid would have been $1.43 if the interest had been taxable. The saving to the issuing jurisdiction is, therefore, $.43, the price paid for the exemption privilege by the purchaser. The gain to the 70 per cent–bracket taxpayer is $1.90, and the cost to the federal government, in terms of tax receipts foregone, is 70 per cent of $3.33, or $2.33.

bonded indebtedness is not a particularly compelling basis for the distribution of a federal subsidy, but assuming that this kind of subsidy is to continue, it could be provided much less offensively if it were done directly, through federal assumption of a portion of state-local interest costs in lieu of the exemption of interest paid. Various alternatives are possible, all of which could eliminate the excess of federal costs over state-local gains and the horizontal and vertical inequity associated with the exemption of municipal-bond interest.

Imputed rental income. Compare the positions of two households, each with $20,000 available for investment. One invests in a house that it occupies; the other purchases bonds yielding 7 per cent and leases an identical house, paying $1,400 per year in rent.[16] Until the income tax is brought into the picture, these households would seem to be in identical circumstances. The only difference is that one realizes the yield on its investment directly, in the form of a flow of services provided by the house it has purchased; whereas the other obtains the services of an identical house but pays for those services with the interest it receives on its investment in bonds. Clearly, each has an annual income from its investment of $1,400.

Under the income tax, however, the bond interest is fully taxable; but the imputed rental income on the owner-occupied home is excluded from the tax base, although mortgage interest and the property tax are deductible. Thus, assuming that each of the households is subject to a marginal tax rate of 22 per cent (taxable income of $10,000), the bondholder-renter is left with only $1,092 of his bond interest, while the owner-occupier retains the entire $1,400 in imputed rental income. In addition, if the property tax on each of the two homes is $600, raising the annual rent to $2,000, the owner gains a further advantage in after-tax income of $132 (22 per cent of $600), making him $440 better off than the renter.[17] His gain is even greater if the homes are mortgaged. The owner then is able to deduct mortgage interest, whereas the renter, carrying the interest in his rent, is not permitted to deduct any part of his rental payments.

The total of net (after mortgage interest) imputed rental income

---

[16] Such details as responsibility for maintenance, repairs, and insurance are not included in this computation.

[17] The calculation is: ($1,400 − $1,092) + $132 = $440. This illustration assumes the tax to be passed on to the renter.

realized is currently estimated at about $16 billion,[18] most of which accrues to families with incomes of over $10,000 per year. Deductibility of property taxes adds another $13 billion[19] to the value of preferential treatment (in terms of reduced tax base) afforded to homeowners under the income tax. The resulting tax saving depends, in turn, on the taxpayer's marginal rate and hence rises with income.

The horizontal and vertical inequities associated with the exclusion of imputed rental income on owner-occupied housing need no elaboration. The exclusion also tends to induce people to own rather than rent dwellings, even where renting would otherwise be preferred. It is also conducive to the diversion to housing of funds and resources from higher-yielding (pretax) investment opportunities, thus giving rise to over-investment in housing.

Public transfer payments. Personal exemptions and the low-income allowance are now at levels sufficiently high to ensure that people with incomes below the poverty line (1972) are not subject to the federal individual income tax. Under these circumstances, there is no justification for the continued exclusion of social security benefits in excess of the beneficiary's contributions, veterans' disability benefits, unemployment and workmen's compensation, or even income-conditioned public assistance. Adding these transfer payments to income subject to tax would increase adjusted gross income by $79.8 billion and taxable income by $55.1 billion.[20]

The present law's exclusion of transfer payments has often been supported on the ground that beneficiaries have no capacity to pay taxes and that taxing benefits would simply force Congress to increase them. Such merit as this argument may have, however—and it seems meagre indeed—is more than outweighed by the fact that the exclusion makes the net value of benefits turn on the amount of other taxable income the beneficiary receives. For example, $100 in social security benefits is equivalent to $200 in other income to the taxpayer subject to a 50 per cent marginal tax rate, but it equals only $100 to the individual whose income consists exclusively of such benefits. Most obviously, as well,

---

[18] Pechman and Okner, "Individual Income Tax Erosion by Income Classes," p. 23.

[19] Ibid. The deductibility of mortgage interest is taken into account in estimating *net* imputed rental income at $16 billion.

[20] Ibid.

earned income and, to a lesser extent, property income[21] are discriminated against. It would seem obvious that whether or not an individual's income is too low to warrant his paying taxes depends on the *amount* of that income, not its source.

The dividend exclusion. The Revenue Act of 1954 provided what was regarded as a beginning for integration of the individual and corporate income taxes in the form of a $50 dividend exclusion ($100 for joint returns) and a credit against tax liability of 4 per cent of dividends received. By 1963, it was clear that this was an inappropriate means of alleviating so-called double taxation of corporate dividends; and in response to President Kennedy's recommendation, the 4 per cent credit was dropped. But sentiment in Congress favored encouraging the small investor to own corporate shares, and in its eagerness to "help the little fellow," the Congress, in the Revenue Act of 1964, doubled the dividend exclusion.

The dividend exclusion is now estimated to amount to $2.2 billion,[22] more than 60 per cent of it accruing to the benefit of taxpayers with adjusted gross incomes of over $10,000.[23] It is certainly difficult to identify benefits flowing from this measure that are of sufficient weight and merit to justify their cost to the Treasury of more than $600 million.

Interest on life insurance policy reserves. The payout on life insurance policies consists in part of the return of premiums paid and in part of the interest accumulated on the invested reserves. The annual amount of such interest (which seems indistinguishable in principle from taxable interest on bonds, savings accounts, and so forth) is currently estimated at $9.9 billion.[24] This is the amount (over and above net premiums) that is added each year to policyholders' cash surrender value

---

[21] The retirement-income credit now reduces substantially the discrimination between transfer payments received by older people and property or investment income. Needless to say, of course, if social security benefits were subject to tax, the justification for the retirement-income credit would disappear.

[22] Pechman and Okner, "Individual Income Tax Erosion by Income Classes," p. 23.

[23] Estimated from data presented in *Statistics of Income, 1969, Individual Income Tax Returns,* p. 37.

[24] Pechman and Okner, "Individual Income Tax Erosion by Income Classes," p. 23.

of life insurance in force. Its reporting to policyholders and the Internal Revenue Service through information returns presents no major problems. Whether it would be desirable to press harder in questioning the exclusion from income of interest plus "pure insurance gains" as measured by the difference between the cash value and the face value of policies held at the time of death is debatable, but allowing the interest element to escape the tax net does not bear even cursory examination.

The following tabulation summarizes the amounts of income excluded under the six major categories discussed, together with the associated revenue cost at 1972 levels.[25]

	Amount of Exclusion from AGI	Revenue Cost
	(billions)	
Capital gains—one-half of realized gains	$ 17.1	$ 9.3
—gains accrued on assets transferred by gift or at death	10.4	4.4
Municipal-bond interest	1.9	1.2
Net imputed rent	15.5	5.1
Public transfer payments	79.8	13.1
Dividend exclusion	2.2	.7
Interest on life insurance reserves	9.9	2.7
Total	$136.8	$36.5

Personal deductions. In 1970, $88.2 billion in itemized personal deductions was claimed on 35.5 million income-tax returns. Approximately 90 per cent of this total was accounted for by the four major categories of itemized deductions: state and local taxes, interest, charitable contributions, and medical expenses.[26] On the other 38.4 million tax returns, the optional standard deduction was taken. For 1970, it was claimed either as the lower of $1,000 or 10 per cent of adjusted gross income[27] or in the form of the low-income allowance, now (Revenue Act

---

[25] As estimated in ibid.

[26] U.S. Department of the Treasury, Internal Revenue Service, *Preliminary Statistics of Income, 1970, Individual Income Tax Returns* (Washington, D.C.: Government Printing Office, 1972), p. 40.

[27] For 1972 and subsequent years, the percentage standard deduction is the lesser of $2,000 or 15 per cent of adjusted gross income (Revenue Act of 1971).

of 1971) equal to $1,300. The total standard deduction amounted to $32.4 billion.[28]

For the most part, the itemized deductions represent uses of income that are favored relative to those that do not give rise to deductions. The deductibility of a particular household expenditure is of increasing importance as income rises. A contribution of $1 to one's church, for example, is given at a net cost of $1 if the individual is not subject to tax or if he elects the standard deduction, $.86 if he is subject to the first bracket rate of 14 per cent, and as little as $.30 if his top marginal tax rate is 70 per cent. Still another way to look at the issue is to note that a nondeductible expenditure of $1 requires $1.66 in pretax earnings if the marginal tax rate is 40 per cent; whereas if the expenditure is deductible, $1 in pretax earnings will cover it.

Obviously a set of deductions that removes more than $120 billion from the tax base deserves careful scrutiny.

State and local taxes. The state and local taxes that qualify for deduction are the income, general sales, property, and motor-fuel taxes. General justification may be found in the desirability of reducing inter-jurisdictional competition for wealth and population based on tax differentials. In addition, it mitigates differences that arise because an individual's state-local tax liability may depend as much on the wealth or income of his neighbors as on the quality and quantity of public services offered to him. In this instance, as well as with respect to all exclusions and the other deductions, the value of deductibility rises with income and marginal tax rate, from zero to 70 cents per dollar. Thus, only some are helped, and some much more than others.

Least defensible is the deductibility of the gasoline tax. This tax is essentially a user charge, and since there is surely no national interest in encouraging people to use automobiles, there is no reason to allow the tax to be taken as a deduction against income otherwise subject to tax. With respect to the property tax and general sales and income taxes, the connection between benefits enjoyed and tax paid is, of course, much more remote. Nevertheless, state and local taxes paid constitute a disposition of income that differs from other dispositions primarily because their payment involves less discretion. But even this difference is limited, particularly with respect to sales and property taxes, because the payment

---

28 *Preliminary Statistics of Income, 1970, Individual Income Tax Returns,* p. 3.

of these taxes is as much the subject of the individual's choice as are the value of the home to be occupied or the amount spent on taxable goods and services. Perhaps the best case can be made for the deductibility of the income tax, the payment of which is a nondiscretionary disposition of income. This position is enhanced if one takes the view that it is in the national interest to encourage the substitution of this tax for others at the state-local level.

Interest paid. When interest is paid on debt incurred for the purpose of acquiring or holding income-yielding assets, its deductibility is required in order to arrive at net income of the taxpayer. Such interest should be deductible in arriving at adjusted gross income, rather than as an itemized deduction, irrespective of whether the taxpayer itemizes or takes the standard deduction.

Well over half of all interest deducted is interest on mortgages on owner-occupied homes. If imputed rental income on the total value of the home were to be included in income subject to tax, mortgage interest would be properly deductible in the same manner as interest on other debt incurred for the purpose of holding an income-yielding asset. But as long as imputed rent is excluded, there is no justification for deductibility of mortgage interest.[29]

Other interest payments are related to borrowing to finance more or less current consumption. Justification for their deduction for income-tax purposes, when the purchase price of the item financed is not deductible, has thus far eluded all those who have studied the matter. Deductibility in this instance does not appear to serve any overriding social purpose. Interest payments cannot be said to represent extraordinary, unbudgetable expenses; and the deductibility of interest on consumption loans is not required in order to arrive at the net income of the taxpayer.

Contributions. The deductibility of contributions to charitable, religious, hospital, and educational institutions generally dates back to the fear expressed during World War I that high wartime income-tax rates would dry up charitable giving. Its advocates continue to argue that deductibility is an important spur to giving. That contributions are higher

---

[29] Except, perhaps, as a means of avoiding preferential treatment of the "free and clear" owner as opposed to the mortgagor. This argument, however, is suggestive of the line of reasoning that leads to policy designed to seek equity by extending, rather than restricting, special privileges.

with deductibility than they would be without it is probably indisputable. What is not at all clear is whether they are higher by at least as much as the revenue cost to the Treasury ($5 billion in 1972).

In 1970, the amount of charitable contributions claimed on returns with itemized deductions was 2.9 per cent of the adjusted gross income reported on those returns.[30] Among income brackets, contributions ranged from 5 per cent of AGI for those with incomes of less than $5,000, down to 2.5 per cent in the $25,000-to-$30,000 bracket, and then up to 3.3 per cent for returns in the $50,000-to-$100,000 bracket and 7.2 per cent for those with AGI of $100,000 or more.[31] If, however, the excluded half of long-term capital gains is added to the income base, the variance among brackets in the proportion of income contributed to charity is very small. It is, therefore, difficult to discern evidence suggesting that deductibility, which should increase in influence as income and tax rates rise, plays a substantial role in stimulating charitable giving.[32]

The case for permitting the deduction of charitable contributions from income otherwise subject to tax is most convincing with respect to contributions in excess of amounts representing average or "normal" giving. This would suggest allowing the deduction of contributions only to the extent that they are "extraordinary," say in excess of 3 per cent of adjusted gross income. Even with this limitation, however, the deduction can be justified only if one is convinced that it does in fact stimulate additional giving in an amount that is greater than the revenue cost, that the purposes served thereby are of overriding social importance, and that these purposes cannot be better served in any other way.

Medical expense. Medical expense in excess of 3 per cent of adjusted gross income is now implicitly regarded in the tax law as being sufficiently burdensome to impair the household's capacity to contribute to the support of government. Whether or not this is so at 3 per cent,

---

[30] *Preliminary Statistics of Income, 1970, Individual Income Tax Returns.* $12.9 billion in contributions and adjusted gross income reported was $448.7 billion.

[31] Derived from data contained in ibid., p. 40.

[32] One interpretation of this finding is that the income elasticity of supply of contributions is approximately equal to 1 with respect to before-tax adjusted gross income plus excluded capital gains. Since the price or cost to the taxpayer of a contribution of $1 declines as his taxable income rises and is always equal to $1 - t$, where $t =$ marginal tax rate, this suggests that there is no price effect. Another interpretation is that the income effect leads to a declining rate of giving offset by a rising and positive price effect.

clearly it is true at *some* level, and the deductibility of extraordinary medical expense is readily justified.

The extension in recent years of the availability of medical and hospital insurance raises the question of whether deductibility of medical expenses serves in substantial part as a subsidy to the self-insured or the noninsured. Because only expenses in excess of 3 per cent of adjusted gross income are deductible and, for most people, all or almost all of insurance costs will lie below that level, insurance is discouraged. The effect is probably of minor consequence, however, because of the widespread provision of medical and hospital insurance as a fringe benefit afforded to employees and because the law permits the deduction of one-half of health insurance premiums (up to $150) independently of the 3 per cent floor.

Child-care deduction. Until 1972, the child-care deduction was of little consequence for anyone. The amount deductible was limited to $600 per year for one child age twelve or under (or for one incapacitated dependent) and $900 for two or more. For married taxpayers (if neither spouse was incapacitated), these limits were reduced by one dollar for each dollar of adjusted gross income in excess of $6,000.

The Revenue Act of 1971 substantially revised and broadened these provisions. The deduction is now available for expenses for household services and child care of up to $400 per month incurred in order to permit the taxpayer to be gainfully employed.[33] Employed single taxpayers who have dependent children age fourteen or under or disabled dependents of any age and married couples both of whom work or one of whom is disabled are eligible for the deduction. The same income limit applies to both married and single taxpayers. The full amount of the allowable deduction may be taken if AGI is $18,000 or less. Beyond $18,000, the allowable amount is reduced by $.50 for each dollar of income in excess of $18,000, so that by $27,600, it disappears entirely. As under the old provision, the deduction for "expenses to enable individuals to be gainfully employed" may be taken only if personal deductions are itemized. The revenue cost of this new feature of the tax law is difficult to predict, but it is unlikely to exceed $200 million.

---

[33] The taxpayer may deduct $400 per month for services provided in the home. The deduction is limited to $200 per month for one child, $300 for two, and $400 for three or more in the case of child-care services outside the home. "Gainfully employed" means employed for three-quarters or more of the normal workweek.

In most respects, the new terms of this deduction seem preferable to the old. It provides a more substantial means of reducing the strong bias in the income tax in favor of wives working in the home and producing nontaxable services, rather than working outside the home for taxable wages. But its impact would be enhanced if it were made available to all taxpayers as a deduction from income in arriving at adjusted gross income, rather than to only those who itemize personal deductions. It is difficult, however, to justify confining allowable expenses to those incurred for household services and child care. Surely other costs of employment outside the home, such as commuting expenses, are equally worthy.

Other itemized deductions. Among the other personal deductions, alimony and expenses relating to one's job (such as union dues and work clothes) are either not properly part of the taxpayer's income or are costs of earning that income. They should be deductible for all taxpayers, whether or not deductions are itemized.

Permitting a deduction for casualty losses only to the extent that each loss exceeds $100 seems hard on low-income taxpayers, but it is preferable to permitting all such losses to be deducted. Quantitatively, it is of small importance.

The standard deduction. The low-income-allowance form of this deduction, now at $1,300, does much to enhance progressivity at the lower end of the income scale. It is a means of relieving low-income people from liability for tax at relatively small cost to the Treasury. In conjunction with the percentage standard deduction, the low-income allowance is, in effect, an extra "disappearing exemption." For example, at an income level of $5,000, the percentage standard deduction would be $750; thus the low-income allowance adds $550 to deductions otherwise allowable. But the difference between the low-income allowance and the 15 per cent standard deduction declines as income rises, disappearing entirely when adjusted gross income reaches $8,667.

The percentage standard deduction of whichever is smaller, 15 per cent of AGI or $2,000, may be defended as a means of simplifying compliance with and administration of the income tax. But since it negates a large proportion of the effect of permitting the itemized deductions, both cannot be defended simultaneously. Assume that there are two taxpayers, each with AGI of $13,333. Under the present law, suppose that one of them has incurred medical expenses of $1,000 (of which $1,000 — .03($13,333) = $600 deductible), has paid state and local taxes of $1,000, and has given $500 to charity. The other has incurred medical expenses of less than $400, paid state and local taxes of $1,000, and given nothing to charity. Each of these taxpayers may take a standard deduction of $2,000 (15 per cent of $13,333). The first has the option of deducting $2,100 in itemized deductions, $1,100 more than the second taxpayer. But the standard deduction has wiped out all but $100 of his personal deductions for medical expense, taxes, and contributions. Thus, the standard deduction in large part washes out or offsets the itemized deductions, and the higher the standard deduction, the less the merit that may be found in the arguments favoring itemized deductions. On the other hand, without the itemized deductions, the standard deduction would make no sense at all, except as a means of adding an element of progressivity to the income tax.

Rough estimates of the amount of the itemized and standard deductions to be taken on 1972 tax returns and the revenue cost associated with them are as follows:

	Amount Deducted	Revenue Cost
	(billions)	
Itemized deductions		
Taxes	$ 38	$13
Interest	29	10
Contributions	15	5
Medical expense	12	3
Other and not specified	9	3
Subtotal	103	34
Standard deduction		
Low-income allowance	24	3
Percentage standard deduction	21	7
Subtotal	45	10
Total personal deductions	$148	$44

Other structural issues. Problems relating to depreciation and depletion are quantitatively of far greater importance for corporations than for individuals, but they may be of major consequence for some high-income taxpayers. Joseph A. Pechman and Benjamin A. Okner have estimated that at 1972 levels of activity, the excess of percentage over cost depletion plus the excess of accelerated over straight-line depreciation reduce adjusted gross income by about $1.2 billion, at an annual cost to the Treasury of $560 million.[34]

Another issue of some consequence for equity concerns the extra personal exemptions allowed to taxpayers age sixty-five and over and to those who are blind. In 1969, on 7.2 million returns, 9.3 million extra exemptions were taken for age, 3.7 million of them on returns reporting AGI of $5,000 or more. The extra exemptions for blindness were taken on only 161,000 returns, with total AGI of $1 billion.[35] Extra exemptions under the income tax appear to be a peculiar means of aiding older or blind people. Under present law, to an elderly couple with AGI of $2,800, the extra exemptions are worth nothing. On the other hand, over 31,000 extra exemptions were claimed on returns reporting AGI of $100,000 or more; and for these taxpayers, each extra $750 exemption may be worth as much as $525.

Age and blindness are only two among the great many disabilities from which people suffer. Why not extra exemptions for diabetes, peptic ulcer, angina pectoris, and so on? That Congress has not chosen to extend the list of disabilities entitling the taxpayer to extra exemptions may, in fact, be seen as tacit admission of error.

In summary, the estimated amount of the reduction in income subject to tax for 1972 attributable to the exclusions discussed here, the personal deductions, extra exemptions for age and blindness, excess depletion, and accelerated depreciation is $298 billion. The revenue cost is $84 billion.

The indicated revenue costs or a large part thereof may be viewed as appropriations by indirection or as tax expenditures. Judgment concerning the desirability of continuing any category of personal deductions must rest in part on whether or not there are uses for the funds that warrant a higher priority. The higher priority may be seen either in the public sector through expansion of existing programs or the introduction

[34] Pechman and Okner, "Individual Income Tax Erosion by Income Classes," p. 23.

[35] *Statistics of Income, 1969,* p. 115. Pechman and Okner have estimated the 1972 revenue cost of the additional exemptions for age and blindness at $2.7 billion ("Individual Income Tax Erosion by Income Classes," p. 34). Their figure of $2.9 billion includes some $200 million for the cost of the retirement-income credit.

of new ones or, alternatively, in the private sector, through a distribution of tax reductions that differs from what is now provided by the allowable itemized and standard deductions and the exclusions.

The distribution of these amounts among their various elements is shown in this table:

	Reduction in Income Subject to Tax	Revenue Cost
	(billions)	
Exclusions	$137.0	$36.0
Personal deductions	148.0	44.0
Exemptions for age and blindness	12.0	3.0
Excess depletion and accelerated depreciation	1.2	0.6
Total	$298.2	$83.6

The Individual Income Tax from 1962 to 1973

The past decade has been an extremely busy period for the tax-writing committees of the Congress. The years 1962 to 1971 saw five major revenue bills enacted and the relative importance of the principal components of budgetary receipts shift considerably. What has happened to the individual income tax in the context of the federal revenue system as a whole during these ten years?

Major tax legislation. The most noteworthy enactments were the Revenue Acts of 1962 and 1964, the Excise Tax Act of 1965, the Tax Reform Act of 1969, and the Revenue Act of 1971. It is not the purpose of this chapter to review or summarize this huge mass of tax legislation. This discussion shall touch primarily on the high points as they affect the level and distribution of liabilities and receipts under the individual income tax.

One major development of the decade has been the removal from the income-tax rolls of people with incomes below the poverty level. This has been accomplished in part through the increase in the personal exemption from $600 to $750 in three stages between 1970 and 1972 under provisions of the Tax Reform Act of 1969 and the Revenue Act of 1971.

The low-income allowance has been of even greater significance in its provision of tax relief to low-income households. Its beginning is to be found in the minimum standard deduction introduced in the Revenue Act of 1964. This minimum standard deduction, set at $200 per return plus $100 for each exemption claimed, was designed to raise the level of tax-free income without extending relief to higher-income people. It raised the amount of income below which the tax would not apply from $667 to $900 for single individuals, from $1,320 to $1,600 for two-person families, from $2,640 to $3,000 for four persons, and so on. At least with respect to families, the minimum standard deduction had the effect of relieving those with incomes below the poverty line (as of 1962) of any income-tax liability.

By 1969, however, inflation had substantially raised the poverty line. In the Tax Reform Act of 1969, and as revised in the Revenue Act of 1971, the minimum standard deduction was converted to a low-income allowance at a fixed amount of $1,300, thus correcting the gap between the poverty line and exempt income that had obtained under the minimum standard deduction. Effective for 1972, the amount of income free of tax and the poverty line will approximately coincide for all family sizes. For single persons, no tax liability is incurred until adjusted gross income exceeds $2,050; for two persons, $2,800;[36] for three, $3,550; for four, $4,300; and so forth, rising by $750 for each additional exemption claimed. The federal government is, therefore, no longer engaged in the practice of recognizing that people are too poor to meet basic subsistence needs and at the same time demanding that they pay income tax.

The percentage standard deduction, fixed at the lower of 10 per cent of AGI or $1,000 since 1944, was raised under the Tax Reform Act of 1969 to 15 per cent of AGI, with a limit of $2,000. This change was expected to reduce substantially the proportion of returns claiming itemized deductions, thus reducing the costs and complexity of compliance with, and administration of, the income tax. At an estimated revenue cost of $1.64 billion, however, this "simplification" has been purchased at a cost that exceeds by over $200 million the total annual expenditures of the Internal Revenue Service for all purposes.[37]

---

[36] An additional $750 exemption is allowed if the taxpayer or his spouse is age sixty-five or over or is blind.

[37] See Staff of the Joint Committee on Internal Revenue Taxation, *General Explanation of the Tax Reform Act of 1969* (Washington, D.C.: Government Printing Office, 1970), pp. 215–218; and *The Budget of the United States Government, Fiscal Year 1973* (Washington, D.C.: Government Printing Office, 1972), p. 387.

The increases in the personal exemption and the standard deduction or low-income allowance are of major importance to families and individuals with low to moderate incomes. On the other hand, the tax-rate reductions provided in the Revenue Act of 1964, although extending throughout the taxable-income range, are of greatest importance to those in the higher-income brackets. Tax rates that had ranged from 20 per cent to 91 per cent from 1954 to 1963 were reduced to a range of 14 to 70 per cent. And for earned income only, the maximum marginal rate in effect for 1972 and subsequent years was cut to 50 per cent under the Tax Reform Act of 1969.

On the basis of income reported on 1969 individual returns, for that year the revenue cost of the rate reductions provided in the Revenue Act of 1964 amounted to $17.7 billion, or about 22 per cent of total individual income-tax liabilities.[38] The reduction of the maximum marginal rate on earned income to 50 per cent is estimated to cost a further $170 million.[39] Projecting these estimates forward to 1972[40] raises the annual revenue loss associated with rate reductions for individuals since 1964 to $22 billion.

By 1972, the rate reductions, the increase in the personal exemption, the increase in the percentage standard deduction, and the introduction of the low-income allowance will have reduced individual-income-tax liabilities by some $32 billion below what they would have been in the absence of these changes. Ball-park estimates of the components of this reduction, equal to more than one-third of anticipated fiscal 1973 individual income-tax receipts, are as follows:

	Amount of Tax Reduction, 1972 Levels (billions)
Reduction in marginal tax rates	$22
Increase in exemption from $600 to $750	5
Increase in percentage standard deduction	2
Low-income allowance	3
Total	$32

---

[38] Estimated on the basis of data presented in *Statistics of Income, 1969, Individual Income Tax Returns*, pp. 128–130.

[39] *General Explanation of the Tax Reform Act of 1969*, p. 227.

[40] On the basis of Pechman and Okner, "Individual Income Tax Erosion by Income Classes," p. 23, the projection of taxable income for 1972 is $478 billion.

Reductions in tax liability of up to 100 per cent have been effected for millions of low- and moderate-income people, whereas the percentage reduction has been much less for higher-income taxpayers. Nevertheless, rate reductions coupled with increases in exemptions and the low-income allowance have not increased the redistributive impact of the income tax but have reduced it substantially. Such at least is the case if "redistributive impact" is defined as resulting changes in the distribution of *after*-tax income.

This may, perhaps, be best illustrated by example. Suppose two families of four persons each, one of which has an adjusted gross income of $4,000 and the other, $100,000. Under the pre-1964 law, the low-income family would have paid an income tax of $240,[41] leaving it with income after tax of $3,760. Under present law, this family would pay nothing, thus saving $240. Tax reduction is equal to 100 per cent, and the increase in after-tax income is 6.4 per cent. The high-income family would have paid $38,514 under the 1963 law, assuming that its itemized deductions were equal to the average of 19 per cent of the adjusted gross income for its income bracket. After-tax income would have been $61,486. If all the income is earned, the tax liability on the $100,000 AGI in 1972 will be $31,060,[42] leaving after-tax income of $68,940. This family's tax reduction is $7,454, or 19.4 per cent; but its after-tax income has increased by 12.1 per cent, almost twice as much as in the case of the low-income family.

In order to maintain a constant redistributive effect, the percentage increase in after-tax income would have to have been the same for both families. This result would have obtained if the tax reduction for the high-income family had been limited to $3,935, or 10.2 per cent. Only if the reduction had been even smaller than this would the distribution of disposable income have become more equal. With higher initial average effective rates of tax at higher income levels, an equal percentage reduction in tax liabilities will result in an increasingly large percentage increase in disposable income as income rises.[43]

---

[41] It is assumed that the standard deduction was taken.

[42] The tax liability will be $32,220 if the 50 per cent maximum marginal rate does not apply.

[43] For equal percentage changes in disposable income to result, it is necessary to have $\Delta DY/DY = \Delta DY^*/DY^*$, where DY is disposable income and Y^* refers to the income of the higher-income taxpayer. This may also be written in terms of average tax rates and changes in them, as $\Delta t^* = \{(1 - t)/(1 - t^*)\}\Delta t$, where t

In addition to changes in the income tax during this past decade, excise taxes have been sharply cut; the effective corporate-income-tax rate has been much reduced by introduction of the investment credit, liberalization of depreciation, and a 4-percentage-point reduction in the statutory rate; and the base and rate of the social security taxes have been substantially increased. What are the effects of these and other changes on the relative position of the individual income tax as a source of federal budgetary receipts?

Relative importance of the individual income tax. As Table 1 shows, the individual income tax is expected to yield $93.9 billion in fiscal 1973, somewhat more than twice as much as it did in 1962. The proportion of total budgetary receipts accounted for by this tax has dropped, however, from 45.7 per cent in 1962 to an estimated 42.5 per cent for 1973, with all the change occurring between 1971 and 1973. Far more dramatic have been the changes in the relative importance of the three other major sources of revenue: the corporate income, employment (largely FICA), and excise taxes.

The corporate income tax has been reduced by some $4 billion as a consequence of the reduction in the tax rate under the Revenue Act of 1964 and by a further $3 billion and $4 billion, respectively, because of the investment credit and liberalized depreciation, for a total reduction of about $11 billion (at 1972 levels).[44] Its yield has gone from $20.5 billion in 1962 to an estimated $35.7 billion in fiscal 1973, but its share of budgetary receipts has dropped from 20.6 to 16.2 per cent.

During the decade under review, corporate income-tax receipts as a fraction of corporate profits before taxes have declined from about 40 per cent to just over 35 per cent. At the same time, corporate profits have fallen from near 10 per cent of the gross national product (GNP) to an average of 8 per cent for the fiscal years 1971 to 1973. Thus, the drop in the corporate tax share of budgetary receipts appears to be a result, in large part, of the reduction in the proportion of GNP represented by corporate profits. If profits in 1972 were expected to be equal to $114 billion, or 10 per cent of forecast GNP, the corporate-income-tax yield

---

and *t** are the initial average effective tax rates for the lower- and higher-income taxpayers, respectively.

[44] Corporate profits before taxes are assumed to be $95.9 billion in 1972, the level forecast by the Research Seminar in Quantitative Economics of The University of Michigan.

Table 1. Federal Budget Receipts, by Major Source, 1962 to 1973, Selected Fiscal Years (billions)

	1962	1964	1966	1968	1969	1970	1971	1972[a]	1973[a]
Individual income tax	$ 45.6	$ 48.7	$ 55.4	$ 68.7	$ 87.2	$ 90.4	$ 86.2	$ 86.5	$ 93.9
Corporate income tax	20.5	23.5	30.1	28.7	36.7	32.8	26.8	30.1	35.7
Employment taxes	12.8	17.0	20.7	29.2	34.2	39.1	41.7	46.4	55.1
Unemployment insurance	3.3	4.0	3.8	3.3	3.3	3.5	3.7	4.4	5.0
Excise taxes	12.5	13.7	13.1	14.1	15.2	15.7	16.6	15.2	16.3
Estate and gift taxes	2.0	2.4	3.1	3.1	3.5	3.6	3.7	5.2	4.3
All other receipts	3.0	3.4	4.7	6.6	7.7	8.6	9.7	10.0	10.5
Total	99.7	112.7	130.9	153.7	187.8	193.7	188.4	197.8	220.8
Individual income tax as percent of total	45.7	43.2	42.4	44.7	46.5	46.7	45.8	43.7	42.5
Individual income tax as percent of personal income[b]	10.6	10.1	9.8	10.4	12.1	11.6	10.4	9.7	9.8

[a]The figures are estimates.
[b]Fiscal-year personal income is estimated as the mean of the two calendar years in which it lies.

Source: Economic Report of the President, 1972, pp. 211 and 270–271.

would amount to approximately $43 billion, equal to 18.9 per cent of budgetary receipts. Thus, of the 4.4-percentage-point drop in this proportion between 1962 and 1973,[45] 1.7 points may be said to be attributable to statutory reductions in the effective tax rate while the remainder, 2.7 percentage points, is a result of the shrinkage of corporate profits relative to the total value of output in the economy.[46]

Despite the repeal of the automobile excise tax and the manufacturers' excise taxes, the excise tax yield rose from $12.5 billion in 1962 to $16.3 billion in 1973, and its share of total receipts fell from 12.5 to 7.4 per cent.

Thus, all three of these major tax sources have declined in relative importance. The one source that has grown most dramatically, both absolutely and relatively, is the social security tax. Since 1962, the payroll base has been increased from $4,800 to $9,000 and the combined employer-employee rate has gone up from 6.25 to 10.4 per cent. At the same time, revenues have risen from $12.8 billion to $55.1 billion, to account in 1973 for 25.0 per cent of total budgetary receipts, compared with 12.8 per cent in 1962.

There has been a slow but fairly steady decline in the proportion of personal income represented by the individual income tax. In 1962, individual income-tax receipts were equal to about 10.6 per cent of personal income. By 1971, this proportion was down to 10.4 per cent; and it is projected to decline further to 9.8 per cent by 1973. This decline, coupled with the nature of the changes affecting the individual income tax enacted since 1962 and the changes in the relative importance of the various major sources of budgetary receipts, point to an overall impact of the federal tax structure that is less progressive now than it was a decade ago.[47]

---

[45] From 20.6 to 16.2 per cent.

[46] Because of the liberalization of depreciation since 1961, corporate profits plus depreciation have held up better as a percentage of the gross national product than have corporate profits alone. In 1961 and 1962, corporate profits plus depreciation and other capital consumption allowances amounted to 14.7 and 15.3 per cent, respectively, of the gross national product. In 1971 and 1972, the corresponding percentages are 14.1 and 14.2.

[47] "Less progressive" is used here to mean that the tax system contributes less now to reduction in inequality in the distribution of disposable income than it did ten years ago.

The Income Tax as a Source of Additional Revenue

What are the alternatives under the individual income tax that might be pursued if it is decided that some $20 billion of federal receipts is needed over and above the expected yield of the existing revenue system?

As demonstrated on p. 23, a tax levied on income as comprehensively defined might add approximately $300 billion to income subject to tax and, at 1972 tax rates, more than $80 billion to revenues.[48] From the standpoint of political feasibility and in the interests of vertical equity, however, there is much appeal in a less ambitious program of base broadening. For example, as Pechman and Okner have shown, it would seem possible to add $15.5 billion to tax liabilities at present rates by means of measures that would impinge primarily on the rich and near rich. These measures would entail the inclusion of the whole of long-term capital gains in adjusted gross income, constructive realization of capital gains at death or gift, taxing municipal-bond interest, and allowing only straight-line depreciation and cost depletion.[49]

On close examination, however, much of the $15.5 billion disappears. Traditionally, Congress has been careful to avoid appearing to impose taxes retroactively or to break implicit contracts. This will almost certainly mean that the most that can be hoped for in the capital-gains area is the taxation of *future* gains in full on realization during life or constructively at death. Thus, in the first few years after enactment, the annual addition to revenue is more likely to fall short of $2 billion than to reach the $13.7-billion level suggested by Pechman and Okner.

If interest on state and local bonds were to be taxed, these bonds would no longer be particularly attractive to high-income individuals and would be particularly unattractive to exempt institutions, pension funds, and so forth. The shift in holding patterns would certainly reduce the revenue yield well below the level of $1.2 billion suggested on the

---

[48] See Pechman and Okner, "Individual Income Tax Erosion by Income Classes," Table 3, p. 23. They add $138 billion to adjusted gross income, $166 billion to taxable income, and $55 billion to tax liabilities. They also find an additional $22 billion in elimination of the rate advantages of income splitting. The principal sources of the difference between their $166 billion and the $300-billion figure indicated in this chapter is in the fact that the latter amount includes all the personal deductions of $148 billion, compared with only $44 billion, and it takes no account of some $25 billion in leakages between additions to income subject to tax and taxable income.

[49] Ibid., p. 36.

assumption that nothing but taxability changes. Moreover, it is widely recognized that it is extremely unlikely that the Congress would be willing to withdraw the present indirect subsidy without replacing it with a substitute that is equally attractive from the point of view of state and local jurisdictions. Thus, the gains to be realized may be great indeed, but they will almost certainly take the form of improved equity and efficiency. This is not a promising source of new revenue.

Excess depletion and depreciation remain as possible sources, together with the taxation in full of future capital gains realized during life and on constructive realization at death or gift. Within the first five years after passage of these reforms, new revenue is likely to be in the neighborhood of $3 billion.

If large sums are to be realized through base broadening, measures must be taken that will affect individuals throughout the income range, with most of the new revenue coming from people with moderate to high-middle incomes (i.e., $10,000 to $50,000), where close to 55 per cent of income, 28 per cent of tax returns, and 58 per cent of tax liability are to be found.[50] Base broadening might add the following to income subject to tax, with estimated revenue gains as indicated:[51]

	(billions)
Imputed net rental income on owner-occupied homes	5.1
Interest on life insurance reserves	2.7
Dividend exclusion	.7
State and local taxes	13.0
Charitable contributions limited to excess over 3 per cent of AGI	4.0
Medical expenses limited to excess over 5 per cent of AGI	1.5
Interest limited to property income, including imputed rent	2.0
Percentage standard deduction (amount in excess of low-income allowance)	2.0
Extra exemptions for age and blindness	2.7
Total additional revenue	$33.7

---

[50] See *Statistics of Income, 1969, Individual Income Tax Returns*, p. 9.

[51] The estimates are as reported in Pechman and Okner, "Individual Income Tax Erosion by Income Classes," p. 23, except for some modifications and additions.

Taxing transfer payments, primarily in the form of social security benefits, would add some $13 billion to the yield of the tax, to bring the total
that might be gained through all the indicated measures to close to $50
billion.

This potential revenue gain is large enough so that almost any net
distributive effects that might be desired could be achieved by means of
the rate reductions made possible if $30 billion of the $50 billion could
be used for that purpose, leaving a net revenue gain of $20 billion.[52]
Rate cuts totaling $30 billion might be provided by reducing all bracket
rates by about 25 per cent or, alternatively, in order to achieve a more
progressive effect, by 5 percentage points.

The history of tax-reform efforts over the past twenty-five years
does not offer much hope, however, for enactment of legislation that will
remove from the tax laws some of the most strongly entrenched special
privileges, particularly those that accrue primarily to the advantage of
middle-income (broadly construed) homeowners, the elderly, and others
whose voices carry political weight.

However, the recognition that taxes, howsoever levied, ultimately
come out of the incomes of individuals and families suggests that the
choice of tax instrument for raising new funds is essentially a choice in
terms of distribution of tax burdens. The great attraction of the individual
income tax, despite its many shortcomings, and even if its base remains
unreformed, is that the new revenue can be drawn from readily identifiable groups and under whatever distribution scheme the Congress
chooses. If, for example, it is believed that the tax structure is excessively
progressive, this defect can be corrected more readily and precisely by
adjusting income-tax rates than by introducing new consumption taxes or
relying more heavily on other nonincome taxes.

Thus, given the income-tax base as presently defined, some $22
billion in additional revenue could be raised simply by restoring tax rates
to their 1963 levels. But, of course, there is no magic in the 1963 rate
structure; and it should be noted that given the 27 per cent decline in the
consumer value of the dollar, retaining 1963 rates would have meant, in

---

[52] For detailed estimates of the impact by income bracket of various base-
broadening measures, see ibid., Table A–2, p. 34. Of the $55.7 billion of additional
revenue realized through their base-broadening program, $7.2 billion falls on
taxpayers with adjusted gross income of less than $10,000; $34.5 billion on those
with between $10,000 and $50,000; and $14.1 billion on taxpayers whose adjusted
gross income exceeds $50,000.

effect, a substantial increase in tax rates applicable at given levels of real income. Increasing all present rates by 4 percentage points or, alternatively, by 20 per cent across the board would yield $20 billion. The first of these alternatives would weigh more heavily on lower-income taxpayers and would produce rates ranging from 18 to 74 per cent; whereas they would range from 17 to 84 per cent under the second alternative.

The Future Role of the Income Tax

Foreseeable fiscal circumstances suggest that more, rather than less, revenue than the existing tax system will yield will be needed over the next few years, based on the assumption that the federal government will assume some new responsibilities in such areas as income maintenance, education at all levels, mass transportation, improving the quality of the environment, and substantial untied grants to state and local jurisdictions. It presupposes as well that fiscal policy will play a major role in stabilizing the economy. All this suggests that budgetary receipts required by fiscal 1974 will be between $250 and $270 billion, perhaps $20 to $30 billion more than the existing revenue system could be expected to produce.

There are, as already noted, several alternative routes through which the individual income tax might be pursued as a means of raising additional revenue. If equity and economic efficiency are to be sought in the tax structure, and especially if the nation is less certain than it was a decade ago that rapid economic growth must be a high-priority goal, then there is no attractive substitute for the income tax, whichever of these routes may be chosen. Moreover, the individual income tax may well be called upon to expand its functions into two new areas: extension of its role in income distribution through the addition of the negative income tax and assumption of the responsibility for taxing profits directly in the hands of the individuals to whose benefit they accrue.

The negative income tax. The income-tax-collection system, including withholding at the source, is well adapted to extension to the administration of a negative income tax. Such a tax would consist, basically, of an income grant to qualifying individuals and families, coupled with a special tax on income earned, incorporated in the regular income tax in a way that would provide for smooth transition from the

application of the one to the application of the other as income moves up
or down.

The superiority of this general approach to income maintenance
as a substitute for the existing public-assistance programs appears to be
widely agreed upon. People, including most politicians, seem to be
divided largely on matters of detail, such as the appropriate level of the
basic grant and work requirements or incentives.[53]

Taxing corporate profits. Recognition of the fact that taxes, howsoever levied, are paid by people through either their sources or their uses
of income necessarily raises questions about the role of the corporate
income tax in the revenue system and its relation to the individual income
tax.

At present, there is no agreement among economists concerning
whether the corporate tax is shifted forward to consumers or is not
shifted forward and is, instead, borne by stockholders or investors generally. If it is shifted forward, the corporate income tax may be viewed as
a selective sales tax that carries effective rates relative to product prices
that vary widely and capriciously with the ratio of profits to market
prices. Such a sales tax would surely never command a place in a rational,
equitable tax system.

On the other hand, if the tax is not shifted forward but reduces
profits available for distribution and reinvestment, it is borne by owners
of equity interests in corporate enterprises or, after long-run adjustments
in capital markets, by the recipients of capital income in general. In this
instance it is, in effect, a supplementary income tax, imposed upon
stockholders without regard to their overall economic circumstances.
Thus, the tax borne on this part of income carries the same rate for the
retired person of modest means as it does for the wealthiest individuals.
Moreover, because interest, rents, and royalties are deductible but dividends are not, among types of property income, only the return on invest-

---

[53] This is not the place for detailed discussion of the negative income tax in the
various forms in which it has been proposed. For an excellent summary of the
earlier literature, see Christopher Green, *Negative Taxes and the Poverty Problem*
(Washington, D.C.: Brookings, 1967). Also very useful are James Tobin, Joseph
A. Pechman, and Peter M. Mieszkowski, "Is a Negative Income Tax Practical?"
Yale Law Journal (November 1967); President's Commission on Income Main-
tenance Programs, *Poverty Amid Plenty, the American Paradox* (Washington, D.C.:
Government Printing Office, 1969); and Harvey E. Brazer, "The Federal Income
Tax and the Poor," *California Law Review* (April 1969).

ment in corporate equities is subject to the corporate income tax as well as the individual income tax. This results in a shift of capital from the incorporated to the unincorporated sector and implies a public policy designed to discriminate against investment in the incorporated sector of the economy, the reasons for which must remain most elusive.

Opposing either of these views of the corporate income tax is the view that is based on the belief that the corporation is an income-earning, tax-paying entity that quite properly may be expected to bear its fair share of taxes. In this view, taxes may be paid by people *or* by corporations; and to the extent that corporations pay taxes, people are relieved of that part of the total tax bill. Frequently, the corporate income tax is seen as the obvious means of reaching profits through the tax system. Support for the tax can be explained only in these terms.

But the question of incidence cannot be avoided. Any tax, including the corporate income tax, must come out of the incomes of individuals or households. If it does so through consumption expenditures because of forward shifting, its replacement by the individual income tax or a general sales tax seems clearly called for. If the corporate tax is not shifted forward, then uniform treatment of income irrespective of source and neutrality with respect to form of business organization and debt versus equity financing demand that profits be taxed directly through the individual income tax.

With comprehensive averaging and full taxation of capital gains, including gains deemed to be realized on transfer of assets at death or by gift, true corporate profits would be reached under the individual income tax. Dividends would be taxed as received, and retained corporate profits would be reflected in capital gains. Enormous simplifiction of the tax system as well as large gains in equity and economic efficiency would be achieved. This rather purist approach has much appeal, but the initial revenue loss entailed would probably approach $30 billion, to be reduced only gradually over time as dividend payouts increased and capital gains were realized.[54]

---

[54] The $30-billion figure is based on 1972 levels of profits and personal income. It is arrived at by assuming that repeal of the $36-billion corporate income tax would, within say three years, bring an increase in dividends paid to individuals of $10 billion and in *realized* capital gains of $5 billion. The estimated tax on this $15 billion is $6 billion, leaving a net revenue loss of $30 billion. Ultimately, dividends might be expected to rise by as much as $20 billion and realized capital gains (including constructive realization at death or gift) by another $20 billion, to cut the net revenue loss to about $20 billion.

A less radical approach involves retaining the corporate income tax but either allowing dividends to be deductible for corporate-tax purposes or treating the tax paid on profits represented by dividends as having been withheld for the stockholder. The stockholder, on receipt of $1 in dividends paid out of profits subject to a corporate tax of 48 per cent (the current rate on corporate income in excess of $25,000), would be required to "gross up" the $1 to $1.92 [$1/(1 — .48)], the corporate profits before tax represented by the dividend. He would add $1.92 to his adjusted gross income, compute his tax liability, and claim a credit for the $.92 in tax paid on his behalf by the corporation. Either of these methods of integrating the corporate and personal income taxes leaves undistributed profits subject to tax at a rate that is either too low or too high for almost all stockholders. But this may be a minor problem as long as at least rough justice is ultimately achieved through the taxation of capital gains.

There remains the problem of making up the revenue loss. Under either the gross-up-and-credit or the dividend-deduction approach, that loss is likely to amount to about $9 billion, unless dividends paid were to increase sharply.[55] In that event, the revenue loss could reach perhaps $12 billion. Making up this sum through the individual income tax should not pose serious difficulties. If $10 billion were to be raised among income groups in proportion to the share of total dividends that they receive, $7.3 billion would be allocated to taxpayers with adjusted gross incomes of more than $15,000 and $2.7 billion to those with less than $15,000. On the basis of taxable income reported for 1970, this would suggest an average increase in statutory tax rates of about 1 percentage point for the income brackets below $15,000 and 4 percentage points for those above $15,000. Among the highest-income taxpayers, those with AGI of $100,000 or more, who reported 23.4 per cent of all dividends in 1970, the increase in tax rate indicated would be about 16 percentage points.[56]

---

[55] Assuming dividends of $16 billion paid to individuals, the grossed-up amount would be $31 billion. The additional individual-tax liability would be about $6 billion and the credit, $15 billion, for a net loss of $9 billion. If dividends paid out amounted to $25 billion, the revenue loss would be approximately 45 per cent of this sum, or $11 billion.

[56] These estimates are based on data presented in *Preliminary Statistics of Income, 1970, Individual Income Tax Returns,* pp. 29–33.

The outlook. Bracket rates under the individual-income-tax rates may have to be increased appreciably, may remain unchanged, or may even be reduced substantially and $20 billion to $30 billion still be added to budgetary receipts. The answer turns on the extent to which the tax base is to be broadened. Bold moves toward the achievement of a comprehensive tax base could permit rates to be cut from the present range of 14 to 70 per cent to a range of, say, 10 to 50 per cent and still allow attainment of a substantial increase in revenue.[57] But any such reform program will impose higher taxes on a large proportion of tax-payers with incomes of between $10,000 and $50,000. There simply is not enough income, let alone untaxed income, accruing to the very rich to permit any other result. To believe otherwise is to harbor an illusion. Major gains in equity and economic efficiency are the important gains to be realized.

However, the obstacles to reform are formidable. Privileged treatment of various sources and uses of income are well entrenched, some originating with the adoption of the modern income tax in 1913. And there is simply no way in which a comprehensive tax base coupled with reduced statutory tax rates can be achieved without imposing higher tax liabilities on presently privileged groups. Unfortunately, such groups are always quick and effective in their protests against any move to delete their favored treatment, whereas little, if anything, is heard from those who would gain. They are less readily self-identified and therefore not politically articulate or organized for effective political action.

---

[57] Reducing tax rates by about 30 per cent to the level indicated in this chapter while increasing individual income-tax receipts by $20 billion would require an increase in the tax base of close to $250 billion above the present level of about $450 billion.

PROPERTY TAX

Helen F. Ladd

THE ROLE OF THE PROPERTY TAX: A REASSESSMENT

HISTORICALLY, THE PROPERTY TAX has played a significant role in the American tax system. Although property-tax revenue as a per cent of total tax revenue has declined from 51.4 per cent in 1902 to 11.9 per cent in 1970 because of the growth of the federal income tax and state sales and income taxes, it is still the primary source of tax revenue for local governments. In 1970, local property-tax collections were $32.9 billion, or 85 per cent of the total local tax revenue for that year. As a local tax, however, it has recently come under attack as the source of inequitable differentials in educational opportunity across communities. This current criticism plus traditional criticisms of the property tax based on its poor administration, presumed regressivity, discrimination against housing expenditures, and effect on urban slums have cast renewed doubt on the desirability of continued heavy reliance on it.

This chapter does not deal at length with the important issues of property-tax administration; rather, it examines the other issues raised by these criticisms in order to reassess the future role of property taxation in the American fiscal structure.[1] A comparison of the increase in property-tax revenue and that of other taxes reveals that the property tax has increased at a lesser rate. However, there are certain peculiarities

[1] The limited emphasis on property tax administration in this chapter is not intended to imply that inequities in the tax assessment process are not a serious deficiency of the tax. An underlying assumption throughout the discussion is that property tax administration can and will be improved. (See section on "Criticisms of the property tax.")

of the property tax that explain why this tax should have become the hub of an alleged taxpayer revolt, especially among homeowners. This chapter presents an analysis of who pays the property tax. Modifications of the traditional approach to property-tax incidence suggest that the burden is not so regressive as it is generally assumed to be. In fact, it may be substantially progressive in the middle- and upper-income ranges.

Is housing, especially owner-occupied housing, currently overtaxed in comparison with other forms of investment or consumption? Examination of aggregate U.S. data and consideration of the impact of the entire tax system (including the individual income tax, the corporate tax, and the excise taxes, as well as the property tax), demonstrate that on the average, owner-occupied housing is undertaxed, in spite of the residential-property tax, because the corporate income tax excludes the housing sector and because homeowners are granted favorable income-tax provisions. Moreover, looked at from the consumption side, sales taxes exclude housing services.

A major conclusion of this chapter is that local financing of public services, rather than the property tax itself, creates tax-base differentials and service-level inequalities across communities. This implies that the current concern about education disparities is a question not of the merits of the property tax but rather of what level of government is the most appropriate to finance education expenditures, whether from the property tax or from other sources. The answer involves both efficiency and equity considerations.

Finally, the property tax is evaluated both as a local tax and as a statewide tax. To the extent that local fiscal autonomy is considered desirable in spite of its costs in terms of tax-base disparities, the local property tax is no worse than any other local revenue source and better than most. To the extent that less reliance on local revenue sources is deemed desirable, whether for financing education or for other functions, this chapter concludes that there is a substantial case for use of the property tax at the combined state-local level rather than for its replacement by other revenue sources.

Is There Excessive Reliance on the Property Tax?

A large part of the current concern about property taxation arises from the general impressions that excessive reliance is presently being placed on property-tax revenue in relation to other sources of revenue and that property-tax revenue is rising more rapidly than other sources of tax revenue. It is, therefore, relevant to see to what extent these impressions are substantiated by the data.

Table 1 presents data for 1960 and 1970 on the major types of tax revenue raised by all three levels of government, including the per cent increase of each source during the period. Although total state and local tax revenues increased more rapidly than federal tax revenue during this period, state and local property-tax revenues increased by less than both the federal individual income tax and the payroll tax, whether considered as a per cent or in absolute terms. At the state and

Table 1. Growth of Tax Revenue (in millions)

Source of Revenue	1960	1970	Per cent Increase
Federal government			
Individual income	$40,715	$90,412	122
Corporation income	21,494	32,829	53
Sales and gross receipts	12,603	18,297	45
Payroll[a]	12,712	41,980	230
Other taxes	2,191	4,544	107
Total tax revenue	89,715	188,062	110
State and local			
Property	16,405	34,054	108
Individual income	2,463	10,812	339
Corporation income	1,180	3,738	217
Sales and gross receipts	11,849	30,322	156
Payroll[a]	4,896	10,732	119
Other taxes	4,220	7,868	86
Total tax revenue	41,013	97,530	138
Local			
Property	15,798	32,963	109
Other taxes	2,832	7,169	153
Total tax revenue	$18,630	$40,132	115

[a]Payroll taxes represent insurance-trust revenue.

Sources: U.S. Bureau of the Census, *Governmental Finances in 1969–70* (1971), Table 4; and idem, *Governmental Finances in 1960* (1961), Table 1.

local levels, the 108 per cent growth in property-tax revenue is less than the per cent growth of each of the other major tax sources. In addition, the absolute growth is less than the growth of sales and gross-receipts revenues.

Table 2 relates state and local property-tax revenues to various aggregate measures for the same two years (1960 and 1970). The table shows that as a per cent of tax revenue collected by all levels of government and as a per cent of state and local tax revenues, property-tax revenue has declined during the decade. As a per cent of the gross national product, however, property-tax revenue has increased slightly, from 3.3 to 3.5 per cent; and as a per cent of personal income, from 4.1 to 4.2 per cent. What has clearly been happening is that total tax revenues and, therefore, expenditures have been increasing substantially in relation to the gross national product but that property-tax revenue has not risen fast enough to maintain its 1960 relationship to either state and local tax revenues or total tax revenues. Hence, the general impression that relative reliance on the property tax has increased over the last decade is shown to be invalid.

Table 2. State and Local Property Taxes as a Per Cent of Base Items

Base Items	1960	1970
Total tax revenue (all levels)	12.5	11.9
State and local tax revenue	40.0	34.9
Gross national product	3.3	3.5
Personal income	4.1	4.2

Sources: U.S. Bureau of the Census, *Governmental Finances in 1969–70,* Table 4; and idem, *Governmental Finances in 1960,* Table 1; and U.S. President, *Economic Report of the President* (1972), Tables B-1 and B-14.

There might still be cause for concern, however. If property-tax *rates* had to rise substantially in order to allow property-tax *revenue* to rise at the rate it did, the growth in revenue might be less acceptable to taxpayers than it would be if it were derived from an increase in the taxable base, which was, for example, the primary source of revenue increase of the federal individual income tax.

The most relevant rate comparisons over time are for owner-occupied housing because it is the homeowner who is most vocal in his criticisms of the rising property-tax burden. Aggregate data on property-tax revenue from owner-occupied housing and property tax rates are not directly available, but crude estimates may be made (see Table 3).

Table 3. Estimated Increase in Effective Property-Tax Rates, 1956–1966[a]

Year	Property-Tax Revenue, Single-Family Homes (in millions)	Estimated Value of Single-Family Homes (in millions)	t_n	t_e (in per cent)	A/S
1956	$4,361	$302,016	4.58	1.44	31.5
1961	6,661	423,187	4.90	1.57	32.1
1966	9,720	570,012	4.94	1.70	34.5

Note: t_n = nominal tax rate (taxes/assessed value)
t_e = effective tax rate (taxes/market value)
A/S = assessment-sales ratio, where A is assessed value and S is sales or market value.

[a]Based on the distribution of the taxable base and estimated assessment ratios from the U.S. Bureau of the Census, *Census of Governments,* Vol. 2 for 1957 (Table 7), 1962 (Table 8), and 1967 (Table 11).

Although property taxes on single-family homes increased substantially between 1956 and 1966, the table shows that over half the increase can be attributed to the increase in the market value of such homes and that the remainder is a result of the increase in effective rates from 1.44 per cent in 1956 to 1.70 per cent in 1966. It is interesting to note that the increase in effective rates was primarily a result of an increase in the nominal tax rate between 1956 and 1961; whereas in the later period, the average nominal tax rate stayed constant, but the assessment-sales ratio increased from 32.1 to 34.5 per cent.

For the period since 1966, a similar comparison is difficult to make without an explicit assessment-sales ratio for 1970. The following figures are of some interest as a rough approximation:

	Estimated Property-Tax Revenue, Single-Family Homes	Net Imputed Rent and Mortgage Interest
	(per cent growth)	
1963–1966	30	25
1967–1970	33	21

Housing values are viewed here as the capitalized value of net imputed income from housing; this is approximated by national income accounts data on net return on equity and mortgage-interest payments. If the rate of growth of these is assumed to be a reasonable measure of the rate of growth of the tax base, the figures suggest that effective property-tax rates increased by about 4 per cent in the period from 1963 to 1966 and by about 10 per cent in the period from 1966 to 1970. Although the tentative nature of these calculations should be recognized, it is evident that effective rates have risen with the result that a $20,000 house pays more in taxes in 1970 than a $20,000 house in 1960.

This increase in rates may be particularly disturbing to the taxpayer in the case of property taxation because he will tend to charge the higher taxes against "the same house," without realizing that the major part of the increase in the tax payment is only a reflection of the rising market value of the house. A homeowner who bought a house in 1960 for $20,000 and paid $400 in taxes on it that year and $600 on the same house in 1970 might think that property-tax rates had increased by 50 per cent. In fact, the property-tax rate might well have stayed constant at 2 per cent, with the entire rise in absolute tax resulting from the increase in the value of the house from $20,000 to $30,000. In the case of the property tax, the increase in the money value of the tax base may remain hidden, whereas with the income tax, for example, increasing tax liabilities are accompanied by a visible rise in income.

The discussion up to this point has been in terms of nationwide averages; these figures hide the fact that property-tax rates may have risen faster in some areas than in others. This, plus absolute differences in tax rates in different areas, may make homeowners in areas with high or rapidly rising tax rates more concerned about property taxation than they would be if all rates were similar. Table 4 shows that property-tax rates on middle-income homes vary significantly across states and that a major reason for this, especially for high- and low-rate states, is varying degrees of reliance on property-tax revenue in the state and local tax structures. The five states with the highest effective rates (2.75 per cent or more) also derive the largest share of total revenue (above 50 per cent) from the property tax.

It remains to be noted that the significance of property taxation cannot be evaluated without reference to corresponding expenditure benefits. An increase in tax rates may be matched by an increase in expenditure benefits, and rate differentials among jurisdictions may reflect differentials in expenditure levels. However, because the property tax finances many services that have general rather than property-related benefits, taxpayers may fail to link the two sides of the fiscal picture.

Table 4   State-by-State Comparison of the Average Property-Tax Rate on Middle-Income Homes and Relative Reliance on Property-Tax Revenue (in per cents)

State	Effective Tax Rates 1969[a]	Property Taxes as Per Cent of State and Local Taxes, Fiscal Year 1970	State	Effective Tax Rates 1969[a]	Property Taxes as Per Cent of State and Local Taxes, Fiscal Year 1970
New Jersey	2.99	54.08	Missouri	1.72	40.09
Nebraska	2.89	52.63	Indiana	1.70	46.98
Massachusetts	2.86	50.30	Ohio	1.49	47.23
New Hampshire	2.84	62.30	New Mexico	1.49	22.60
South Dakota	2.75	54.98	Nevada	1.48	34.39
New York	2.61	36.37	Utah	1.48	36.00
Vermont	2.48	34.88	Idaho	1.41	36.43
Wisconsin	2.48	43.36	Wyoming	1.41	47.47
Iowa	2.31	48.85	North Carolina	1.40	25.29
Colorado	2.29	42.68	Washington	1.38	35.09
Maine	2.27	45.70	Oklahoma	1.38	30.46
Connecticut	2.26	49.19	Georgia	1.33	30.54
California	2.23	46.87	Florida	1.32	34.01
Oregon	2.16	47.23	Tennessee	1.31	27.52
Kansas	2.16	51.17	Delaware	1.25	18.57
Maryland	2.11	32.44	Kentucky	1.21	22.94
Rhode Island	2.11	40.51	Virginia	1.17	28.25
Pennsylvania	2.03	29.55	Arkansas	1.14	25.76
Illinois	2.01	41.21	Hawaii	1.05	17.18
Montana	1.98	54.25	Mississippi	0.91	27.07
North Dakota	1.93	46.57	West Virginia	0.74	23.32
Arizona	1.90	38.92	Alabama	0.72	15.21
Alaska	1.81	24.37	South Carolina	0.68	22.38
Michigan	1.81	40.32	Louisiana	0.43	19.76
Texas	1.75	40.53			
Minnesota	1.72	38.66	U.S. average	1.81	39.24

[a] Calculated by the New Jersey Taxpayers Association from U.S. Federal Housing Administration, "Characteristics of FHA Operations Under Section 203, 1969."

Source: *Report of the New Jersey Tax Policy Committee* (Trenton: February 23, 1972), pt. 2, Tables 2–5 and 2–11.

Who Pays the Property Tax?

In order to determine who ultimately pays the property tax, it is useful to have some idea of the relative importance of the various sources of property-tax revenue. It is difficult to determine the exact revenue from each type of property tax, but a crude breakdown can be estimated on the basis of the distribution of the taxable base as presented in Table 5. If average nominal rates were the same for each type of property, the assessment data would imply that 47 per cent of the total property-tax revenue is derived from nonfarm residential property, both single-family and rental; that 39 per cent, including the state-assessed share, is from commercial, industrial, and farm realty; and that 14 per cent is from personal property, the major portion of which is business machines and inventories.

The traditional approach. The different sources of property-tax revenue complicate the issue of incidence because for each source, different assumptions must be made about whether the tax is shifted forward to consumers or backward to other factors of production or is borne by the payers of the tax. Traditional analysis assumes that the tax on the land component of each type of reality is not shifted, that the tax on structures is borne by the homeowner in the case of owner-occupied residential property, by the tenant for rental units, and by the consumer in the case of business property. The tax on business personalty is usually assumed to be shifted forward to consumers, and the tax on consumer durables is assumed to remain on the owner of the durables.[2]

As shown in column 1 of Table 6, these traditional assumptions lead to the conclusion that the property tax is regressive. The major part of the tax falls on housing expenditures and general consumption expenditures, both of which decline as a per cent of income as the level

---

[2] See, for example, Tax Foundation, Inc., *Tax Burdens and Benefits of Government Expenditures by Income Class, 1961 and 1965* (New York: 1967); W. Irwin Gillespie, "Effect of Public Expenditures on the Distribution of Income," in *Essays in Fiscal Federalism,* ed. by Richard A. Musgrave (Washington, D.C.: The Brookings Institution, 1965); Dick Netzer, *Economics of the Property Tax* (Washington, D.C.: The Brookings Institution, 1966), chap. 3; and Richard A. Musgrave et al., "Distribution of Tax Payments by Income Groups, A Case Study for 1948," *National Tax Journal* 4 (March 1951): 1–53.

of income rises. This evidence is derived from cross-sectional data showing household-expenditure patterns by income brackets, where income is defined in terms of current income. As noted in "A modified traditional approach," the patterns might differ and prove less regressive if

Table 5. Property-Tax Base, by Type of Property,
Assessed Values, 1966

Type of Property	Amount (billions)	Per Cent of Total
Realty		
Locally assessed		
Residential: single-family houses	$197	39
Residential: rental	40	8
Acreage and farms	43	9
Vacant lots	10	2
Commercial property	60	12
Industrial property	37	7
Other	6	1
Total	393	78
State assessed		
Total	42	8
All levels		
Total	435	86
Personal Property		
Tangibles		
Commercial and industrial	42	8
Agricultural	7	2
Households	3	1
Motor vehicles	8	2
Other	3	1
Intangibles	1	—
Total	64	14
All Property		
Total	499	100

Sources: U.S. Bureau of the Census, *1967 Census of Governments*, vol. 2: *Taxable Property Values*, p. 2, 7. The estimated breakdown in personal property is based on the 1961 distribution given by Dick Netzer, *Economics of the Property Tax* (Washington, D.C.: The Brookings Institution, 1966), p. 147.

similar data were available for households grouped in accordance with
permanent income.[3]

Table 6. Incidence of the Property Tax, 1961

Income Class[a]	Property Taxes as Per cent of Money Income Before Taxes		
	Crude Traditional Approach[b] (1)	Modified Traditional Approach[c] (2)	Capital-Income Approach[d] (3)
Under $2,000	9.1	8.0	6.0
$2,000–$2,999	6.9	6.7	6.3
$3,000–$3,999	6.3	6.2	6.1
$4,000–$4,999	5.6	4.8	4.1
$5,000–$5,999	5.5	4.5	3.4
$6,000–$7,499	5.2	4.2	3.3
$7,500–$9,000	4.8	4.2	3.6
$10,000–$14,999	4.4	4.7	5.1
$15,000 and over	3.3	8.9	14.6
Total	5.2	5.2	5.2

[a]Income classes defined in money income after personal taxes.

[b]One-half of property tax allocated in line with housing expenditures; one-half,
in line with consumption expenditures.

[c]One-half of property tax allocated in line with housing expenditures; one-half,
in line with income from capital.

[d]Total property taxes allocated in line with income from capital, calculated by
subtracting wages and salaries, public assistance, and social security benefits
from money income for each class.

Source: Calculated from data in Tax Foundation, Inc., *Tax Burdens and Benefits
of Government Expenditures by Income Class, 1961 and 1965* (New York:
1967).

A modified traditional approach. More recent analysis has argued
that the property tax is essentially a tax on land and capital. This being
the case, its incidence should be similar to that of a tax on capital income because there is a direct relationship between income from capital
and the value of that capital. Only if the assumption of profit maximiza-

---

[3] *Permanent income* means income averaged over a number of years. In some
economic analysis, it refers to lifetime average income. For most purposes, however, averaging over three to five years is usually sufficient to remove the major
transitory components of current income.

tion does not apply is there leeway for the full shifting of the tax that is implicit in the traditional analysis. Table 5 suggests that the scope for such behavior is limited to industrial and commercial property, state-assessed property, and residential rental property.

For commercial and industrial firms, the traditional hypothesis of forward shifting to consumers implies that instead of profit maximizing, the firms follow a policy of administered pricing in which the property tax is considered a cost. Because administered pricing requires a substantial degree of market power or implicit collusion, the amount of shifting of the tax on commercial and industrial property is likely to be quite limited and for various reasons may be expected to be less than in the case of the corporate income tax. Thus, there is a better case for distributing the tax on business realty and personalty in line with capital income than there is for distributing it in line with general consumption expenditures. Because capital income rises as a share of income, the incidence of this component of the property tax thus becomes progressive.

There is a stronger possibility of forward shifting in the case of state-assessed property, composed in large part of public utilities, because price commissions generally include taxes as a cost to be included in the price charged to consumers. However, this applies to only about 8 per cent of the total property-tax base.

With respect to property taxes on residential rental property, which also accounts for about 8 per cent of the total property-tax base, a case can be made for forward shifting in some situations, especially where rent-control administrators allow rents to increase as costs, including taxes, increase. In other situations, collusive or oligopolistic behavior in urban rental markets may also lead to some short-run shifting. Rising property-tax rates may then be used as a signal for landlords to raise rents simultaneously without the fear of a substantial decrease in rental demand that each landlord might expect if he raised his rents unilaterally.

The major modification that these considerations suggest is that the tax on commercial and industrial property should be distributed in line with income from capital rather than on the basis of consumption expenditures; whereas taxes on residential structures should still be distributed in line with housing expenditures. The resulting distribution of the property-tax burden is shown in column 2 of Table 6. Although the tax is still regressive in the low-income range, it now becomes progressive in the higher ranges, in contrast with the distribution in column 1, which is regressive throughout.

In both column 2 and column 1, taxes on owner-occupied housing are assumed to be borne by the homeowners. This, by itself, means that 39 per cent of the total property-tax revenue is distributed regressively in terms of current-income classes because cross-sectional studies show that expenditures on owner-occupied housing decline as a per cent of income as incomes rise. In view of the fact that homeowners can deduct property-tax payments in calculating their federal income-tax liability, this regressivity is intensified. Because the value of the deduction depends on the marginal tax bracket of the homeowner, the net property tax on owner-occupied housing becomes more regressive than is allowed for by the data in Table 6. Assuming that the federal government wishes to continue subsidizing homeowners, these undesirable distributional side effects might be avoided by giving tax credits that would not vary in amount with the marginal tax bracket of homeowners, rather than by allowing deductions.

The applicability of cross-sectional expenditure data based on current-income classes is open to question. Expenditures on durable goods, especially owner-occupied housing, may well be governed more by expectations of normal or permanent income than by current income, with its transitory components. Both Richard Muth and Margaret Reid have found permanent-income elasticities of housing expenditures to be significantly greater than one, thus suggesting that the tax burden on owner-occupied residential property may be progressive in terms of the more meaningful permanent-income concept.[4]

This consideration, especially in connection with the argument that the tax on commercial and industrial property is borne by the owners of business, suggests that except perhaps for the taxes on residential

---

[4] Richard Muth, "The Demand for Non-Farm Housing," in *The Demand for Durable Goods,* ed. by Arnold C. Harberger et al. (Chicago: University of Chicago Press, 1960); and Margaret G. Reid, *Housing and Income* (Chicago: University of Chicago Press, 1962). For a summary, review, and criticism of the studies by Muth and Reid, see Frank DeLeeuw, "The Demand for Housing, a Review of Cross-Section Evidence," *Review of Economics and Statistics* 53 (February 1971): 1–10. In reviewing much of the empirical work that has been done, he, too, concludes that the income elasticity of demand for owner-occupied housing is greater than one. It should be pointed out, however, that this conclusion has been verified for the middle-income range only. If better data were available, it would be desirable to test the hypothesis for very low permanent-income and very high permanent-income groups as well.

rental property and state-assessed public utilities, the income-distribu-tional implications of the property tax are not so adverse as is tradi-tionally assumed.

The perfect-markets approach. Recent developments in tax-in-cidence theory have suggested that in a world of flexible capital markets and perfect competition, the property tax, looked at from a national point of view, should be analyzed in a general equilibrium framework as a tax on capital income, the implication of which is that its incidence will be similar to that of a profits tax.[5] This approach will be considered here first on the assumption of a comprehensive and national tax and then on the assumption of exclusions and differentiation by jurisdiction.

Nationwide uniform-rate tax. Provided that the tax applies equally to all forms of land and capital, its burden in the short run, when the stock of capital is fixed, will fall on the owners of property at the time the tax is introduced (or raised). The incidence in the long run, when the capital stock may be changed, will depend on the elasticity of savings with respect to the net rate of return on investment. To the extent that there is some responsiveness of savings to the property-tax rate, the burden of the portion of the tax on man-made capital will fall in part on other factors because a smaller capital stock will reduce the rate of return to other factors. Without much evidence in favor of a high responsiveness of savings to the net rate of return on capital, it seems safe to conclude that even in the long run, the distribution of the burden of a general tax on property would be essentially in line with property ownership. Because the value of property reflects the capital-ized value of property income, this distribution would be similar to that of a tax on property income.

The implication of this can be seen in column 3 of Table 6, where total property-tax revenue is distributed in line with income from property wealth. The burden is distributed progressively except at the lower end of the income scale, where it remains regressive be-cause a sizable number of low-income families, particularly the aged,

---

[5] See, specifically, Arnold C. Harberger, "The Incidence of the Corporation In-come Tax," *Journal of Political Economy* 70 (June 1962): 215–40; Peter Miesz-kowski, "On the Theory of Tax Incidence," *Journal of Political Economy* 75 (June 1967): 250–62; *idem,* "Tax Incidence Theory," *Journal of Economic Literature* 7 (December 1969): 1103–24; and *idem,* "The Property Tax: An Excise Tax or a Profits Tax?" *Journal of Public Economics* 1 (April 1972): 73–96.

receive a substantial share of their income in the form of capital income as opposed to wage or salary income. This picture is repeated in Table 7, where the data from columns 1 and 3 of Table 6 are restated on the basis of more recent and satisfactory data.[6] As can be seen most

Table 7. Incidence of the Property Tax, 1972

| | Property Taxes as per cent of income assuming that tax on improvements is borne by | |
Income Class[a]	Renters and Consumers[b] (1)	Capital[c] (2)
Under $3,000	13.0	7.2
$3,000–$5,000	8.0	5.4
$5,000–$10,000	5.9	3.6
$10,000–$15,000	4.9	2.6
$15,000–$20,000	4.7	2.9
$20,000–$25,000	4.4	3.7
$25,000–$50,000	4.4	5.7
$50,000–$100,000	3.7	14.1
$100,000–$500,000	3.5	22.4
$500,000–$1,000,000	3.0	24.5
$1,000,000 and over	2.1	18.2
All classes	5.0	5.0

[a]Income is equal to the sum of adjusted gross income, transfer payments, state and local government bond interest, and excluded realized long-term capital gains.

[b]It is assumed that the tax on land falls on the landowner, that the tax on owner-occupied houses falls on the homeowner, that the tax on apartments rests on tenants, and that the tax on commercial and industrial is borne by the consumer in line with general consumption expenditures.

[c]All property taxes other than levies on nonfarm motor vehicles and agricultural property were distributed among families on the basis of total property income; the tax on cars was distributed using the value of cars owned by the family; and agricultural taxes were distributed on the basis of gross farm value.

Note: The table is based on the Brookings MERGE File of 30,000 family units for the year 1966, with incomes projected to the 1972 level.

Source: Adapted from Charles L. Schultze et al., *Setting National Priorities: The 1973 Budget* (Washington, D.C.: The Brookings Institution, © 1972), p. 445.

---

[6] Table 6 is derived from a 1961 Tax Foundation study; Table 7 is based on the Brookings tax file, with incomes projected to the 1972 level. No comparison can be made of the absolute per cent calculated because the definitions of income differ in the two tables. Table 7 is more satisfactory than Table 6 in that it employs a more comprehensive definition of income, covers a wider range of incomes, and is more up to date. Table 6 has been included because the data provided in the Tax

clearly in column 2 of Table 7, the major effect of interpreting the property tax as a tax on capital income is to increase the progressivity in the higher-income classes substantially.

Thus, as long as the tax is a general tax applied uniformly to all land and capital and as long as the assumption of perfect markets approximates the real world, the burden of the property tax is essentially progressive.

Is the property tax a partial tax? This conclusion will be modified only slightly if the fact that the property tax does not apply uniformly to all forms of land and capital is taken into consideration. This section examines a nationwide property tax that does not include all capital in its base. (For a discussion of nonuniformity resulting from local differentials, see the section "Local differences in tax rates." (With plant and structures generally covered by the property tax, the question arises whether business machinery and inventory (usually referred to as business personalty) are covered to the same extent. The data in Table 5 indicates that business personalty (including agricultural) accounts for only 10 per cent of the total assessed tax base, or approximately $48 billion. A comparison of this assessed value with an estimate of total producer durables and inventories of $464 billion in 1966 suggests that only a fraction of business personalty is covered, even if the fact that business personalty may be assessed at only part of its market value is taken into consideration.[7] This conclusion is reinforced by the knowledge that four states (New York, Pennsylvania, Hawaii and Delaware) exempt business personalty completely and that many of the remaining states provide partial exemptions for business personalty. Although exemptions are applied to other types of property as well, especially to owner-occupied housing in some of the southern states, the general assumption is that real property in the form of land and structures is more fully taxable than personalty.[8]

Foundation study, which in turn is based on the Bureau of Labor Statistics Survey of Consumer Expenditures, 1960–61, makes it possible to calculate the burden under alternative assumptions.

[7] The source for the 1966 estimate is *Institutional Investor Study: Report of the Securities and Exchange Commission,* supplementary vol. 1, 92d Cong., 1st Sess., H. Doc. 92–64 (1971), pt. 6, app. 1, p. 281. The figures in 1958 dollars were adjusted to 1966 dollars by using the relevant GNP price deflators.

[8] Note that the incomplete coverage of the property tax differs from that of the corporation income tax in that the property tax discriminates between the types of

The effect of this somewhat partial nature of the property tax is probably minor. Even if no substitutability between realty and personalty in production is assumed, the main impact of the tax will still be to reduce rates of return equally on all forms of capital in a world of perfect capital markets because capital will flow from the more heavily taxed realty-intensive sectors of the economy to the less heavily taxed personalty-intensive sectors until after tax rates of return are equalized.[9] This may, however, cause some additional excise or price effects as resources are shifted out of one sector into another. In consequence, the prices of realty-intensive goods will rise, and other prices will fall, resulting in gains to some consumers and losses to others. Only to the extent that realty-intensive goods occupy a larger part of the budgets of low-income families, relative to high-income families, will there be a minor regressive impact from the uses-of-income point of view, which would modify slightly the burden distribution given in column 3 of Table 6 and column 2 of Table 7.[10]

Local differentials in tax rates. Clearly, the American property tax is not a uniform-rate nationwide tax. In fact, it is administered by over 70,000 taxing jurisdictions, each with its own definition of taxable property, assessment ratios, and nominal rates. Tax-rate differentials across communities in metropolitan areas are primarily a function of the interaction between consumer preferences for public goods and the tax-

---

capital; whereas the corporation income tax discriminates between forms of business organization.

The exclusion of intangibles from the property-tax base should also be noted. This does not matter to the extent that intangibles are claims to real assets. In the case of a personal net-worth tax as opposed to an *in rem* property tax, however, the structure of claims would need to be considered.

[9] This is equivalent to Arnold C. Harberger's analysis of the incidence of the corporation income tax. Although it is true that the total burden of a partial (as opposed to a general) tax on capital may not fall completely on capital, the fact that the housing sector is very capital-intensive without much factor substitutability suggests that most of the burden will in fact fall on the owners of capital. For a precise formulation, see Harberger, "The Incidence of the Corporation Income Tax."

[10] This discussion examines only the distributional implications of incomplete property taxation. Although the partial nature of the tax suggests excess burden or efficiency problems of the type discussed in "Is Housing Overtaxed?" it should be pointed out that attempts to tax business personalty, especially at the local level, also give rise to inefficiencies caused by efforts to avoid the tax. These administrative difficulties have generally led experts to argue against including business personalty in the property-tax base.

able capacity of the community. (This is discussed in detail in "Implications for Local Public Finance.")

This interaction between benefit levels and tax-rate differentials makes it difficult to analyze the incidence implications of differential tax rates without also bringing in expenditure-level considerations. For the moment, however, let us abstract from benefit differentials across communities.[11] In addition, it is assumed first that there are no non-tax-related location advantages for firms. In the long run, capital will then move among jurisdictions in a way that will yield higher gross rates of return in the high-tax-rate communities than in the low-rate communities. This in turn tends to raise the prices of local outputs, including those of housing services, and to lower the return to immobile or relatively immobile local factors of production in the high-rate communities. Analogously, low-tax-rate communities will experience lower-than-average output prices in relation to wages and land rents because of a lower-than-average required gross rate of return on capital.

After the adjustment is completed, consumers and workers in high-tax areas will be relatively worse off than consumers and workers in low-tax areas.[12] As a group, consumers and workers will not be burdened, however, because although some suffer lower real wages from working and consuming in high-tax areas, others gain through higher real wages from working and consuming in low-tax areas. This does not mean that these effects must be distributionally neutral. Large cities tend to have higher tax rates than suburban communities.[13] Thus, to the extent that there is a greater concentration of low-income tenants and workers in the central cities than in the suburbs, the tax-rate differentials may impose some regressivity, primarily because low-income families tend to be less mobile in response to tax-rate differentials than high-income families and are therefore less able to migrate from the high-rate cities than high-income families are.

Two qualifications are necessary to this argument, however.

---

[11] This follows Mieszkowski, "The Property Tax: An Excise Tax or a Profits Tax?"

[12] They will not bear the full effect of the tax-rate differentials, however, because part of the effect will be shifted backward to the owners of land. The effect of these differential capital-tax rates on landowners as a class will wash out in the aggregate because landowners in low-tax towns will gain, but landowners in high-tax towns will lose.

[13] See Appendix A for data pertaining to central-city and suburban tax rates.

First, it is necessary to allow for the fact that tax-related considerations are only one factor in location decisions. Given the strong advantages of being located in a central city, for instance, higher tax rates need not induce an outflow of capital. Instead, the higher tax liabilities may be absorbed out of location rents. Second, no capital flow will occur where a higher tax rate is the result of higher benefit levels in the form of municipal services for firms.

In summary, the implications for incidence of tax-rate differentials across communities are somewhat inconclusive. They do not appear to modify significantly the previous conclusion that the incidence of the property tax should be considered as similar to that of a uniform national tax on property income and, therefore, should be allocated in line with the distribution of income from wealth.

Property-tax relief for low-income families. Although the property tax is generally progressive, it may still impose significant burdens on low-income families. This may be the case either because of imperfections in the rental-housing market or because of the large concentration of retired people who have low incomes and who own their own homes. These burdens could be reduced by the adoption of credits against state income taxes for low-income families.

The case for sweeping property-tax exemptions of the homestead variety is weak. Such exemptions substantially reduce the local tax base, furnish a hidden subsidy that should be evaluated in comparison with other expenditures, and increase the administrative burden of the property tax.[14] These considerations are much less applicable to the type of property-tax relief now being offered to low-income elderly families in several states including Wisconsin, Minnesota, and Vermont. Under the circuit-breaker plan, elderly low-income homeowners and renters can claim a credit or receive a rebate against their state income-tax liability if they pay an excessive amount of property tax. Unlike the homestead exemptions introduced in the 1930s, which were given to all homeowners regardless of income, this new form of relief deals directly with the low-income problem by having an upper-income limit and by including low-income renters as well as homeowners.[15]

---

[14] For a complete presentation and evaluation of different types of exemptions, see Advisory Commission on Intergovernmental Relations, *The Role of the States in Strengthening the Property Tax* (Washington, D.C.: U.S. Government Printing Office, 1963), vol. 1, chap. 8.

[15] For renters, a given per cent of gross rent is assumed to constitute the property

Various methods are possible to determine whether excessive property taxes have been paid, and varying per cents of that excessive burden, depending on income level, may be relieved.[16] Justification for such relief depends, of course, on the view of where the final burden of the tax comes to rest; but provided that the relief is limited to those who are indeed impoverished, it may not be objectionable even if it errs on the generous side.

A major advantage of this approach, given local property taxes, is that it does not reduce the local tax base because credits or rebates would be at the expense of the state government. Since it is generally accepted that redistribution of income should be accomplished at as high a level of government as possible, it might even be desirable to have the federal government (rather than the state governments) eventually bear the burden of such property-tax relief.[17]

Who would benefit from property-tax reduction? The discussion of who pays the property tax has direct implications for the question of who would gain from property-tax reduction. Consider first a reduction in a hypothetical national tax, which is the same as an across-the-board reduction in all local taxes. If the property tax is viewed as a tax on capital in perfectly competitive markets, the answer is unambiguously that property owners would benefit from a nationwide reduction in the property tax because the after-tax rate of return on property would rise with the reduction of the tax. The distributional implication would be to render the tax structure less progressive.

Even if perfect markets are not the rule, as is perhaps the case with residential rental property, this does not imply that renters would reap the benefits of a reduction in property taxes even though they may currently bear part of the burden. There is nothing compelling in the theory to suggest that landlords who have shifted the burden of

---

tax paid, the assumption being that landlords fully shift the tax forward to tenants in the short run.

[16] For an analysis of the Wisconsin plan, see Kenneth E. Quindry and Billy D. Cook, "Humanization of the Property Tax," *National Tax Journal* 22 (September 1969): 357–67.

[17] A possible drawback to the scheme is that many people eligible for relief will not be paying any income taxes and, therefore, would be eligible for a rebate rather than a credit against their tax liability. It is unclear how many of them would actually apply for the rebate.

property taxes forward to tenants through some form of administered pricing would lower rents when those taxes were reduced.

The situation differs if property taxes are lowered in just one community or city relative to another. At the time of the tax reduction, local property owners would benefit because the lower taxes would be capitalized in the form of higher prices that potential buyers would be willing to pay for property in that community. In the longer run, residents and consumers of locally produced goods might benefit as a result of the capital inflow induced by the lower tax rates. At the same time, however, residents and consumers of capital losing jurisdictions might lose. The distributional implications will differ depending on whether the tax-reducing jurisdiction is a high- or a low-income community. Again, it is necessary to note that changes in property-tax rates in any particular jurisdiction are likely to be accompanied by changes in expenditure levels and that the distributional effects of benefit changes must also be allowed for.

Is Housing Overtaxed?

In this section, the discussion will focus on the effects of the property tax on resource allocation, rather than on its distributional implications. The question to be considered is whether housing is taxed less or more severely than other forms of investment or consumption, so that resource allocation to housing exceeds or falls short of what it would be under neutral tax treatment. For this purpose, the property tax must be considered as part of the whole tax structure, rather than as an isolated tax.

Homeowners as investors. The focus of this discussion is owner-occupied housing, but rental housing will also be considered briefly. The nature of homeownership is such that homeowners are both investors in housing capital and consumers of housing services. On the one hand, the homeowner can be thought of as making a portfolio decision between investing more heavily in his home and investing in other nonhousing forms of capital, the major difference between housing and nonhousing investment being that housing investment carries an imputed return which must be consumed in the form of owner-occupied housing services but that nonhousing investment carries a return which is usually in the form of money income not tied to any particular use. On the other hand, the homeowner can be analyzed in his role as a consumer, in which his problem is to allocate current income between owner-occupied housing and other types of consumption. It is necessary to consider the homeowner from both points of view in order to give a complete picture of the allocative effects of the average property tax on owner-occupied housing.[18]

Relative tax burden on home investment. If homeowners are considered as investors in housing capital, homeownership is discriminated against when the tax rate on imputed income from housing is greater than the tax rate on other forms of investment income. Underlying this definition of discrimination is the implicit assumption that investors equalize net after-tax rates of return adjusted for risk on all types of investment. This means that relative to a situation in which all sectors of the economy were taxed *equally*, too few resources would be allocated to the more highly taxed sector because of the higher-than-average required gross rate of return. If, on the other hand, it is found that the return from housing capital is less heavily taxed than other capital income, then the implication is that housing is favored in the sense that there is an overallocation of resources to that sector.

For purposes of this analysis, it is thus necessary to return to the model of perfect capital markets used in the section "The perfect markets approach" in the incidence discussion. The assumption that risk-adjusted after-tax net rates of return are equalized at the margin is a very demanding one in that it requires a long-run adjustment period and perfect capital markets throughout the economy. Although generally used in recent models of capital-income taxation,[19] this assumption is

---

[18] For the investment approach, see Leonard Rosenberg, "Taxation of Income from Capital, by Industry Group," in *Taxation of Income from Capital,* ed. by Arnold C. Harberger and Martin J. Bailey (Washington, D.C.: The Brookings Institution, 1969); for the consumption approach, see Netzer, *Economics of the Property Tax,* p. 30. Both David Laidler, "Income Tax Incentives for Owner-Occupied Housing," in *Taxation of Income from Capital,* p. 27, and Henry Aaron, "Income Taxes and Housing," *American Economic Review* (December 1970): 789–806, deal with the investment-consumption issue with respect to housing, although not specifically with respect to the property tax.

[19] See, in particular, Harberger, "The Incidence of the Corporation Income Tax"; Mieszkowski, "The Property Tax: An Excise Tax or a Profits Tax?"; and Rosenberg, "Taxation of Income from Capital, by Industry Group."

particularly questionable with respect to owner-occupied housing because of the long life of the existing housing stock and the fact that
homeowners are responding to imputed (as opposed to monetary) returns. Without such an assumption, however, a general equilibrium approach is not manageable and calls for complexities far beyond the
realm of this chapter. It is fortunate, therefore, that in spite of existing
imperfections, capital markets are sufficiently close to the competitive
model to make these results of practical interest.

As a first approximation of whether homeowners are discriminated against in their role as investors in housing capital, the personal
income tax is disregarded, and it is assumed that there are only two taxes
in the economy: the 48 per cent corporation income tax and the property tax on owner-occupied housing at the current average rate for the
United States.[20]

The first task is to calculate the relevant tax rate in the housing
sector. Expressed as a per cent of the market value of single-family
homes, the tax is estimated to be 1.8 per cent in 1969 on the basis of
an estimated $11.9 billion paid in property taxes on single-family homes
and an estimated total value of those structures of $674 billion.[21]

In order to compare this rate with the rate of tax on corporate
shares, however, it is necessary to translate it from a capital tax to a

---

[20] This is similar to the approach taken by Leonard Rosenberg in that he also
ignores the personal income tax. It differs in that his study is empirical and includes a much finer breakdown of the economy, whereas the approach here is
more analytical and consequently is more simplified and abstract. The advantages
of this approach are that it bypasses the many difficult data problems Rosenberg
encountered (such as having to separate the Commerce Department real estate
figures into residential and all other) and more easily allows for the inclusion of
the personal income tax.

[21] Total taxes paid on single-family homes were estimated by multiplying total
(both state and local) property-tax collections of $30.7 billion in 1969 by 39 per
cent, which is the per cent of the total tax base accounted for by single-family
residential structures. An implicit assumption in this method is that the same
nominal tax rates apply for different types of property. In order to derive the
total value of single-family residential structures, the 1967 assessed value for that
category ($197 billion) was raised to a market value by dividing by the average
assessment-sales ratio for that category (.345) to reach a 1966 market value of
$571 billion. This was then raised to $674 billion for 1969 by multiplying by
1.18 the 1966–1969 increase in the GNP price deflator for residential structures.
This final figure is slightly biased downward because it takes no account of new
structures built between 1966 and 1969. All data (except the price deflator) are
from U.S. Bureau of the Census, *1967 Census of Governments* (1968), vol. 2:
Taxable Property Values, pp. 2, 7 and Tables 9, 11.

capital income tax. If it is assumed that the investor requires an after-tax imputed annual return of 5 per cent to induce him to invest in housing, the tax rate on the imputed income from housing can be calculated as:

$$\frac{\text{Property tax}}{\substack{\text{Imputed income} \\ \text{gross of property} \\ \text{tax}}} = \frac{\text{Property tax}}{\text{value }(0.05) + \text{property tax}}$$

$$= \frac{\text{Property tax}}{\text{value }(0.05 + 0.018)} = 26\%$$

The property tax has been included in the base to make the rate comparable with the other taxes on capital income that are generally expressed as a per cent of capital income gross of taxes.[22] It should be noted that under certain assumptions consistent with this analysis, it makes no difference to the calculated tax rate to what extent homeowners own their homes outright or have mortgaged them to banks or other lending institutions.[23]

Now consider the investor's choice of investing in a larger house versus investing in corporate equity. The tax rate per dollar of income earned on corporate equity is 48 per cent because, by assumption, the corporate-profits tax is the only tax affecting that sector.[24] Again, assuming perfect capital markets, it makes no difference to the calculated

---

[22] The choice of the 5 per cent after-tax rate of return is somewhat arbitrary, yet it obviously affects the results. It was chosen on the basis of work done by Henry Aaron, who uses a 4 per cent and a 6 per cent imputed net return but prefers the 4 per cent for his 1966 study, "Income Taxes and Housing," and work done by David Laidler, who uses the 6 per cent rate in "Income Tax Incentives for Owner-Occupied Housing." Since it is also used as the mortgage-interest rate (see note 22), it is most likely to be downward-biased, which would lower effective tax rates throughout the analysis, thus strengthening the argument.

[23] The basic assumption required is that the mortgage-interest rate is the same as the after-tax required rate of return on the equity portion alone, in this case 5 per cent. The reader is reminded that personal-income-tax considerations have not yet been introduced.

[24] For this conclusion to be valid, it must be assumed, in line with traditional microeconomic theory, that the corporate-profits tax is not shifted either forward to consumers or backward to other factors in the short run. See Marian Krzyzaniak and Richard A. Musgrave, *The Shifting of the Corporation Income Tax* (Baltimore, Md.: Johns Hopkins Press, 1963), for an alternative view. Their empirical result implies an administered-pricing policy on the part of corporate firms, in contrast with the profit-maximization assumption implicit in the present analysis.

[25] Rosenberg, "Taxation of Income from Capital, by Industry Group," Table 14, pp. 174–77.

tax rate whether the investor buys the corporate shares outright or on margin. From this, it can be concluded that the homeowner is under-taxed on his investment in housing capital relative to his investment in corporate equity because the 26 per cent tax rate on imputed income from housing is substantially below the 48 per cent corporate rate.

In order to make the analysis more realistic, the property tax paid on the return to corporate equity should also be included. Assuming, on the basis of data presented by Rosenberg,[25] that this rate is approximately 15 per cent, and allowing for the fact that property taxes are deducted before the corporate income tax is applied, the total tax on gross income from corporate equity is about 55 per cent, or 0.15 + 0.48 (1 − 0.15), even before adjustment for the personal income tax.

The addition of the provisions of the federal personal income tax further strengthens the argument that on the average, investment in homeownership is undertaxed relative to other forms of investment. In general, the income tax raises the total tax rate on investment income; but in the case of housing income, it does just the reverse. This happens because imputed income from housing services is not taxed; whereas homeowners are allowed to deduct both their property-tax and their mortgage-interest payments from taxable income derived from other sources.[26] Assuming that all homeowners use the option of itemizing deductions, that 40 per cent of the total value of single-family owner-occupied homes is mortgaged, that the mortgage-interest rate is 5 per cent, and that the average marginal personal tax rate for homeowners is 23 per cent, the combined income- and property-tax rate on income from investment in housing may be calculated as follows:[27]

---

[26] At the same time, introduction of the income tax raises the homeowner's total tax liability if the tax bill on his total income including income from other sources is considered.

[27] The assumption that 60 per cent of the total value of owner-occupied housing is not mortgaged is based on 1962 data in Dorothy S. Projector and Gertrude S. Weiss, *Survey of Financial Characteristics of Consumers* (Washington, D.C.: Board of Governors of the Federal Reserve System, 1966), and on more recent data in George Katona et al., *1969 Survey of Consumer Finances* (Ann Arbor, Mich.: University of Michigan, 1970). The average marginal tax rate for homeowners is a weighted average of marginal tax rates, weighted by the per cent of the value of real estate tax deductions in each adjusted gross income class for all itemized individual tax returns in 1968. The marginal tax rates for each AGI class were calculated for joint returns of husbands and wives.

$$\frac{\text{Property tax} + \text{income tax}}{\text{Value} (0.05) + \text{property tax} + \text{income tax}}$$

$$= \frac{\text{property tax} - 0.23 \, (\text{property tax} + I_m)}{\text{value} (0.05) + (\text{property tax} - 0.23 \, \text{property tax} - 0.23 \, I_m)} = 15\%$$

where I_m = mortgage-interest payments = 0.4 (0.05) value

Since the income-tax component is negative, the combined rate of 15 per cent falls short of the rate of 26 per cent applicable if the income tax is not considered.

In contrast, the addition of personal-income-tax considerations raises the relevant tax rate on the return to corporate equity (ignoring the property tax on corporate equity) from t_c to $t_c + d(1 - t_c)t_p$, where t_c is the corporate tax rate, d is the dividend-payout ratio, and t is the average marginal personal tax rate. If t_c equals 0.48, t_p equals 0.23, and d equals 0.5, the tax rate on income from this source is approximately 54 per cent. In order to take account of the property tax on corporate equity as well, t_c must be reinterpreted as the corporate income-tax rate plus the property-tax rate of approximately 15 per cent. This raises the total tax on corporate equity to about 61 per cent, or more than four times the rate on income from homeownership.[28]

Thus, it is clearly demonstrated that on the average, homeowners are not discriminated against in their role as investors in housing capital vis-à-vis investment in corporate equity. This conclusion also holds for alternative forms of investment. Rosenberg has calculated that the average rate of tax on income from capital, ignoring the personal income

---

[28] It would be even higher if the effect of retained earnings on the price of the stock and, therefore, on capital gains that are taxable were considered. Another consideration that affects the rate in the other direction is the possibility of buying stock on margin. If i equals the required gross of corporate income-tax rate of return on corporate equity E_c, x equals the fraction of corporate equity bought on margin, and d equals 1, then, allowing for interest deductibility, the tax rate can be calculated as follows:

$$t = \frac{[t_c + (1 - t_c)t]iE_c - (1 - t_c)xiE_c t_p}{iE_c} = [t_c + (1 - t_c)t_p] - (1 - t_c)xt_p$$

Given that in 1969 only 1 per cent of the total corporate stock outstanding was purchased on margin, so that x equals 0.01, the downward adjustment required by the second term is inconsequential.

tax, for the economy as a whole is 37.3 per cent.[29] If this is adjusted upward by the average marginal personal income-tax rate of 23 per cent for homeowners, the average rate is approximately 45 per cent, or three times the rate on homeownership.

Significance of preferential treatment of home investment. The finding that homeowners as investors are not discriminated against but, rather, are given favorable treatment implies that from an efficiency point of view, there is an overallocation of resources to the owner-occupied-housing sector. It can be roughly calculated that this overinvestment is of the order of $150 billion, which is substantial in relation to the estimated existing value of the housing stock of $674 billion.[30]

The efficiency or welfare loss of this misallocation can be calculated, following Harberger's methodology, to be about $1.5 billion.[31] In other words, if the income from owner-occupied housing were taxed at the same rate as other income from capital, there would be a resource-cost saving or welfare gain of well over $1 billion. This figure is much smaller than the total overallocation of resources to housing because the resources that would be released from the housing sector with the shift to a neutral tax system would be used in other sectors. The welfare gain from such a shift is derived from the fact that the gross rate of return is

---

[29] Rosenberg, "Taxation of Income from Capital, by Industry Group," p. 174.

[30] The estimate of the overinvestment in the housing sector and of the efficiency loss discussed in the following paragraph is based on the methodology of Arnold C. Harberger in "Efficiency Effects of Taxes on Income from Capital," in *Effects of the Corporation Income Tax,* ed. by Marian Krzyzaniak (Detroit, Mich.: Wayne State University Press, 1966), particularly pp. 114–115. The estimates vary depending on the assumed elasticity of substitution in the housing sector and in the rest of the economy. Although a variety of assumptions were tried, the preferred assumptions were that the elasticity of substitution was 0 in the housing sector and that the elasticity of substitution in the rest of the economy was −½ or −1. For all the estimates, it was assumed that the elasticity between the products of the two sectors was −1. In order to use Harberger's framework, it was necessary to calculate the difference between the tax rate in the housing sector and the average tax rate on income from capital in the economy as a whole, where taxes include corporate income taxes, property taxes, and income taxes. The tax rate in the housing sector was assumed to be the 15 per cent derived from the calculations in the text. The average tax rate for the economy as a whole was estimated to be 45 per cent by adjusting upward Rosenberg's calculations of the average rate of taxation on income from capital for the effect of the personal income tax (Rosenberg, "Taxation of Income from Capital, by Industry Group," p. 174).

[31] See note 30.

presently higher in those other sectors and that, therefore, the shift in resources would increase overall productivity.

At the same time, it should be noted that this view of the matter reflects only the private valuation of housing benefits. To the extent that there are social as well as private benefits from homeownership, such as the encouragement of a more stable society, not all this would be considered a misallocation of resources. But it is unlikely that the social benefits would be large enough to negate the conclusion that the present tax system causes an economically excessive amount of resources to be used in owner-occupied housing.

Is the efficiency loss a result of the property tax? As is well known, the corporation income tax by itself creates an efficiency loss because of its exclusion of the unincorporated sector. This preferential treatment of the unincorporated sector is compounded by the failure to tax the imputed return on owner-occupied housing under the personal income tax. The property tax, on the other hand, assuming it to be national and general, does not create an excess burden of the kind that results from partial taxation. Even property-tax deductibility from the income-tax base does not greatly affect the overall excess burden because it applies across the board to all payers of the property tax.[32] Therefore, it can be concluded that the efficiency loss which results from the undertaxation of housing is a matter not of property taxation but rather of the combined impact of the provisions of the corporation income tax and the personal income tax that affect housing. Thus, a general property tax by itself does not cause an efficiency loss, and a property tax that taxes residential property at a higher rate than corporate property would tend to offset in part the efficiency loss caused by the overtaxation of the corporate sector. On the other hand, a property tax that excluded residential property completely (which has sometimes been proposed) would compound the efficiency loss resulting from the undertaxation of the housing sector.

Homeowners as consumers of housing services. Implicit in these calculations of the overinvestment in owner-occupied housing is the fact that the price of services for owner-occupied housing is *lower* than it

---

[32] There are some allocation effects by tax-bracket class, however, because deductibility from the income-tax base benefits high-bracket taxpayers more than low-bracket taxpayers.

would be if all income from capital were taxed at the same rate.[33] Thus, the consumer of housing services, instead of being taxed on his consumption, as is usually assumed by critics of the property tax, is in fact being subsidized. This means that as consumers of housing services, homeowners receive a net benefit from the present tax structure.

This analysis of the effect of the tax on imputed income from housing has been based on the assumption that there were no other distortions beyond taxes on capital income in the economy. In fact, there are also taxes that apply directly to the consumption of goods and services, for example, sales and excise taxes. If all such taxes applied equally to all forms of consumption, including the consumption of housing services, then there would be no resource-allocation effects in addition to those already discussed.

But state and local sales taxes and excise taxes on items such as cigarettes and gasoline do not in general apply to the consumption of housing services. Only insofar as they apply to such items as goods used for housing maintenance and repair, which represent only a minor fraction of housing outlays, do they apply to housing services at all.[34] This introduces another distortion in favor of consumers of owner-occupied housing by increasing the size of the wedge between the price paid for housing services and the prices, gross of excise taxes, paid for other goods and services. The effect of this is to increase the overallocation of resources to the housing sector beyond the $150 billion already cal-

---

[33] The exact amount of relative price reduction is difficult to calculate, however, because it depends on the supply and demand elasticities in the different sectors, which in turn depend on the elasticities of substitution in production and consumption.

[34] From the homeowner's point of view, the value of annual housing services can be expressed in the following form:

$$GR = NR + I_m + M + D + T$$

where GR is gross rental services; NR, the imputed net return on equity invested in the house; I_m, mortgage-interest payments; M, maintenance expenditures; D, depreciation; and T, annual property taxes paid. Because there is no direct sales tax on GR, the only way current sales taxes can affect GR is through its components. It might be argued, however, that to the extent that excise taxes were applied in the past to the materials used in the construction of the housing stock currently yielding housing services, housing services are in fact subject to excise taxes. But this type of reasoning requires an analysis of the effects of excise taxes on capital goods used in other sectors as well and as such yields no unambiguous conclusion.

culated and to increase the implicit welfare loss or excess burden associated with that overinvestment in housing.

In summary, the quantity of resources allocated to the housing sector is greater than it would be under a neutral tax system for two reasons: the undertaxation of income from capital invested in housing and the lower relative price resulting from the existence of sales and excise taxes on nonhousing goods and services. It has been shown that this misallocation of resources causes a sizable excess burden or efficiency loss. To the extent that this tax subsidy is the result of a conscious societal judgment that housing deserves to be subsidized, however, only part of the overallocation calculated here can be interpreted as a welfare loss from society's point of view.[35]

Rental housing. Finally, the perfect markets model may be extended to the analysis of rental housing. Assuming again that all markets including the rental-housing market are perfectly competitive, there can be no short-run shifting of the tax to tenants. To the extent that this basic assumption is invalid, the conclusions derived here would need to be modified.

Again, it is necessary to compare tax rates without allowance for the personal income tax. As long as the tax rate on income from residential rental property is the same as that on owner-occupied property, about 26 per cent, rental property is undertaxed relative to income from other forms of capital that pay an average rate of 37.3 per cent.[36] The reason for this difference is the fact that other forms of capital income are subject to both property and corporate-profits taxes, but rental housing is subject to the property tax only. The personal income tax does not bestow the same preferential treatment on rental housing as it does on owner-occupied housing because no imputed rent can be excluded; therefore, inclusion of the personal income tax now has no major additional impact on the relative rate of taxation of income from rental housing vis-à-vis income from other nonhousing forms of investment.[37]

---

[35] It should be noted that this analysis deals exclusively with the tax system. The analysis could be broadened to include the effects of other indirect subsidies to housing such as mortgage insurance on the one hand and the effects of tight monetary policy on the other.

[36] See p. 62.

[37] One tax break for rental housing ignored in this analysis is the possibility of depreciating rental property for tax purposes at rates in excess of true economic

The relative undertaxation of investment in rental housing again means that there will be an overallocation of resources to rental housing as compared with a neutral tax system. This, in turn, implies that rents will be lower than they would otherwise be. To the extent that rents are lower, the renter, as a consumer of housing services, receives a subsidy and is, therefore, better off under the present structure of taxes than he would be under a system that taxed all income from capital at the same rate. As before, the overallocation of resources to rental housing results in an efficiency loss. In addition, however, there is a distortion in allocation in favor of owner-occupied housing, as opposed to rental housing, because of the favorable income-tax treatment of homeowners.

Implications for Local Public Finance

Tax-base differentials. As a local tax, the property tax is charac-terized by a high degree of diversity, both in the level of the per capita tax base and in the level of tax rates. This diversity holds across states and especially across communities within states. In this section, these differentials are noted and their significance is examined.

Table 8 shows the variation in the property-tax base per capita across states, calculated from data presented by the Advisory Commis-sion on Intergovernmental Relations (ACIR). According to a standard-ized definition of the tax base, six states plus the District of Columbia have per capita tax bases more than 20 per cent higher than the U.S. average, and eleven states have per capita bases less than 80 per cent of the average. With the exceptions of Maine and Vermont, those with low per capita bases are concentrated in the South.

Of even greater magnitude are property-tax-base differentials across communities. With 70,726 separate property-taxing jurisdictions in the United States and well over 100 separate political units with property-taxing power in many metropolitan areas, it would indeed be surprising to find all units equally balanced in industrial and commercial establishments and both high- and low-income residential areas. Instead, many suburban communities are either primarily high- or low-income residential or dominated by clusters of factories, warehouses, and other

depreciation. For a discussion of this, see Aaron, "Income Taxes and Housing," pp. 801–02.

nonresidential installations.[38] This urban political fragmentation alone explains why wide disparities in tax bases per capita or per pupil may exist.[39]

Table 8. Property-Tax Base per Capita Across States in Relation to the U.S. Average[a]

U.S. average	1.00		
Alabama	0.65	Missouri	0.95
Alaska	0.96	Montana	1.09
Arizona	0.95	Nebraska	1.20
Arkansas	0.74	Nevada	1.57
California	1.32	New Hampshire	1.07
Colorado	1.02	New Jersey	1.07
Connecticut	1.18	New Mexico	0.84
Delaware	1.27	New York	1.17
District of Columbia	1.23	North Carolina	0.75
Florida	1.07	North Dakota	0.91
Georgia	0.72	Ohio	1.01
Hawaii	1.12	Oklahoma	1.03
Idaho	0.86	Oregon	1.07
Illinois	1.18	Pennsylvania	0.89
Indiana	0.97	Rhode Island	0.82
Iowa	1.10	South Carolina	0.50
Kansas	1.10	South Dakota	0.96
Kentucky	0.77	Tennessee	0.73
Louisiana	0.85	Texas	0.89
Maine	0.73	Utah	0.87
Maryland	1.00	Vermont	0.74
Massachusetts	0.93	Virginia	0.89
Michigan	1.03	Washington	1.20
Minnesota	0.89	West Virginia	0.73
Mississippi	0.61	Wisconsin	0.94
		Wyoming	1.38

[a]The tax base per capita relates to a consistently defined tax base across states rather than to the actual property-tax base used in each state.

Source: Calculated from Advisory Commission on Intergovernmental Relations, *Measuring the Fiscal Capacity and Effort of State and Local Areas* (Washington, D.C.: U.S. Government Printing Office, 1971), Tables G-1 and G-2.

---

[38] An extreme example of the latter is Teterboro, New Jersey, where 98 per cent of the assessed valuation is nonresidential property.

[39] For further development of this point, see Lynn Stiles, "Multiplicity of Governmental Units," in Tax Institute of America, *The Property Tax, Problems and Potentials* (Princeton, N.J.: 1967); and idem, "A New Role for the State Property

Data on equalized valuation per pupil across communities in each of the New England states bear this out. The fraction given for each state in Table 9 shows the ratio of the tax base per pupil in the 90th-percentile community to the tax base per pupil in the 10th-percentile community. Thus, the ratio for each state is essentially a measure of the range in the value of the property-tax base per pupil across communities, with the very highest and lowest communities ignored in order to abstract from atypical situations.

The ratios presented in Table 9 may be compared with a ratio for state averages calculated from Table 8 for all states. The interstate ratio is 1.6 to 1, which is significantly lower than the within-state variations for the New England sample.

Table 9. Ratios of Property-Tax Base per Pupil, New England States: Disparities Across Communities

Connecticut	7.1/1
Maine	7.1/1
Massachusetts	2.9/1
New Hampshire	4.1/1
Rhode Island	1.8/1
Vermont	3.6/1

Source: Calculated from Steven J. Weiss, *Existing Disparities in Public School Finance and Proposals for Reform,* Federal Reserve Bank of Boston, Research Report no. 46 (February 1970), p. 17.

Tax-rate differentials and their relationships to tax-base differentials. The average property-tax rates on middle-income homes for each state (presented in Table 3) vary from less than 0.5 per cent to almost 3 per cent. Although tax-base differentials are a factor in explaining these tax-rate differentials across states, they are not the major factor. As shown in Table 3, differences in relative reliance on property-tax revenue are of crucial importance. For example, although Alabama's property-tax base per capita is significantly lower than average, the fact that only 15 per cent of its state and local revenues are derived from the property tax allows it to have one of the lowest property-tax rates in the country. In contrast, New Jersey has a higher-

Tax," in *Revenue Administration* (Chicago, Ill.: Federation of Tax Administration, 1959), pp. 9–12.

than-average property-tax base per capita, but at the same time it has the highest property-tax rate largely because it derives 54 per cent of its state and local revenues from the property tax.

In general, average effective property-tax rates tend to be higher in large cities than in their surrounding suburbs (see Appendix A). Moreover, there is a great variability in effective property-tax rates across communities within states and within metropolitan areas. For example, in New Jersey, even if the three highest- and lowest-tax-rate communities are excluded, the range of effective tax rates across the state is 9 to 1. In the Boston metropolitan area, which includes seventy-eight communities, the range of effective tax rates in 1971 was 2.4 to 1 when the extremely high rate cities of Boston and Chelsea and the low-rate towns of Dedham and Wenham were excluded. This means that the average tax payment on a $20,000 house in the jurisdictions in the Boston area in 1971 varied between $700 and $1,680, depending on its location. If the comparison included the excluded two high-rate cities and the two lowest-rate towns, the tax-liability range would be even greater.

Again, tax-base differentials do not appear to be the primary determinant of tax-rate differences between cities and their suburban communities. This is verified by the data on the relationship between tax rates, expenditure levels, and tax bases of large cities and their suburban communities (presented in Appendix A). In general, those data show that large cities tend to have higher tax rates than their suburban communities because of their large noneducational expenditure requirements even though they place relatively less reliance on the property tax and have larger tax bases than their suburban communities.

Within states or within metropolitan areas, however, the tax base per capita does appear to be the major determinant of the tax rate of a given community because the larger the property-tax base, the lower the property tax required to finance a given level of expenditures. Hence, an inverse relationship between the size of the tax base and the tax rate across communities is to be expected. Table 10 gives the correlation coefficient between the equalized valuation per pupil and the effective school-tax rate across communities for each of the New England states. All the coefficients are negative, thus verifying that this is in fact the case.

Of course, differences in the preferences for public services in each community also affect the tax rate through their effect on the level of public services provided. To the extent that high-tax-base communities provide a higher level of services than low-base communities, less variation is to be expected in tax rates than in tax bases across communities. The degree of variation in rates across New Jersey and across the Boston metropolitan area, however, suggests that rate differentials may still be very substantial.

Table 10. Relationship Between New England Valuation per Pupil and the Effective School-Tax Rate[a]

Connecticut	−0.68
Maine	−0.58
Massachusetts	−0.60
New Hampshrie	−0.69
Rhode Island	−0.59
Vermont	−0.56

[a]Simple correlation coefficients. All are significant at the 1 per cent level.

Source: Weiss, *Existing Disparities in Public School Finance and Proposals for Reform*, p. 21

Significance of tax-rate disparities across communities. An interpretation of the significance of tax-rate disparities poses a variety of issues, including location effects, preference differentials, and equity considerations.

Location effects. Unless offset by corresponding benefit differentials across communities, tax-rate disparities tend to distort location decisions by creating a pecuniary incentive for firms and households to migrate to low-tax-rate communities. Only if the lower tax rates result from lower real resource costs of production of public services would such migration be economically efficient.

Although empirical research has tended to find tax factors to be relatively unimportant if compared with other considerations such as transport or labor cost, property taxes may be significant in a firm's location decisions. This is especially true within a metropolitan area and for firms not highly dependent on product and material markets.[40]

---

[40] See John F. Due, "Studies of State-Local Tax Influences on Location of Industry," *National Tax Journal* 14 (June 1961): 163–73; and Netzer, *Economics of the Property Tax*, pp. 109–16.

For example, one recent study found a significant negative relationship between the gross density of manufacturing employment and effective property-tax rates within the Boston metropolitan area.[41] This suggests that manufacturing companies may be responsive to local tax-rate differentials if all other things, including the municipal expenditure level, are held constant. As a counterpart to effects of tax-rate differentials on location decisions, the potential response of firms seeking a location may affect tax policy at the local level and may thereby distort the provision of local public services.[42]

Households, as well as firms, may migrate in response to tax-rate incentives, especially when they are not tied to their present location by employment, neighborhood, or demographic factors. This holds true particularly for tax-rate differentials between cities and their suburbs. Higher tax rates in the cities tend to induce middle- and high-income families to leave the cities in favor of the suburbs, leaving the less mobile low-income families behind, thus creating undesirable location and income-distributional effects.

Benefit and preference differentials. Tax-rate disparities across communities need not result in inefficiencies in the location of households and firms. If tax-rate differentials correspond to benefit differentials, the existence of a multiplicity of communities with differing tax rates (and hence differing expenditure levels) is not objectionable. Rather, it may reflect differences in preferences between private and public goods among the residents of various jurisdictions. Freedom to express such preference differentials is desirable. The most favorable situation would be one in which all households and firms were freely mobile, and able to locate in the community with the particular tax-and-benefit package that best suited their preferences. Even without complete mobility, local provision of public services allows each community to vote and pay for its own desired level of public services. This results in a provision of public services more in line with consumer (or voter) sovereignty than would be the case under centralized provision of a uniform level of public services to all communities.

---

[41] Larry L. Orr, "Municipal Government Policy and the Location of Population and Industry in a Metropolitan Area: An Econometric Study" (Ph.D. diss., Massachusetts Institute of Technology, 1967).

[42] See discussion relating to "fiscal mercantilism," in the section "Criticisms of the property tax."

Equity considerations. Although local provision of public services with primarily local benefits is more efficient than centralized provision, there may be a cost in terms of undesirable equity effects. Communities with a small tax base may end up with very low levels of public services as compared with wealthier communities because a higher tax rate is required to finance a given level of services. It might be argued that this situation does not differ essentially from inequalities in the provision of private goods: Low-income families must make do with small amounts of consumer goods. The merits of the resulting distribution of goods and services are open to debate in either case. The outcome in both cases depends on the fairness of the original income distribution.

For a variety of reasons, the resulting inequality may be more serious, however, with respect to the provision of public goods and services than with respect to private goods. To the extent that public goods are assumed to meet needs of particular importance, great disparities in provision across communities may be deemed especially undesirable. This type of argument is probably most compelling with respect to education, but it applies as well to other public services, such as recreation facilities and police and fire protection. Furthermore, the level of public services is determined through the political process rather than through individual choice in the marketplace (as is the case with private goods). Hence, families that are immobile either because of their limited employment opportunities or because of discriminatory policies against them by other communities are not able to purchase a higher level of public services than that provided by the community in which they live, even if their tastes and ability to pay differ from those of the majority. It is not the individual family income or family property wealth alone that determines the relative cost to the family of the public services provided; it is the wealth of the community as a whole. This means that the larger the tax base of the community in which a given family lives, the better off that family is. As a result, two families with the same income and housing expenditures but living in different communities are not treated equally by their respective local public sectors. Finally, policies aimed at fiscal equalization among communities may be defended as substitutes (albeit inferior ones) for equalizing measures among individuals.

Thus, a case can be made that the present system of local financing of locally consumed public services can result in substantial inequities across communities. Whether these inequities are sufficient to outweigh the efficiency gains from local provision cannot be answered in this chapter. The outcome depends on how compelling the equity arguments are, on the weights attached to equity and efficiency considerations, and on the particular public service in question.

Implications of the Serrano decision. The major point to be made in a study of property taxation is that it is local financing of public services rather than the property tax itself that is the primary cause of service-level disparities across communities. If local income taxes were used instead of property taxes, there would still be large disparities in the tax base.[43] If the property tax were used on a statewide basis, property taxation would no longer give rise to local differentials.

Suppose it is decided on equity grounds that local financing of many services currently financed at the local level is no longer desirable. This is the basis of the recent state supreme court decisions with respect to property-tax finance of elementary and secondary education. Starting with the *Serrano* v. *Priest* decision in California in the fall of 1971, the general conclusion of these cases has been that the present system of educational finance is inequitable because of the differential levels of services it provides or because of the large disparities in the tax base across communities which give rise to the service differentials.[44] Although the *Serrano* v. *Priest* case and subsequent decisions in other states did not provide an explicit answer, the consensus is that one of two solutions would be acceptable: either assumption by the state of most current expenditures for education, which may well call for a shift of the property tax to the state level, or a system of power equalizing, which would essentially equalize the property-tax base across communi-

[43] Limited data suggest that the tax-base disparities might be even greater with the use of a local income tax than with a property tax. In a sample of 110 towns and cities in Massachusetts, for example, the variation in median income levels was substantially greater than the variation in the equalized property valuation per pupil across communities. Also, for the 21 counties in New Jersey, a comparison of the variability in the income base with that of the property base showed that the range of variation was slightly greater in the income base than in the property base.

[44] For an excellent discussion of the recent legal decisions dealing with educational finance, see Ferdinand P. Schoettle, "Judicial Requirements for School Finance and Property Tax Redesign: The Rapidly Evolving Case Law," *National Tax Journal* 25 (September 1972): 435–72.

ties by guaranteeing to each community the same level of funds for educational purposes for each mill of its tax rate regardless of the size of its tax base. Without delving into the complexities that an evaluation of these two approaches would involve, the point remains that the difficulty with the present system of educational finance is a function of the desire for local autonomy rather than of the property tax itself. Both solutions, it should be noted, would allow continued use of the property tax as the major source of revenue, in the former at the state level and in the latter in a modified form that would end tax-base disparities for educational expenditures.

Evaluation of the Property Tax as a Local Tax

Within each community, the property tax is paid by its residents, and the proceeds are used to finance services, the benefits of which also accrue to these residents. It is in this sense that the local property tax is often justified on grounds of benefit taxation. But the property tax cannot be justified as a user charge or as a strict benefit tax within a particular community because most of the benefits received bear no close relationship to property values. Instead, the local property tax must be interpreted as a general tax that everyone in the community must pay for local provision of public goods such as education and fire protection, regardless of whether their children go to public or private school or whether they live in wooden or brick houses. A system of local user charges would differ in that payments would be made only for specific benefits received. Although a strong case can be made on efficiency grounds for increased utilization of user charges to finance local goods and services, it is unlikely that increased reliance on user charges could completely replace the local revenue currently raised by the property tax.

Is a local tax wanted? Leaving user charges aside, the basic question is whether a local tax is wanted at all. The answer depends not on the merits of the local property tax but rather on the desirability of local fiscal autonomy. Although there are costs as well as benefits connected with local fiscal independence, most people would agree that the benefits of local fiscal autonomy are sufficiently great to outweigh these costs and that, therefore, a substantial degree of local autonomy should be maintained.

Merits of the property tax. Local fiscal autonomy, by definition, requires a major local own-revenue source.[45] The question concerns the merits of the local property tax vis-à-vis other forms of local taxation such as income or sales taxes. Major reliance on local retail-sales taxation can be immediately ruled out, especially for small jurisdictions, because high tax rates are easily avoided. By shopping in a neighboring low-rate town, an individual may retain the benefits of a high-expenditure community and at the same time avoid its tax burden.

The use of income taxes at the local level also presents difficulties. It is not at all clear which definition of income is appropriate: income earned in the community or the total personal income of residents. In the case of income earned in the community, avoidance of high tax rates and consequently inefficient location effects on economic activity are likely to occur as residents shift their place of work from high-rate areas to low-rate areas. In addition, the nexus between local benefits received from residing in a given locality and taxes paid would again be broken. In the case of total personal income, the more comprehensive income definition would present major enforcement and administrative problems. Moreover, it might be even less acceptable to the general public than the local property tax because of the more ambiguous relationship between the level of income derived from all sources and local benefits received than between local property values and local benefits.

In order to avoid a high local income-tax rate, the resident must move to a different community, which makes avoidance of the income tax more difficult than avoidance of the retail-sales tax. Yet, it would be easier to avoid a local income tax than to avoid a local property tax. The reason is that differential property-tax rates are more likely to be capitalized in property values than differential income taxes are. This means that if property-tax rates rise in the central city, for example, the owner of a house will not be able to avoid the tax by moving because the tax increase will have been capitalized into a lower house value.

Another advantage of the property tax over a local income tax is that the property-tax base is cyclically more stable than the income-tax base. This is important for local communities that, unlike the federal government, cannot run recession deficits. It should be pointed out, how-

---

[45] This view is taken although it is realized that expenditure autonomy is compatible with finance by untied grants. However, own revenue is needed to give local independence in determining the total level of public services.

ever, that some of this cyclical stability is derived from infrequent and delayed property assessment, which is not necessarily desirable from other points of view.

Thus, for a variety of reasons, the local property tax appears to be superior to other forms of local general taxation. At the same time, however, the tax has shortcomings, including poor and inequitable administration, detrimental effects on urban development, and its use for "fiscal mercantilism." These defects should not be overlooked.

Criticisms of the property tax. The major criticism of the local property tax is its poor administration, leading to wide variations in the relationship of assessed value to market value of properties within a single community. As a result, the tax liabilities of properties with the same market value may differ substantially, thereby causing horizontal inequities. In addition, there is some evidence to suggest that high-value properties tend to be less highly assessed than low-value properties, thus making the effective tax rate on low-value property higher than the effective rate on high-value property and thereby causing vertical inequities as well.[46] Although these are valid criticisms of the tax, it should be possible to rectify them substantially. More state government involvement in the assessment process through frequent statewide studies of assessment-sales ratios and pressure for assessment at 100 per cent of market value should help to reduce the present inequities. In addition, assessment could be carried out by a level of government higher than the government imposing the tax, such as the county or the state level. This would make the use of computers more economically feasible and would promote professionalism in the assessment process.

A second common criticism of the local property tax is that high tax rates in the central cities have an undesirable effect on urban development by providing a significant tax disincentive for rehabilitation, especially of urban slums. That slums do exist and that structures are often allowed to run down to the point of having to be abandoned are undebatable. How much of this underinvestment in low-income housing in the central cities can be attributed to the property tax, however, re-

---

[46] For example, see *Report of the New Jersey Tax Policy Committee* (Trenton: February 23, 1972), pt. 2: *The Property Tax,* chap. 10; and Oliver Oldman and Henry Aaron, "Assessment-Sales Ratio under the Boston Property Tax," *National Tax Journal* 17 (March 1965): 36–49.

quires more empirical work.[47] There are other reasons that may explain the insufficient investment in low-income urban housing, and removal of the property tax on improvements might not greatly change the situation. Even if an individual landlord upgrades his property, he may not be able to raise his rents correspondingly because of the external diseconomies that result from location in a blighted neighborhood. This and similar effects make the private rate of return on investment in blighted areas lower than it should be from society's point of view and would seem to be substantially more important than the marginal disincentive effect of the property tax.

More specifically, it is argued that although improvements in central cities are overtaxed, land values are undertaxed. The result is to withhold land from its most productive uses, encouraging both under-utilization of land in central cities and urban sprawl in the suburbs. Thus, the policy recommendation for central cities is to reduce the property-tax rate on improvements and increase it on land values. The higher tax on land values, it is argued, is desirable both on efficiency grounds in order to improve land use and on equity grounds in order to recapture for the community as a whole the benefits of higher land prices resulting from the growth of the community and increased government investment in social overhead.

This suggested modification of the property tax in the direction of site- or land-value taxation, although theoretically acceptable, needs further study. Its impact on particular properties in a given area must be studied, and the windfall capital gains and losses caused by such a change should not be incurred unless the policy has a reasonable chance of achieving its objectives. In particular, such a policy change may be undesirable for suburban areas where the major policy goal is preservation of open spaces rather than the more intensive development desired for the cities. It is significant to note that the New Jersey Tax Policy Committee, which recently completed a major study of the New Jersey tax system, was hesitant to accept the desirability of increased reliance on land-value taxation and recommended that higher taxation of land relative to improvements be allowed only in the six major cities

---

[47] One example of the type of research that is required can be found in "A Study of Property Taxes and Urban Blight," draft report submitted to the U.S. Department of Housing and Urban Renewal by Arthur D. Little, Inc., H-1299, December 31, 1971.

and then only if it is adopted by a municipal referendum and introduced gradually over a period of five years.[48]

The third criticism of the local property tax is that it invites what Dick Netzer has referred to as "fiscal mercantilism,"[49] that is, an attempt by individual communities to maximize their tax bases in relation to the demand for public services. This is most often done by zoning regulations that are aimed at keeping out low-income families who, although adding to the public-service burden, would add only insignificantly to the tax base. Although the property tax may lend itself especially to such practices, the basic problem is one of local financing of public services rather than of the property tax itself. Even with a local income tax, there would be an incentive for local communities to pursue zoning policies of this type. Thus, it is a cost of local decision making rather than a criticism of the local property tax per se.

In spite of these shortcomings of the property tax, the conclusion remains that the local property tax is no worse and no better than other forms of local taxation. Attempts should be made to improve administration, to minimize the impact in urban areas, and to reduce the effect of nonresidential property on the ability of localities to raise revenue for explicitly resident-related services. None of these would require a significant reduction in the reliance on property-tax revenue; and given their achievement, there remains a strong case for continued use of property taxation as a source of local finance.

The Property Tax as a Statewide Tax

Although substantial reliance on local financing of local services is likely to continue, equity considerations may militate in favor of reduced emphasis on local revenue sources, especially with respect to educational finance. If this occurs, the states will need additional revenue sources to replace revenues presently raised at the local level. The magnitude of these additional demands on state revenues will depend on how much of the financing of services is shifted to the state level. If, for example, state governments were to take over the financing of 90 per cent of

---

[48] *Report of the New Jersey Tax Policy Committee* (Trenton: February 23, 1972), pt. 2: *The Property Tax.*

[49] Netzer, *Economics of the Property Tax,* pp. 131–32.

education expenditures currently financed at the local level, the required per cent increase in state revenues would be substantial. As shown in Table 11, the required increase differs among states, primarily because of differing degrees of current reliance on local revenue sources to finance local education expenditures.[50]

Inevitably, the question then is: What statewide revenue sources would be appropriate to replace the local property-tax revenues lost from reduced emphasis on local financing? The general thrust of this chapter is that a statewide property tax would be a prime contender to provide such a major revenue source, especially since the transfer of functions would greatly reduce local use of the tax. The desirability

Table 11. Additional Revenue Required for State to Assume 90 Per Cent of Public School Financing, Selected States (1969-1970 School Year)

State	Amount (in millions)	Per Capita	As Per Cent of Total State Taxes
High additional proportion of state revenue			
South Dakota	$ 81.9	$123	72.7
New Hampshire	65.8	91	69.4
Nebraska	152.8	104	58.5
Oregon	244.2	118	56.7
New Jersey	750.3	106	56.3
Ohio	861.3	82	50.1
Low additional proportion of state revenue			
North Carolina	23.0	5	1.9
Mississippi	18.0	8	3.7
New Mexico	11.1	11	4.1
Alabama	43.0	12	6.5
Delaware	13.0	24	6.6
Florida	114.0	17	8.0

Source: Adapted from Charles L. Schultze et al., *Setting National Priorities: The 1973 Budget* (Washington, D.C.: The Brookings Institution, © 1972), p. 341.

---

[50] Actually, the required increases in state revenues are likely to be greater than those shown in Table 11 because a major goal of state take-over of education finance would be to equalize expenditures across communities. This would more likely involve raising the expenditure levels of low-expenditure communities up to the levels of the others, rather than equalizing at the present average level of expenditures that is implicit in the table.

of reducing reliance on local revenue sources whether for educational or for other purposes must be kept separate from the issue of whether to reduce reliance on property taxation in general.

The conclusion that statewide property-tax revenue is an appropriate alternative to increased revenue from state income or sales taxation follows from the discussion earlier in this chapter. There it was argued that property-tax revenue has not been increasing as fast as other sources of revenue and that the tax is not so regressive as is generally assumed and may well be substantially progressive for most of the income range. Moreover, it may be concluded that on the average, the property tax does not result in an overtaxation of housing because of its coexistence with the corporate income tax, favorable income-tax provisions for owner-occupied housing, and sales taxes that exclude housing services.

It should be remembered, however, that what may be valid in general may not be applicable to all states because of the present differing degrees of reliance on the property tax. For states that currently do not have statewide income taxes and do have high property-tax rates (such as New Jersey and New Hampshire), a shift from local financing to statewide financing of education expenditures in response to constitutional or equity pressures would seem to call first of all for the introduction of a broad-based income tax in order to provide a more balanced revenue structure at the combined state and local level. For states that already have broad-based state taxes and do not now have average property-tax rates substantially out of line with service-level disparities across states, however, there is a good case for the use of a statewide property tax to replace the major portion of whatever reduction in local property-tax revenue occurs. Adequate provision should be made, however, for low-income families overburdened by the property tax as was outlined in the section "Who Pays the Property Tax?" and improvements in the assessment process should be realized through increased state involvement with the property tax.

In concluding, an even broader aspect of property taxation may be noted. It has been implicit in this discussion that the ownership of property and wealth constitutes an ability to pay beyond money income that can be legitimately taxed. Logically, however, this implies that the property tax should be a personal tax rather than an *in rem* tax on gross property value. The theoretically correct approach to wealth taxation would be to tax the net worth of each individual, where net worth is defined as the total value of the individual's assets, both tangible and intangible, minus his liabilities. For various reasons, such a net-worth tax would be administratively difficult to employ at the state level, although not impossible. If progressive rates are used, such a tax could most successfully be employed at the federal level. Ultimately, it might thus be desirable to transform the property tax into a net-worth tax at the state or even the federal level. But clearly, this will not occur soon. For the foreseeable future at least, the property tax will remain a matter of state and local finance, with the state playing an increasingly important role in its administration and use.

APPENDIX
Central-City Versus Suburban Tax Rates

Table A-1 presents data to show that tax rates are generally higher in the cities than they are in the surrounding suburbs. Column 1 of the table was calculated from *1967 Census of Governments* data by dividing the median effective tax rate on single-family houses in the central city by the median effective rate for the balance of the county in which the city is located. The cities were chosen to correspond to those for which the Advisory Commission on Intergovernmental Relations gives the somewhat-comparable data that have been included as columns 2 to 4. Of the forty-two cities listed in the table, column 1 indicates that all but ten show higher effective rates in the city than in surrounding communities, and eleven of these have effective rates more than 20 per cent higher in the city portion of the county. It should be pointed out that in many cases these rate differentials would be even larger were it not for the fact that large cities tend to rely more heavily on non-property-tax sources of revenue than the suburban communities do. For example, only 60 per cent of the total tax revenue in the twenty-five largest cities in the United States is derived from the property tax, in contrast with over 80 per cent for all local governments.

The general conclusion that property-tax rates are higher in cities than in surrounding areas is reinforced by the ACIR data in column 4 of Table A-1 as well as by the data in Table A-2. A figure of over 100 in column 4 of Table A-1 or column 3 of Table A-2 means that the ratio for the city of actual revenue collected to its hypothetical

Table A-1. Relative Revenue Effort of Cities and Suburbs, 1966–1967

| | Census | Per Cent Relation of City-Area Measure to Balance-of-County Measure | | |
| | | ACIR | | |
City	Effective Property-Tax Rate[a] (1)	Revenue Capacity per Capita (2)	Revenue per Capita (3)	Relative Revenue Effort (4)
Birmingham, Ala.	118	97	142	146
Mobile, Ala.	117	90	147	163
Phoenix, Ariz.	110	102	109	107
Tucson, Ariz.	103	69[b]	155[b]	226
Little Rock, Ark.	91	166	172	103
Anaheim, Calif.	94[c]	111[d]	141[d]	126
Fresno, Calif.	133	94	107	114
Los Angeles, Calif.	105[c]	108	124	114
Oakland, Calif.	99	116	127	109
Sacramento, Calif.	96	141	155	110
San Diego, Calif.	105	105	109	104
San Jose, Calif.	107	88	97	109
Miami, Fla.	144	112[d]	134[d]	120
St. Petersburg, Fla.	144	112	148	132
Chicago, Ill.	95	97	116	120
Peoria, Ill.	107	108	99	92
Rockford, Ill.	113	164	167	102
Kansas City, Kans.	93	317[b]	202[b]	64
Louisville, Ky.	146	105	158	150
Omaha, Nebr.	108	e	e	89
Albuquerque, N. Mex.	148	129[b]	219[b]	170
Charlotte, N.C.	194	81[b]	135[b]	166

City				
Greensboro, N. C.	82	126	153	121
Winston-Salem, N. C.	181	119	164	137
Akron, Ohio	102	102	123	121
Canton, Ohio	107	97[c]	118[c]	122
Cincinnati, Ohio	110	102	197	193
Cleveland, Ohio	101	96	109	113
Columbus, Ohio	97	92[b]	108[b]	117
Dayton, Ohio	105	124	168	136
Toledo, Ohio	107	119[b]	147[b]	124
Youngstown, Ohio	115	102	116	113
Oklahoma City, Okla.	117	84	106	126
Tulsa, Okla.	123	73[b]	135[b]	184
Portland, Oreg.	99	124[b]	165[b]	132
Chattanooga, Tenn.	138	226	323	143
Knoxville, Tenn.	276	208[b]	421[b]	202
Memphis, Tenn.	192	199[b]	236[b]	119
Salt Lake City, Utah	107	106	136	128
Seattle, Wash.	86	104	138	133
Spokane, Wash.	114	109	165	150
Tacoma, Wash.	122	176	254	144

[a] Ratio of median effective property-tax rate of city to balance of county for single-family houses involved in measureable sales during a six-month period.

[b] Cities with at least twice as much estimated population as the balance of the county.

[c] Ratio of city-area tax rate to balance-of-county tax rate, excluding other large cities in county.

[d] Cities with an estimated population less than half that of the balance of the county.

[e] Data not available.

Sources: U.S. Bureau of the Census, *1967 Census of Governments*, vol. 2: *Taxable Property Values*, Table 21; and Advisory Commission on Intergovernmental Relations, *Measuring the Fiscal Capacity and Effort of State and Local Areas*, Table A-6.

revenue capacity is greater than the similar ratio for the balance of the county or the SMSA (Standard Metropolitan Statistical Area). These are not strictly comparisons of property-tax rates because revenue from sources other than property taxes is included in actual revenue and because the hypothetical capacity figures were calculated assuming nationwide averages of revenue from various sources. But since property taxes are the major source of local revenue, the results are somewhat comparable to those in column 1 of Table A-1. The use of these

Table A-2. Relation Between City-Area and Balance-of-SMSA Measures of Revenue Capacity, Revenue, and Relative Revenue Effort, for Nine Selected Major Cities, 1966–1967

	Per Cent Relation of City-Area Measure to Balance-of-SMSA Measure		
City	Per Capita Revenue Capacity (1)	Per Capita Revenue (2)	Relative Revenue Effort (3)
New York, N. Y.	108	109	101
Philadelphia, Pa.	103	111	108
Baltimore, Md.	104	118	113
Washington, D.C.	69	100	126
St. Louis, Mo.	129	141	109
Boston, Mass.	107	125	118
New Orleans, La.	106	113	107
Denver, Colo.	98	121	124
Nashville-Davidson, Tenn.	107	108	101

Source: Advisory Commission on Intergovernmental Relations, *Measuring the Fiscal Capacity and Effort of State and Local Areas,* Table A-5.

data also points up the fact that both revenue capacity and the need for public service determine the tax effort. Thus, although three quarters of the cities have a higher revenue capacity per capita than their suburbs, the greater per capita revenue requirements in the cities result in only three cities showing a lower relative tax effort than their surrounding communities.

PAYROLL TAX

Nancy H. Teeters

THE PAYROLL TAX AND
SOCIAL-SECURITY FINANCE

SOCIAL-SECURITY EXPENDITURES are the second-largest expenditure of the federal government, and social-security taxes are the second-largest source of revenues. The social-security system can be separated into two parts: the cash-benefits portion, that is, the old-age, survivors, and disability insurance programs (OASDI); and Medicare for the aged, which comprises hospital insurance and supplementary medical insurance. The two parts are obviously related, but the problems associated with them differ. In March 1971, the Reports of the 1971 Advisory Council on Social Security were submitted to the Congress.[1] Numerous recommendations were made to change the benefit structure and the calculation of the financing. Legislation enacted in 1972 accepted many of these recommendations and has made some fundamental changes in benefits and the calculation of present and future tax rates. This chapter examines the nature of these changes on both the expenditures and receipts for OASDHI (which includes the hospital tax rate), the special problems of Medicare, and additional proposals for reform of the social-security system.*

The provision of social-security benefits reflects the commitment

---

AUTHOR'S NOTE: The views expressed in this chapter are those of the author and do not necessarily represent those of officers, trustees, or other staff members of The Brookings Institution.

* See comments of Wilbur J. Cohen, member of CED Research Advisory Board, under "Memorandum of Comment, Reservation, or Dissent," p. 286.

[1] U.S., Congress, House, *Reports of the 1971 Advisory Council on Social Security*, 92d Cong., 1st Sess., H. Doc. 92–80.

and desire of the American people to provide income for the elderly, the disabled, and their dependents. OASDI benefits are considered an earned right, based on the recorded wage history of individual beneficiaries. If a person works in a job covered by social security (i.e., if he pays social-security taxes) for a specified number of quarters, he is assured of receiving income if he should become disabled; benefits, including allowances for dependents, when he retires; or support for his survivors if he dies.

Such a description of benefits is, of course, a gross oversimplification. There are numerous legal provisions concerning eligibility, age at retirement, number of years to be included in earnings records, treatment of dependents, and so forth. However, if a person meets the standards of eligibility, benefits are paid. No annual appropriation by Congress is needed to pay benefits because the social-security tax receipts are permanently appropriated to the trust fund. Thus, if the law remains unchanged, the federal government is committed to pay benefits to those currently on the rolls and to provide benefits to eligible persons in the future.

However, the total benefits that the average person receives are larger than the amount of taxes paid during his working life. Moreover, the benefits that a person currently in the labor force is likely to receive when he becomes eligible will be larger than the amount specified in existing law. This happens because the social-security law has been amended frequently. Benefits were expanded by liberalizing the legal provisions and by legislating across-the-board increases, such as the 10 per cent increase in benefits passed in 1971. The frequent changes in the law reflected the desire to correct inequities, to provide increases in real benefits, and to protect the beneficiaries from the effects of inflation.

The most important long-range new feature of the 1972 legislation for benefits was the provision of automatic increases in benefits tied to increase in the consumer price index (CPI). In the future, if the CPI increases by more than 3.0 per cent over the base period, there is to be a corresponding increase in benefits to take place at the beginning of the next calendar year. The base period is currently defined as the third quarter of 1972 but will become the quarter that subsequent increases are calculated on. The first such cost-of-living increase cannot take place until 1975. For example, if a 5 per cent increase in the cost of living occurs between the third quarter of 1972 and the third quarter of 1974, OASDI benefits would be raised by 5 per cent, effective

January 1, 1975. The third quarter of 1974 then becomes the new base period. However, such automatic adjustments are not to take place if an across-the-board increase is legislated for that year. These automatic increases in benefits are to be financed by automatic increases in the ceiling on wages subject to tax that will be discussed later.

In addition to providing for automatic increased benefits for cost of living, the June 1972 legislation granted a 20 per cent across-the-board increase in benefits based on a one-time windfall that resulted from changing the actuarial assumptions. Subsequent legislation in October 1972 provided further liberalizations in benefits and extended coverage of Medicare to the disabled. By 1974 when all these provisions are fully effective, the 1972 legislation will have increased social-security expenditures by at least $12.3 billion and will have raised the combined old-age survivors, disability, and hospital tax rate from 10.4 per cent of the first $9,000 of earned income to 11.7 per cent of the first $12,000 of earned income.

What aspects of this system has led to social-security expenditures being one of the most rapidly growing elements of federal outlays and social-security taxes being the most rapidly growing element of federal receipts?

Although there are elements of insurance to the system, it is basically an income-maintenance program, with current benefits being paid out of current tax receipts. Cash benefits, with some exceptions, have been financed entirely by payroll taxes levied in equal percentages on the employer and employee. (A tax is levied on self-employed persons also; in general, this has been about three-quarters of the combined employee-employer tax rate.)

> In connection with the 1950 amendments, the Congress was of the belief that the program should be completely self-supporting from the contributions of covered individuals and employers. Accordingly in that legislation the provision permitting appropriation to the system from general revenues of the Treasury was repealed. Thus, the Congress has always very strongly believed that the tax schedule in the law should make the system self-supporting as nearly as can be foreseen and, therefore, actuarially sound.[2]

So long as these expenditures continue to be financed in this way,

---

[2] U.S., Congress, Senate, *Social Security Amendments of 1960*, 86th Cong., 2d Sess., S. Rept. 1956, p. 37.

the aggregate amount of benefits determines the tax rate. Therefore, current and future tax-rate schedules are based on projections of total expenditures under the program. Two sets of OASDI-cost projections are prepared and presented in each year's annual report of the trustees (Secretary of the Treasury; Secretary of Labor; Secretary of Health, Education, and Welfare; and Commissioner of Social Security). The short-run estimate is for five years, and the long-range estimate covers a period of seventy-five years. In both cases, aggregate benefits are expressed as a percentage of payroll. The short-run estimates of expenditures are based on current law concerning eligibility for benefits, expected changes in the number of beneficiaries, and the impact of rising average wages on new benefits awarded.[3] The short-run revenue estimates are based on projections of wages subject to tax that include assumptions about the increasing number of people in the labor force and rising average wages.[4]

A long-range evaluation of the program is necessary because of the commitment to pay future benefits. Young people entering the labor force today are posting credits toward retirement benefits that will only begin to be paid forty to forty-five years in the future. Therefore, in order to keep decision makers aware of the future costs, projections are made of aggregate benefit payments for the next seventy-five years. The present value (i.e., the discounted value) of the future stream of aggregate benefits over the seventy-five-year evaluation period is then calculated under provisions of the current law. Projections are also made of the aggregate payroll that would be subject to social security taxes, and the future stream of payrolls is also discounted to present value. Social-security costs are then measured as a percentage of present value of the future stream of payroll subject to tax. The system is said to be in actuarial balance when the present value of future benefits is matched by the present value of future revenues. Prior to 1972, the long-run estimates of expenditures were also based on the provisions of current law and expected changes in the number of beneficiaries based on pop-

---

[3] For example, a person retiring in 1971 with earnings equal to or in excess of the ceiling would receive a higher initial benefit than someone with similar earnings who retired in 1969, because his wage history contains two years at higher wages than the history of the 1969 retiree.

[4] Not all wages and salaries are subject to the tax. Some groups are exempt, primarily federal civilian employees. In addition, an individual's wages are taxed only up to whatever the current wage ceiling is.

ulation projections. In order to estimate the number of retired persons and other dependents well into the next century, established actuarial rules concerning mortality can be applied to the age cohorts of the current population. The size of the future working-age population that will support the retired population is already partly predetermined, but it also depends on future fertility rates. The long-run revenue estimates were based on wage projections that reflect only projected changes in the labor force; average wages were assumed constant.

Because of the age distribution of the U.S. population, the tax rates needed to produce the revenues to finance the benefits will have to be raised in the future. The level cost is the tax rate that, if it were in effect during the entire seventy-five-year period, would generate enough income to pay for the benefits during the period as specified by the laws in effect at the time the long-range evaluation is made. The level tax rate would accomplish this by producing revenues in excess of the amount needed to pay current benefits, creating a surplus to be invested in U.S. government securities. The interest earned on those securities was to be used to finance a significant part of the benefits in the period of high costs in the future. The analogy being used in the long-range planning for the social-security programs was that of private insurance.

Are Private Insurance Principles Appropriate?

A private pension plan can transfer resources over time for the individual by currently investing in productive capital that produces real income in the future, whereas the social-security surpluses are invested in government securities. The interest on those securities is a government expenditure that must be financed from current revenues. Creating near-term surpluses to build up large trust funds that will generate large interest payments in the future does not reduce the burden of supporting the dependent population in the year that it occurs. The existence of large trust funds only determines whether the cash-benefit program is going to be financed out of payroll taxes or out of general revenues used to pay the interest on the securities held by the trust funds.

The only way a national retirement program such as social security could transfer resources to a later date without widespread public ownership of productive capital would be to invest the current surplus of the retirement fund in a way that would *raise the national growth rate,* thereby providing a net increment in national income during later years. Even if that surplus could be used to increase the level of productive investment in the country through federal monetary and fiscal policies that adjusted the volume of investment in the light of the surplus in the social security trust funds and even if this added investment raised the growth rate of national income, future generations would be unlikely to associate part of their income with investments made possible in earlier years because of the trust-fund surplus. From the point of view of those future generations, they would still be taxed to pay for current retirement benefits, either through a payroll tax or through other taxes to cover the interest on securities held by the trust funds.

In short, social security is a system under which each working generation is taxed to support the currently retired population. Building up a surplus, investing the surplus in government securities, and using the interest earnings to help meet future benefit payments does not change this relationship.

The real costs of supporting the elderly population depend upon the level of benefits and the number of beneficiaries relative to the working population. Over the next twenty years, the ratio of the beneficiary population to the labor force will rise from 18 to 19 per cent. It will then decline over the following twenty years, reflecting the low birth rates between 1925 and 1945. However, shortly after the turn of the century, the ratio of the retired population will rise sharply, reflecting the very high birth rates of the 1947-1957 period and the drop in fertility in the post-1957 period.[5]

Figures 1 and 2 describe the basic underlying demographic problem facing the system. Although this is called the actuarial problem, it has only a remote and tenuous relationship to the actuarial problems of private insurance. Private insurance contracts to pay specified dollar amounts to policyholders at some future date. Social security promises to replace a certain percentage of preretirement income. The percentage has been modified, usually upward, over time. The amount a person gets back has little to do with the amount he paid in. The massive recording of earnings for each individual and the elaborate calculation of the primary insurance amount are methods of determining the replacement rate.

---

[5] U.S., Social Security Administration, *United States Population Projections for OASDHI Cost Estimates,* Actuarial Study No. 62 (1966).

Figure 1. Number of Live Births (millions)

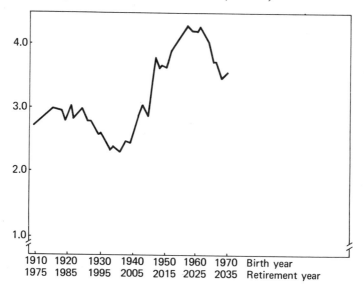

Figure 2. Ratio of Population Over 65 Years of Age to Population Aged 20 to 64 Years

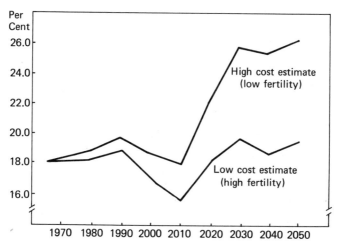

Source: U.S. Social Security Administration, *United States Population Projections for OASDHI Cost Estimates,* Actuarial Study No. 62 (1966).

The social-security system does have a future problem that arises out of the demographic composition of the U.S. population. Figure 1 shows the annual number of live births in the United States since 1910. By adding sixty-five years to the year of birth, it is possible to obtain an approximation of the increment to the retired population for the next sixty-five years. One of the important measures of the burden of supporting the retired population is the ratio of the number of persons over sixty-five to the working-age population. Figure 2 shows the high cost estimate, which assumes low future fertility rates, and the low cost estimate, which assumes higher future fertility rates. If future fertility rates are low, the large number of persons born between 1947 and 1957 will be a relatively larger proportion of the total population after the turn of the century than they will be if the future birth rates are high (low cost estimate). But under either assumption, the ratio of the retired population to the working population begins to rise in the year 2010, and the real costs begin to rise at that time.

The Role of the Level-Wage Assumption

The problems created by trying to prefinance future benefits was compounded by the use of the level-wage assumption in the actuarial calculation. Each time a long-range estimate was made to determine whether the system was in actuarial balance, it assumed that average wages for the next seventy-five years would be the same as in the year the calculations were made. Thus, estimates of future revenues reflected only the increasing numbers of persons in covered employment. Because of the level-wage assumptions, the estimates of future benefits reflected only the increasing number of beneficiaries plus the effect of *past* increases in wages and wage ceilings on future entitlements. The estimates of future benefits were projected to rise because they took into account the deaths of beneficiaries with relatively low benefits and the addition to the rolls of large numbers of persons with higher benefits based on the rising wages up to the time of the actuarial evaluation. The level-wage assumption understated both future revenues and future expenditures, but it understated the revenues by more than the expenditures because the estimated expenditures allowed for turnover of beneficiaries with higher earnings records.

The use of the level-wage assumption in the actuarial calculation had the effect in the short run of producing annual "unexpected" actuarial surpluses because, contrary to the assumption, wages did rise. The higher level of wages was used to recalculate the present value of future revenues. The benefits were also recalculated to reflect the increase in wages, but the difference between the new estimate of benefits and the previous one was smaller than the difference between the two revenue estimates because the feedback on benefits of prior increases in wages was already built into the previous calculation. In the past, the annual "unexpected" actuarial surplus has been used partly to finance cost-of-living increases and partly to expand benefit provisions. These increases in benefits required legislation, and as long as the present value of increased benefits did not exceed the actuarial surplus, no revision in the tax-rate schedules was needed. However, numerous proposals for revising the benefits were usually under consideration, and if the present value of the total benefit increase exceeded the actuarial surplus, new tax schedules were needed. Table 1 shows the eight tax-rate schedules that have been in effect since 1950 and the one scheduled in the October 1972 legislation.

The Advisory Council on Social Security recommended

> . . . that the actuarial cost estimates for the cash benefit program be based—as the estimates for the hospital insurance program now are —on the assumptions that earnings levels will rise, that the contribution and benefit base will be increased as earnings levels rise, and that benefit payments will be increased as prices rise.[6]

The trustees accepted the recommendation with the reservation that a safety margin be introduced into the actual estimates to safeguard against possible changes in the long-run economic assumptions, primarily the estimate of the differential over the long run between rates of wage and price increases. In explaining the effect of the level-wage assumption of an estimate of future costs, the 1972 OASDI trustees report says for the first time:

> The resulting cost estimates . . . are essentially those that would be obtained if Congress acted in such a fashion that the benefit table

---

[6] U.S., Congress, House, *1972 Annual Report of the Board of Trustees of the Federal Old-Age and Survivors Insurance and Disability Insurance Trust Funds,* 92d Cong., 2d Sess, H. Doc. 92–307, p. 25.

Table 1. OASDI, Combined Employer-Employee Legislated Tax-Rate Schedules (percentages)

Year	Ceiling on wages subject to tax	Combined Employer-Employee Tax Rate									
		1950	1954	1956	1958	1961	1965	1967	1969	1971	1972
1950	$3,000[a]	3.0[a]									
1951	3,600										
1952											
1953											
1954		4.0	4.0[a]								
1955	4,200										
1956											
1957				4.5[a]							
1958											
1959	4,800				5.0[a]						
1960		5.0	5.0	5.5	6.0[a]						
1961											
1962						6.25[a]					
1963					7.0	7.25[a]					
1964											
1965		6.0	6.0	6.5							
1966	6,600				8.0	8.25	7.7[a]				
1967							7.8[a]				
1968	7,800					9.25	8.8[a]	7.6[a]			
1969					9.0			8.4[a]	8.4[a]		
1970		6.5	7.0	7.5							
1971								9.2[a]	9.2[a]		
1972	9,000										
1973	10,800[b]						9.7	10.0	10.0	10.0	9.7[c]
1974	12,000[b]										
1975			8.0	8.5							
1976										10.3	

[a] Rates that actually went into effect.

[b] The wage ceiling after 1974 is to be automatically adjusted to reflect the rise in average wages each time benefits are automatically adjusted for increase in the cost of living.

[c] The OASDI tax rate is scheduled to drop 9.6 percent for the years 1978–2011. In 2011, it is scheduled to rise to 11.7 percent. However, scheduled increases in the hospital-insurance rate more than offset the reduction in the OASDI rate.

Sources: U.S. Social Security Administration, *Social Security Bulletin: Annual Statistical Supplement, 1969* (1971), pp. 19–20; *Congressional Record*, Vol. 118 (Oct. 17, 1972), p. H 10205.

were to increase at a rate somewhat slower than earnings but . . . faster than prices . . . The average benefit per beneficiary will increase faster than earnings, because of effect of earnings increases on the level of benefits for beneficiaries coming on the rolls in the future.

. . . . Contribution rates set in accordance with these level-benefit level earnings estimates make it possible for Congress to increase the benefit table at a rate faster than prices without increasing the contribution rates. In this sense financing in accordance with these estimates may be considered to encourage future benefit table increases beyond those necessary to keep up with the cost of living. . . .

Cost estimates [using] . . . dynamic assumptions provide financing needed to increase the benefit table in step with the Consumer Price Index, but do not provide financing for benefit table increases in excess of the increase in prices. . . .[7]

The introduction of dynamic wage and price assumptions produced sizable actuarial surpluses over the seventy-five-year time span and reduced the level cost over the period by nearly 1 per cent. Table 2 shows the impact on the estimated cost by ten-year intervals under the level wage assumption and under dynamic assumptions.

Table 2. Estimated Current Cost of OASDI Expenditures as Per Cent of Taxable Payroll, Selected Years 1975–2045

Calendar Year	Level Earnings Assumption	Dynamic Wage and Price Assumptions	Difference
1975	8.73	8.39	−0.34
1985	10.02	8.42	−1.60
1995	10.53	8.16	−2.37
2005	10.24	7.98	−2.26
2015	11.31	9.19	−2.12
2025	12.74	10.51	−2.23
2035	12.86	10.76	−2.10
2045	12.88	10.98	−1.90
Level/Average Cost	10.16	9.23	−0.93

Source: U.S. Congress. House, *1972 Annual Report of the Board of Trustees of the Federal Old-Age and Survivors Insurance and Disability Insurance Trust Funds*, 92d Cong., 2d Sess., H. Doc. 92–307, pp. 29, 31.

[7] Ibid., pp. 28, 30.

The difference between the costs estimated under the level-wage assumption and under dynamic wage and price assumptions is the windfall actuarial surplus, expressed as a per cent of payroll, that developed from changing the actuarial assumptions. It is the amount that the tax rate could be reduced and still finance the benefit schedule in effect during the first half of 1972, plus the automatic increases to compensate for increases in cost of living. Conversely, this could be used to expand benefits without increasing the tax rate. Apparently no consideration was given to reducing the near-term tax rate. Instead, the windfall was used to finance the 20 per cent across-the-board increase in benefits legislated in July 1972.

Nevertheless, even under dynamic assumptions the "unexpected" actuarial surpluses will again accumulate, although they probably will not be quite as large as they have been. The dynamic wage and price assumptions chosen were, for a 2.75 per cent increase in prices per annum and 5 per cent per annum for wages. The difference between the wage and price assumption is the allowance for the growth in productivity. By subtraction, the actuarial assumption about the rate of growth in productivity can be derived. The implicit rate of growth in productivity used in the 1972 long-run cost evaluation of social security is 2.25 per cent—conservative but creditable.

The contingency margin built into the actuarial calculation is equal to three-eighths of one per cent for each year from 1972 to 2010. The price assumption actually used was not 2.75 per cent but 3.125 per cent. With the recent history of inflation, providing such a margin appears at first glance to be eminently reasonable. However, the higher price assumption was not allowed to affect the wage assumption. Consequently, the implicit rate of growth in productivity actually used was 1.875 per cent.

	Without margin	With margin
	(per cent)	
Assumed average annual rate of price increase	2.75	2.75
Contingency margin	—	.375
Assumed average annual rate of producitivity	2.25	1.875
Average rate of wage increase	5.00	5.00

The relationship between the assumed rates of price and wage increase is unrealistic. The rate of price increase is too high relative to the rate of wage increase. This means that the estimates of future benefits are going to continue to be overstated since the price assumption is applied to the benefits, and the revenues are going to continue to be understated since the wage assumption is applied to calculation of the tax base.

History of OASDI Tax Rates

Until recently, the near-term tax rates appear to have been set so that the revenues and expenditures were approximately equal, with the tax rates needed to keep the system in actuarial balance scheduled far

Table 3. OASDI Benefits as Per Cent of Taxable Payroll, Combined Tax Rate in Effect, and Size of the Trust Funds

Calendar Year	Benefits as Percentage of Taxable Payroll	Tax Rate (percent)	Trust Funds (billions)
1950	1.17	3.0	$13.7
1951	1.61		15.5
1952	1.76		17.4
1953	2.28		18.7
1954	2.83	4.0	20.6
1955	3.34		21.7
1956	3.48		22.5
1957	4.23	4.5	23.0
1958	4.91		23.2
1959	5.26	5.0	22.0
1960	5.89	6.0	22.5
1961	6.60		22.2
1962	7.16	6.25	20.7
1963	7.43	7.25	20.7
1964	7.45		21.2
1965	7.93		19.8
1966	6.88	7.7	22.3
1967	6.92	7.8	26.2
1968	7.03	7.6	28.7
1969	7.01	8.4	34.2
1970	8.06		38.1
1971	9.06[a]	9.2	40.4[a]

[a] Preliminary.

Source: U.S. Congress. House, *1972 Annual Report of the Board of Trustees of the OASDI Trust Funds,* pp. 18, 21, 27.

enough into the future so that reconsideration of the total program could be undertaken before they became effective. Table 3 shows OASDI benefits as a percentage of taxable payroll and the tax rates in effect.

In 1958, the tax rates in effect were not as high as the cost of the program, and the schedule of future rate increases was first shortened in that year's legislation (see Table 1). The number of retirements in the 1956-57 period, especially among groups newly covered by the 1954 and 1956 legislation, was higher than had been expected; thus, the total expenditures were higher than estimated.[8] In 1961 and 1965, the near-term rates were adjusted upward to cover expanded benefits under the program. After 1965, OASDI expenditures as a percentage of taxable payroll declined, partly reflecting the rapid expansion in employment and earnings during this period. However, the tax rates legislated in 1967 did not recognize these lower costs except to shift 0.1 per cent from the combined OASDI tax rate to the health-insurance tax rate.

From 1965 until 1972, the tax rate increases were scheduled so that the level cost—that is, the rate needed to finance the expenditures for the entire seventy-five-year period—would go into effect in the relatively near future (see Table 1). During that period, the tax rates under the wage ceilings in effect have exceeded the cost of the program, generating surpluses and resulting in substantial accumulations in the trust funds (see Table 3). From the point of view of the overall budget, payroll taxes were financing not only OASDI benefits but some portion of other expenditures as well.

However, the Advisory Council recommended that "the financing of the program should be on a current-cost basis, with the trust funds maintained at a level approximately equal to one year's expenditures."[9] Congress accepted this recommendation in passing the 20 per cent increase in benefits in June 1972. Acceptance of this recommendation, in essence, means that large future liberalizations of social-security benefits will have to be financed either by raising the tax rate or by raising the ceiling on wages by more than would occur under the automatic provisions. The additional liberalizations enacted in October 1972

---

[8] U.S., Congress, Senate, *Social Security Amendments of 1960*, p. 39.

[9] U.S., Congress, House, *1972 Annual Report of the Board of Trustees of the OASDI Trust Funds*, p. 26.

were, in fact, financed by an increase in the tax rate. Table 4 shows the rate schedules either enacted or proposed in the last two years under the. level wage-level cost assumptions and those enacted under dynamic wage-price and current cost financing assumptions. Hospital insurance tax rates are in addition to the OASDI rates. The change to current cost financing has shifted the further increases in OASDI tax rates into the future when the real costs of the benefits begin to rise for demographic reasons.

Table 4. Combined OASDI Tax Rates Under Different Assumptions, Selected Calendar Years 1971–2011

Calendar Year	Ceiling on Wages Subject to Tax	Level Wage – Level Cost		Dynamic Assumptions Current Cost Financing	
		1971 Law (enacted)	HRI (proposed)	June 1972 Law	October 1972 Law
1971	$ 7,800	9.2	9.2	9.2	9.2
1972	9,000	10.0	8.4	9.2	9.2
1973	10,800				9.7
1974	12,000				
1975	a		10.0		
1976	a	10.3			
1977	a		12.2		
1978	a			9.0	9.6
2011	a	10.3	12.2	10.7	11.7

a Wage ceiling to be automatically increased.

Sources: *Congressional Record,* Vol. 118 (June 29, 1972), p. S 10785 and *Congressional Record,* Vol. 118 (Oct. 17, 1972), p. H 10205.

The Role of the Wage Ceiling

The ceiling on wages subject to tax was initially established at $3,000; it was not raised until 1951 (see Table 1). Since then, it has been raised six times and currently (1973) is $10,800, an increase from the 1970 ceiling of $7,800[10] and the 1972 ceiling of $9,000. It is scheduled to rise up to $12,000 in 1974. Because of the wage ceiling, total wages subject to tax are smaller than total covered wages. Moreover, if the wage ceiling is not raised periodically, wages are subject to tax decline as a percentage of covered wages because more and more workers have annual incomes in excess of any given ceiling as average wage rises over time. Of course, an increase in the wage ceiling is just as effective increasing revenues as an increase in the tax rates; but it concentrates the effect of the increased tax liability on the middle-income groups.

As mentioned above, the 1972 legislation provides for increasing the ceiling on wages subject to tax to $12,000 in 1974. After 1974, the wage ceiling is to be increased at the rate at which average wages have risen since the last base quarter.[11] The legislation defines the original base quarter as the first quarter of 1973. If an automatic cost-of-living increase in benefits is indicated in 1974 and takes effect in 1975, the $12,000 wage ceiling in 1975 would be increased by the percentage increase in average wages between the first quarter of 1973 and the first quarter of 1974. Such calculated increases in the ceiling are to be rounded up to the nearest $300 increase. Thus, if the 5 per cent average annual increase in wages assumed in the long-range evaluation occurs, the wage ceiling would be raised to $12,600 in 1975 and to $14,000 in 1977. These increases in the ceilings appear to raise enough revenue to finance the automatic increase in benefits.

An increase in the wage ceiling also increases future benefits. Because taxes are paid only until earnings reach the ceiling, the maximum amount recorded in an individual's wage history cannot exceed the ceiling. For example, for a person who had earned at or above the wage ceiling and who retired in 1965, the benefit would be calculated on a wage history reflecting the $3,000 to $4,800 ceilings in effect during his working life. For a similar person retiring in 1970, the benefit would be based on a wage history from $3,000 to $7,800 and would be larger.

---

[10] Social security taxes are paid on covered wages until the ceiling is reached. For example, a person whose annual earnings in 1971 were $15,600, when the ceiling was $7,800, would pay social security taxes only for the first six months of the year but would be credited with being in covered employment for all four quarters as far as his eligibility for future benefits is concerned.

[11] Technically, the average increase in wages is calculated on the average taxable wages reported to social security.

The impact of increasing the wage ceiling on benefits is gradual, but it does increase the commitment to future expenditures.

Future Planning for Social Security

How should we plan for social security? The major reforms that are being made in the methodology for computing the costs of OASDI expenditures in order to determine the tax rates are beginning to clarify some issues that have previously been buried in what appeared to be technical assumptions. Putting the system on current cost financing (pay-as-you-go) recognizes that the trust-fund mechanism cannot shift the real burden over time. It also recognizes that there is a distinct time profile to those costs.

The complexities of the actuarial calculation and the many technical aspects of the eligibility requirements tend to obscure the basic purposes of the program. Four basic questions concerning the benefit structure need to be examined.

First, are the replacement rates adequate, both for people already on the roles and for the future beneficiaries? The replacement rates have developed on an ad hoc basis. Originally, there was a formula that precisely stated what the replacement rates were. That formula has been replaced by lengthy benefits tables that relate average monthly earnings to benefit amounts. The table is extended every time the wage ceiling is increased by what amounts to a rule of thumb—namely, a $1 increase in monthly benefits for each $5 increase in the wage ceiling.

Second, should only earned income, or really the lack of it, be used as the criteria for determining eligibility for benefits? Many retired persons have other sources of income. Counting only earned income in determining eligibility means on the one hand that benefits are being paid to persons who often have substantial incomes from dividends and interest; on the other, it often discourages persons from earning more than $2,100 in cases where social-security benefits and their earnings are their sole source of income.

Third, although the benefits are now automatically adjusted for increases in the cost of living, should society share the increases in real per capita income that result from productivity increases with retired and dependent population? In the past, the ad hoc across-the-board increases have been larger than the increase in prices and real benefits have been increased, especially in the past seven years. However, the older retirees—the ones who have been retired ten to twenty years—receive much smaller benefits than recent retirees. Are their needs really that much less than those of the younger retirees?

Finally, are across-the-board increases in benefits an effective way of providing adequate income to the retirees and dependents? The 20 per cent increase in benefits enacted in July 1972 costs $8 billion. Twenty-seven million people were receiving OASDI benefits in 1972. Only about 20 per cent of those people are poor. Their incomes could have been increased much more adequately at much lower cost if the increase in benefits had been designed specifically to help those most in need.

However, a discussion that focuses on the interrelationship between tax rates, wage ceilings, and benefit payments overlooks the broad and important question of what the role of payroll taxes should be in the overall federal revenue system. This question is becoming increasingly important because the OASDHI tax rate is now so high (11.7 per cent in 1973) that it is the second largest source of revenues and because there are proposals to finance major new programs (primarily national health insurance) through expansion of the payroll taxes.

The Role of Payroll Taxes

Payroll taxes (OASDI only) have grown from 5 per cent of total federal revenues in fiscal year 1950, to 11½ per cent in 1960, to 16 per cent by 1970, and are projected to rise to 19.4 per cent in 1973. Many people already question whether the payroll tax in its present form should continue to be the sole means of financing the social security programs.[12] Legally, half of the tax is paid by the employer and half by the employee. There is fairly strong evidence, however, that especially for nonunion workers, the entire tax burden falls on wages.[13] There is some evidence that in unionized industries, the employer's share is passed forward in the form of higher prices.

---

[12] Joseph A. Pechman, Henry J. Aaron, and Michael K. Taussig, *Social Security: Perspectives for Reform* (Washington, D.C.: The Brookings Institution, 1968).

[13] John A. Brittain, "The Incidence of Social Security Payroll Taxes," *American Economic Review*, Vol. 61 (Mar. 1971), pp. 110–125.

To the extent that the tax falls on wages, it is regressive: a person whose total earnings are above the wage ceiling pays a smaller percentage of his income in payroll taxes than a person whose total earnings are equal to or below the ceiling. There are no exemptions or deductions permitted and no adjustment for the presence of more than one wage earner in a family. In a family with two wage earners whose combined income exceeds the ceiling, both must pay the tax, and their tax liability exceeds that of a family with the same income earned by one person. Thus, a family with one wage earner earning $15,000 pays $631 in OASDHI taxes, but a family with two wage earners, one earning $10,000 and one earning $5,000, pays $877. This is one of the reasons that the tax should be made a tax on family income.

Not only is the tax regressive for the taxpayers but the aggregate revenue is probably not as responsive to variations in economic activity as the income tax is. During the past twenty years, there were only eight years in which neither the tax rate nor the wage ceiling was raised. Table 5 shows the percentage increase in OASDI payroll tax receipts and in wages and salaries for those eight years. Because there are so few years in which the tax rate or wage ceiling remained unchanged, it is impossible to determine exactly the elasticity of the tax; but it appears to be less than 1.0. That is, a 1.0 per cent increase in wages and salaries results in something less than a 1.0 per cent increase in OASDI payroll taxes.

Table 5. Responsiveness of OASDI Receipts

	Percentage Change	
Year	*OASDI Payroll-Tax Receipts*	*Wages and Salaries*
1952	7.0	8.2
1953	6.9	7.1
1956	7.7	7.8
1958	−0.5	0.5
1961	1.2	2.7
1964	5.0	7.2
1967	7.5	7.3
1970	4.1	6.1

Individual income-tax rates were reduced in 1964 and 1965 and raised from mid-1968 to mid-1970. The rates were reduced in mid-1970 because of the expiration of the surcharge and the first stage of the reduction scheduled in the 1969 Tax Reform Act. Effective rates were reduced again in 1971. But the increases in the payroll tax have, and will, offset much of the tax-rate reductions on the individual income. The combined tax liability for a family of four for social security and individual income taxes is shown in Tables 6 and 7.

Table 6. Individual Income and OASDHI Taxes[a], by Income Level, Family of Four with One Wage Earner, Current Law

	Income Tax	OASDHI	Total	As Percent of Income
		$3,000 Wage and Salary Income		
1963	$ 60.00	$108.60	$ 168.60	5.0
1964	60.00	108.60	168.60	5.6
1965	0.00	108.60	108.60	3.6
1966	0.00	126.00	126.00	4.2
1967	0.00	132.00	132.00	4.4
1968	0.00	132.00	132.00	4.4
1969	0.00	144.00	144.00	4.8
1970	0.00	144.00	144.00	4.8
1971	0.00	156.00	156.00	5.2
1972	0.00	156.00	156.00	5.2
1973	0.00	175.50	175.50	5.8
		$5,000 Wage and Salary Income		
1963	420.00	174.00	594.00	11.9
1964	321.00	174.00	495.00	9.9
1965	306.00	174.00	480.00	9.6
1966	306.00	210.00	516.00	10.3
1967	306.00	220.00	526.00	10.5
1968	333.25	220.00	553.25	11.1
1969	341.00	240.00	581.00	11.6
1970	200.90	240.00	440.90	8.8
1971	177.50	260.00	437.50	8.7
1972	98.00	260.00	358.00	7.2
1973	98.00	292.50	390.50	7.8
		$7,000 Wage and Salary Income		
1963	780.00	174.00	954.00	13.6
1964	662.00	174.00	836.00	11.9
1965	603.00	174.00	777.00	11.1
1966	603.00	277.20	880.20	12.6
1967	603.00	290.40	893.40	12.8
1968	648.00	308.00	956.00	13.7
1969	663.00	336.00	999.00	14.3
1970	530.00	336.00	866.00	12.4
1971	492.50	364.00	856.50	12.2
1972	402.00	364.00	766.00	10.9
1973	402.00	409.50	811.50	11.6

	Income Tax	OASDHI	Total	As Percent of Income
	$10,000 Wage and Salary Income			
1963	1,372.00	174.00	1,546.00	15.5
1964	1,200.00	174.00	1,374.00	13.7
1965	1,114.00	174.00	1,288.00	12.9
1966	1,114.00	277.20	1,391.20	13.9
1967	1,114.00	290.40	1,404.40	14.0
1968	1,198.00	343.20	1,541.20	15.4
1969	1,225.00	374.40	1,599.40	16.0
1970	1,122.00	374.40	1,496.40	15.0
1971	1,000.00	405.60	1,405.60	14.1
1972	905.00	468.00	1,373.00	13.7
1973	905.00	585.00	1,490.00	14.9
	$15,000 Wage and Salary Income			
1963	2,616.00	174.00	2,790.00	18.6
1964	2,326.00	174.00	2,500.00	16.7
1965	2,172.00	174.00	2,346.00	15.6
1966	2,172.00	277.20	2,449.20	16.3
1967	2,172.00	290.40	2,462.40	16.4
1968	2,335.00	343.20	2,678.20	17.9
1969	2,389.00	374.40	2,763.40	18.4
1970	2,204.00	374.40	2,578.40	17.2
1971	1,996.00	405.60	2,401.60	16.0
1972	1,820.00	468.00	2,288.00	15.2
1973	1,820.00	631.80	2,451.80	16.3

[a] Includes hospital-insurance tax.

The combined tax liability (individual income and employees' share of OASDHI) on a $7,000 income will be only $142 lower in 1973 than it was in 1963; for a $10,000 income, it will be only $56 lower in 1973 than it was in 1963. The income-tax rate reductions have been larger than the social security tax increases at higher levels of income. It is difficult not to come to the conclusion that payroll taxes are being partially substituted for the individual income tax.

The hospital insurance tax rate has been included in Tables 6 and 7 in order to show total tax payments.

Medicare

As noted at the beginning of this chapter, Medicare consists of two parts: hospital insurance and supplementary medical insurance. Health insurance is financed through the payroll tax; supplementary medical insurance is paid for by a monthly contribution from the beneficiaries that is matched by a contribution from general revenues.

The major financial problem that has arisen with the Medicare program has been the rapidly increasing price of medical services. The

Table 7. Individual Income Tax and OASDHI Taxes,[a] by Income Level, Family of Four, with Two Wage Earners, Current Law

	Income Tax	OASDHI	Total	As Percent of Income
$10,000 Total Income ($3,000 and $7,000)				
1963	$1,372.00	$282.60	$1,654.60	16.5
1964	1,200.00	282.60	1,462.60	14.8
1965	1,114.00	282.60	1,406.60	14.1
1966	1,114.00	403.20	1,517.20	15.2
1967	1,114.00	422.40	1,536.40	15.4
1968	1,198.00	440.00	1,638.00	16.4
1969	1,225.00	480.00	1,705.00	17.0
1970	1,122.00	480.00	1,602.00	16.0
1971	1,000.00	520.00	1,520.00	15.2
1972	905.00	520.00	1,425.00	14.3
1973	905.00	585.00	1,490.00	14.9
$10,000 Total Income ($5,000 and $5,000)				
1963	1,372.00	348.00	1,720.00	17.2
1964	1,200.00	348.00	1,548.00	15.5
1965	1,114.00	348.00	1,462.00	14.6
1966	1,114.00	410.00	1,524.00	15.2
1967	1,114.00	440.00	1,554.00	15.5
1968	1,198.00	440.00	1,638.00	16.4
1969	1,225.00	480.00	1,705.00	17.0
1970	1,122.00	480.00	1,102.00	16.0
1971	1,000.00	520.00	1,520.00	15.2
1972	905.00	520.00	1,425.00	14.2
1973	905.00	585.00	1,490.00	14.9
$15,000 Total Income ($5,000 and $10,000)				
1963	2,616.00	348.00	2,964.00	19.8
1964	2,326.00	348.00	2,674.00	17.8
1965	2,172.00	348.00	2,520.00	16.8
1966	2,172.00	487.00	2,659.00	17.7
1967	2,172.00	510.40	2,682.40	17.9
1968	2,335.00	563.20	2,898.20	19.3
1969	2,389.00	614.40	3,003.40	20.0
1970	2,204.00	614.40	2,818.40	18.8
1971	1,996.00	665.60	2,661.60	17.7
1972	1,820.00	728.00	2,548.00	17.0
1973	1,820.00	877.50	2,697.50	18.0

[a]See Table 6.

health-insurance tax rate has been raised from 0.7 per cent of taxable payroll in 1966 to 1.2 per cent in 1972 and is scheduled to rise to 2.0 per cent in 1973. The wage ceilings are the same as for OASDI taxes. The amount paid by the recipients has been raised from the initial $3.00 a month to the current $5.80. Major efforts are being made to bring medical prices under control, but extensive reorganization of the delivery of health services will probably be required to modify price trends markedly.

The legislation passed in October 1972 extended Medicare to the disabled at an annual first-year cost of $2.0 billion. One of the broad questions concerning Medicare is whether the monthly premium paid by beneficiaries should be shifted to the payroll tax. Shifting the premium to the payroll tax would probably raise the combined OASDHI tax rate from the 11.7 per cent scheduled for 1973 to about 12 per cent. The arguments against such a shift are primarily that the combined tax rate is too high, placing too large a burden on the working population, and that the beneficiaries ought to be kept aware of the cost of their benefits. The arguments for shifting the premium to the payroll tax is that $5.80 a month is a heavy burden for the recipients to bear. There are a multitude of technical problems concerning what services are to be covered, what institutions should be included, what type of care is to be provided, and so on. How these are resolved will undoubtedly affect tax rates, but the major issues are rising prices and methods of financing the program.

The supplementary medical insurance program is not subject to actuarial evaluation. It has so far been treated as a current tax-and-transfer program, with the premium set each year in order to meet anticipated costs. The health-insurance program is actuarially evaluated, but only for the next twenty-five years, rather than for the seventy-five-year span used in the cash-benefits program; and the evaluation assumes rising wages and prices.

The payroll tax is embedded into the OASDHI system and is not likely to be replaced. However, certain reforms of the tax such as personal exemptions or combining the employee portion of the tax with the individual income tax would make it more equitable. The place of the payroll tax in the overall revenue system should be evaluated carefully before new programs are financed with this form of taxation. Even more careful thought should be given to the question of whether the concept of actuarial soundness is relevant to the new programs.

Proposed Reforms of the Payroll Tax

The most direly needed reform now is in the payroll tax itself. It makes little sense to tax the poor and middle-income groups so heavily in order to support the retired population. If it is recognized that the payroll tax is an intergenerational tax-and-transfer system, not an insurance system, it does not make sense to finance the benefits with a regressive tax.

Various reforms have been proposed. If the ceiling on wages subject to tax were removed, the tax rates could be lowered. This would make the tax at least proportional and would create a more elastic tax base in a macroeconomic sense. The employers would continue to pay half the tax. The employees would pay half the tax, but personal exemptions based on family size could be introduced, and husbands and wives would file joint returns.

The removal of the wage ceiling has implications for benefits. Benefits are related (as explained in "The Role of the Wage Ceiling") to the number of quarters of covered employment and the average wage of each individual. A person with earnings at or near the ceiling during his working life receives a larger benefit than a person with lower wages. Thus, the elimination of the ceiling *could* create very large future benefits, even in real terms. However, it does not have to. As mentioned earlier, current social-security legislation contains, what is called, by those who know it exists, the "20 per cent rule." It has been the practice in recent legislation to increase entitlement to future benefits by $1 for each $5 increase in the wage ceiling. A formula that utilizes the 20 per cent rule for the first $5,000 above the current ceiling, 15 per cent for the next $5,000 or $10,000 of income, and so forth, eventually reaching zero or some nominal amount (such as one per cent) would control the size of the future benefits. This proposal leaves in place the mechanism for determining benefits. It has worked well, and there is no reason to replace it.

Even further reductions in the tax rate would be possible if the tax was levied on *all* income with exemptions only, rather than limiting it to earned income. However, taxing all income, including property income, raises possible complications on the benefit side. There seem to be few complications in crediting property income toward future benefits. Self-employed taxes are already paid under the declaration system. The complications come in the application of the retirement test. As the system now works, after a person becomes eligible for benefits at sixty-two or sixty-five, he receives benefits only if his monthly wages are less than one-twelfth of whatever the current annual retirement test is. If unearned income is credited toward benefits, should unearned income be taken into account in the retirement test? Retirement tests, incidentally, apply only until age seventy-two.

This problem can be solved. The level of the retirement test could be generous, with both earned and unearned income included, and minimum benefits could be established. People already on the roles would not be affected because no unearned income would be credited to their accounts. But there is the problem of the transition.

By changing to adjusted gross income minus exemptions, crediting unearned income, and including it in benefit calculations and the retirement test, one glaring inequity in the system would be corrected. Under the present system, a person over sixty-five earning more than $2,100 a year begins to lose his benefits; whereas a person receiving the same amount from property income loses nothing. Those opposed to using total income minus exemptions are concerned about this because they feel it would be a major disincentive to the accumulation of assets. The problem can probably be handled by establishing minimum benefits regardless of the source and size of income.

Until recently, there has been very little pressure for reform of the payroll tax except from academics. However, the grumbling is likely to become more widespread. As Tables 6 and 7 show, many people have had little or no tax relief in the past ten years because of the biannual increase in social security tax rates. In a surprising number of income brackets, the decreases in the income tax rates have been largely offset by increased social security tax rates. Not only has there been very little tax reduction over all but a regressive, inelastic tax is being substituted for a progressive, elastic tax, altering the overall nature of the tax system in a highly undesirable way.

Future Level of the Trust Funds

Because of the long-term commitment that OASDHI makes to future beneficiaries and the variation in the real costs of the program resulting from demographic factors that are known to exist, it is essential that the public and policy makers be kept aware of them. It is not difficult, if reasonable assumptions concerning wages and prices are used, to calculate the cost of the existing program or proposed changes in it for specific years in the future. The change to pay-as-you-go financing and dynamic wage and price is explicit recognition of the period of high cost in the future and will facilitate more rational planning in providing for it.

For the most part, the existing trust funds have built up slowly over the past thirty-five years. The real function of the trust funds is to protect the benefit program from unexpected variations in expenditures and revenues and to maintain public confidence in the system. The report of the economists and actuaries to the advisory council on social security recommended that the trust funds be maintained at levels equal to one year's benefit payments but that this recommendation be reviewed to see whether even that amount is needed in the future.

USER CHARGES

Charles J. Goetz

THE REVENUE POTENTIAL OF
USER-RELATED CHARGES IN
STATE AND LOCAL GOVERNMENTS

STATE AND LOCAL GOVERNMENTS in the United States have generated an extremely high rate of revenue growth in recent years. Because the relatively broad-based taxes on sales, income, and property have been subjected to heavy pressure, attention has naturally turned to possible alternative forms of finance. Among these alternatives, the broad class of user-related benefit taxes and user charges have attracted considerable interest. User-related charges are direct analogues of private-sector prices. Because they are linked to an individual's consumption of specific public services, their payment is in a sense voluntary and directly linked with a benefit. Common sense also dictates extension of this category to taxes on private goods that are essential complements of the consumption of certain public services. For instance, the linkage between consumption of highway services and gasoline is sufficiently strong to suggest the classification of motor-fuel taxes as user-related charges.

An appropriate system of nonrelated charges is capable of easing state and local financial pressures in several ways. Obviously, the charges may serve as a source of revenues that defray part of the cost of some public goods or services. More indirectly, the imposition of charges also actually *reduces* the level of costs to be covered because the demand for public services presumably will fall below the level of demand at no cost. Finally, the demand for public services may be further dampened to the extent that a user-charge system more effectively rations out any

113

given stock of services to those individual users whose demands are most intense.

This chapter focuses primarily on the direct contribution of charges to revenue flows. This in no way excludes the possibility that the rationing or efficiency aspects of public-goods pricing may not ultimately have greater potential importance than the direct revenue contributions. However, recent interest in the strict revenue aspects of public-goods pricing has been high because of an alleged new trend in the utilization of user charges. The impression is that user charges are already much more heavily exploited and are, moreover, destined to play an increasingly heavy role in the future of state-local finance.

However, the actual statistics from recent years cast substantial doubt on the existence of such a trend. Unless technological developments or changes in social attitudes are postulated, it is not clear why state and local governments would be expected to place an increased emphasis on user charges. In most cases, moreover, federal tax deductibility suggests advantages for the more traditional forms of taxation. Even under favorable assumptions, the scope for application of user charges does not seem to be as wide as has sometimes been suggested.

Evidence from the Immediate Past

At any level of government, the deduction of intergovernmental revenues from total revenues yields total own-source revenues generated. Although it is debatable exactly how changes in the relative dependence of governments on any financing source should be measured, this concept of own-source revenue is a plausible base for measuring changes. The period from 1965 to 1969 is both recent enough to reflect current trends and long enough to reduce the danger of possible short-period quirks.

Relative-growth measures. During this four-year period, the major revenue sources with direct user- or beneficiary-related characteristics have, as a group, actually expanded *less* rapidly than total own-source revenues. This is reflected in the separate statistics for all levels of government, state, city, and local. In each case, of course, there are individual categories of user charges, notably higher education, whose growth has exceeded that of overall own-source revenues (see Tables 1, 2, and 3).

It is probable that the contrary impression of relative expansion in the employment of user revenues is the result of uncritical reliance on the Census Bureau definition of "current charges," which excludes not only utility revenues but also certain licenses and taxes (such as those pertaining to automobiles and motor fuel) that clearly have the characteristics of prices for public services.[1]

Table 1. Major User-related State Revenue Sources (millions)

Item	1965	1969	Per Cent Change
All own-source revenue	$38,506	$59,809	55.3
Motor fuel	4,300	5,644	31.3
Auto licenses	2,021	2,685	32.9
Tolls	524	696	32.0
Other auto-related	31	53	70.9
Sum of highway-related revenue	6,876	9,025	31.0
Higher education	1,686	3,041	80.4
Other education	25	50	100.0
Hunting and fishing	138	178	28.9
Hospitals	379	786	107.4
Natural resources	134	189	41.0
Housing, urban renewal	5	8	60.0
Water transport	49	71	44.9
Air transport	16	33	106.2
Liquor sales	1,270	1,663	30.9
Total	10,578	15,044	42.2
Per cent of own-source revenue	27.5	25.1	

Sources: U.S. Bureau of the Census, *State Government Finances in 1965, 1969,* Table 7, pp. 19–26; and *Governmental Finances in 1964–65, 1968–69,* Table 4, p. 20. (Housing and Urban Renewal is a very small part of state revenues and, therefore, not treated separately in *State Government Finances.* It is significant at federal and local levels and, therefore, listed separately in *Governmental Finances.*)

---

[1] In other words, the census classifications are sometimes arbitrary and do not always reflect the true economic character of the levy. As it happens, the subset of charges identified as such by the census has been growing at a faster rate than the more inclusive set of charges that may be identified by applying functional criteria as the basis of classification.

Table 2. Major User-related Local Revenue Sources (millions)

Item	1965	1969	Per Cent Change
All own-source revenues	$38,242	$53,192	39.1
Motor fuel	31	37	19.3
Auto licenses	124	157	26.6
Higher education	148	264	78.4
Other education	351	545	55.3
Hospitals	993	1,879	89.2
Sewerage	519	684	31.8
Nonsewerage sanitation	191	220	15.2
Parks and recreation	155	236	45.8
Natural resources	107	84	−21.5
Housing and urban renewal	453	538	18.8
Water transport and terminals	129	181	40.3
Parking	160	151	− 5.6
Air transport	244	400	63.9
Utility revenue	4,908	5,931	20.8
School lunches	981	1,284	30.9
Liquor sales	177	245	38.4
Total	9,671	12,836	32.7
Per cent of own-source revenues	25.3	24.1	

Sources: U.S. Bureau of the Census, *Governmental Finances in 1964–65, 1968–69,* Table 4, p. 20.

Table 3. Major User-related City Revenue Sources (millions)

Item	1969	Per Cent Change from 1965[a]	Per Cent Distribution in 1969[a]
All own-source revenues	$22,327	33.0	100.0
Charges	2,753	41.1	12.3
Special assessments	310	−5.8	1.4
Utility revenue	4,576	21.7	20.5
Liquor-stores revenue	134	45.6	0.6

[a]Calculated

Source: U.S. Bureau of the Census, *City Government Finances in 1968–1969,* Table 1, p. 5.

Price and cost as measures of use. Relative-growth measures are not the only possible criteria of increased reliance on the pricing of state and local goods and services. Another reasonable measure might be the percentage of costs, attributable to a specific function, that are covered by user revenues drawn from that functional area. Although it is difficult to perform such match-ups between costs and charges, the available evidence for the past five years does not suggest any recent trend of increased efforts to recover costs out of user-related revenues. At the state level, for instance, only hospital fees show a distinct trend toward covering higher proportions of cost (see Table 4). On the contrary, what seems to be a marked expansion of charges for higher education is primarily a consequence of a high expenditure growth

Table 4. User Charges as Per Cent of State Expenditures on Selected Functions[a]

Expenditure Category	1963	1965	1967	1969
Higher education	32.2	32.0	29.9	30.3
Hospitals	15.7	15.5	12.7	20.9
Highways, direct expenditures	82.0	83.7	82.8	86.7
Highways, including local subsidies	68.9	69.8	69.1	72.0
Fish and game	75.1	75.0	70.6	68.4

[a]Calculated

Sources: U.S. Bureau of the Census, *State Government Finances in 1963, 1965, 1967, 1969,* Table 9, pp. 27–37 (expenditures); Table 7, pp. 19–26 (revenues).

rate in that area; in fact, fees have actually declined slightly as a per cent of higher-education expenditures. It is difficult, then, to find evidence that legislators are growing any more eager to charge users for public services. Rather, some of the fastest-growing areas of state-local expenditure happen to involve priceable services, even if such prices are merely keeping approximate pace with costs.

The Applicability of Prices to Government Services

Although recent history may be a disappointing source of evidence of startling departures from trend, it is possible to examine the factors that *might* affect variations in the use of public-service charges. One useful method of shedding light on the potential applicability of user-related charges is to pursue the analogue between such charges and private-sector pricing schemes. Different types of public services differ not only in terms of the *possibility* of being priced but also in terms of the *advisability* of imposing such pricing to the maximum extent feasible. The possibility of pricing is essentially a question of technical feasibility. The advisability of such pricing is a matter of efficiency. Efficient pricing demands that a citizen be discouraged from consuming a unit of public service only when the benefits of such consumption are less than its cost to society.

Necessity of a transferable property right. Prices are normally paid in exchange for a property right to some benefit. Hence, it is almost truistic that a seller cannot collect a price for a right that the potential consumer expects to have even without making any payment. Governments are no exception to this rule. The inability to enforce a property right has been discussed in economic literature under such terms as "indivisibility" or "nonexcludibility" of benefits. Most of the so-called general government functions of state and local units cannot be priced for individual users because of this indivisibility problem; if the benefits are provided to one citizen, they are essentially available to all. Police patrols, mosquito spraying, flood control, and the like are common examples of state-local functions that are impossible to price directly because the property rights to their benefits cannot be effectively transferred among individual purchasers.

However, highway tolls are an excellent reminder that the pricing of public services is not necessarily a matter of inherent qualities of excludibility in the goods involved, but that it depends on economic and technological considerations. Given the present technology of collecting highway tolls, the delays and other costs attendant on the collection process make it impractical to consider pricing city streets but perfectly feasible to levy charges on trunk highways. Nevertheless, it is not impossible to imagine the development of electronic monitoring devices that would bring almost-universal road-usage pricing within the realm of practicality. Where the possibility of technological advance seems promising, a public policy of investment in the research and development of exclusionary devices that would facilitate the pricing of roads and other public services may bear very high returns.

Where direct pricing is impossible, license fees and the taxation of complementary goods constitute opportunities to recoup the costs of government services. Dog licenses and hunting and fishing licenses provide two examples of well-defined areas in which state and local governments attempt to finance benefits by exacting payment for certain rights. A major weakness of licenses as prices is that the payments do not vary with the services consumed, so that it is difficult to ration use according to cost, which efficiency norms demand. Even quite apart from interpersonal equity or efficiency considerations, it is also possible to prove that the state could always collect more fish and game revenue, for example, if the typical lump-sum fee could be supplemented by an incremental fee per hunting or fishing trip. From this standpoint, highways again provide an interesting case because they are in large measure financed by charges to the essential inputs of highway travel: a lump-sum license fee on the vehicle and its operator and then a variable fee on fuel consumption. Obviously, the motor-fuel tax more nearly serves the function of a true price than the various forms of license fees do, but the fuel tax does not properly discriminate among the varying social costs of using different highways at different times. Comparison with the rates of gasoline taxation in Western Europe suggests that the revenue potential of this form of highway user charge has not yet been fully exploited in the United States.

Unfortunately, at the present time, the technological feasibility of pricing happens to be minimal in some of the exact areas where its application is most devoutly desired by state and local governments. For instance, urban governments have been plagued by their inability to recoup what they feel are the service costs imposed on them by individuals who reside and pay their principal taxes in the suburbs.

In summary, a government is like any other seller in that it can only charge for well-defined, enforceable property rights. Some important additional classes of public services are potentially chargeable because of future technological developments; but for others, it is difficult to envision any scheme for creating a salable property right. (See the Appendix for a discussion of an alternative to public pricing.) Among existing pricing schemes, a significant distinction exists between genuine prices and lump-sum license charges that, in essence, make a taxpayer's costs independent of the level of his usage, provided such usage occurs at all.

Voluntary versus involuntary sales. In the private sector, it is normally expected that a price need not be paid unless the thing received is contracted for voluntarily. In the public sector, some prices are charged even when the reception of the benefit is unavoidable. For instance, so-called special assessments have traditionally been levied on real property to defray all or part of the costs of specific public improvements such as street paving, sidewalks, and sewer lines. Such payments constitute a gray area of user charges because they are clearly intended to be connected with the reception of differential benefits. The government, in essence, has decided that the benefits from a certain expenditure are divisible between those who are not being specially assessed and those who are being assessed, but are indivisible within the assessed group. This may not be an unreasonable rule of thumb. Unlike the other types of user charges, however, it is then not possible to be certain that the services provided are really worth the price in terms of the assessment extracted.

Overall, the postwar record is one of secular decline in the use of special assessments by municipal governments. For cities of over 500,000 people, this decline has been absolute as well as relative. For smaller cities, special assessments have grown more slowly than general revenues.

Potentially profitable public services. In the case of local governments, a surprisingly large part of expenditures and revenues is traceable to services whose *potential* priceability is open to little argument. This is the area of utility services, which formed slightly over 20 per cent of local budgets in 1969. The consumption rights being transferred are divisible among consumers and present no special problems of exclusion. In fact, many of these services are potentially providable by private enterprise on a profit-making basis. Besides the major categories of gas, water, electricity, and transport, sewerage and garbage collection are essentially private goods that just happen in many cases to be provided under the aegis of local government.[2] This is also true, at the state level, of the sales of government-owned liquor stores. Although charges from

2 Of course, the pricing of sewerage and garbage collection would have to be coupled with a requirement that disposal in fact be accomplished in a suitable manner. Thus, people should be permitted to adjust the flows of sewerage and garbage they create but should not be permitted to opt for dumping in lieu of paying the proper cost of disposal.

these essentially commercial activities are technically user charges, their role would be relatively noncontroversial if the effect of utilities on government budgets were essentially neutral or exactly break even. But what if publicly owned utilities set charges that generate net profits or losses?

Based on the nationwide average, municipally owned gas and electric utilities produce positive net revenues; whereas water and transportation incur losses (see Table 5). Special comment will be made on transportation in the section "One good distortion deserves another." With respect to water, it should be noted that in the past some cities chose not to invest in an adequate metering capability and have subsequently been reluctant to make the capital investment necessary to implement a reasonable pricing system for this service. Otherwise, the considerations relating to pricing of most government utilities are essentially similar.

Table 5. Finances of City-operated Utilities, 1969 (millions)

Utility	Revenues	Expenditures	Revenue as Per Cent of Expenditures
Water	$2,026	$2,169	93.4
Electricity	1,706	1,644	103.7
Transportation	578	911	115.1
Total	$4,576	$4,954	92.3

a Calculated

Source: U.S. Bureau of the Census, *City Government Finances in 1968-69*, Table 2, p. 6.

Local governments typically enjoy a monopoly position with respect to the goods under discussion. In most cases, therefore, they could significantly enhance their net revenue positions by extracting monopoly profits from utilities operation. However, such utility pricing policies have complex distributional and efficiency implications. If the utility sets prices equal to the marginal cost of the services it is providing, the net profit or loss merely transfers income from citizens in their capacity as utility consumers to citizens in their capacity as taxpayers. If all citizens were identical with respect to both taxes paid and preferences for the public service being provided, the effects would cancel each other out. Normally, however, there will be some effective redistribution of income among citizens. If the user charges are *not* set equal to marginal cost, an economic inefficiency exists because the incremental costs and benefits implied for the two groups (taxpayers and consumers) are not equal. In simple terms, if the costs and benefits to each individual are added up when a user charge is changed from the economically efficient (marginal-cost) level to some other level, a net loss must be involved.

The argument is necessarily oversimplified in the brief space of this chapter, but the fundamental logic of the situation does become clear. A voter should be reluctant to approve any policy of exploiting the full revenue potential of a local utility because, on balance, the net benefits to him of such a policy are likely to be negative. Conversely, it may be desirable, in the case of services with high fixed and low marginal costs, to deliberately set user charges below average cost. It is, in any case, difficult to see why the future should be expected to hold any extremely significant changes in pricing policy in this area except, perhaps, for coming closer to achieving full-cost pricing in the area of water provision.

Finally, it may be noted parenthetically at this point that the large-scale conduct of essentially market-type sales by local governments renders any display of statistics more than a little bit ambiguous. A city with commercial garbage collection that is subject to franchise fees and commercial power provision that is subject to a utilities tax may in actuality confront its citizens with circumstances identical to those in a similar city with completely municipalized services. By shifting from one form of organization to another, a city may affect the statistics themselves but not the substance behind the statistics.

One good distortion deserves another. Mass transportation is a special case of a perfectly priceable service for which pricing at other than strict marginal cost may be justified. In many cases, the subsidization of mass transport is defended on the basis of indirect benefits of the type discussed in the following section. However, it is legitimate to question whether transportation inherently produces any more indirect benefits than, say, electric power. Actually, it is easier to rationalize relatively low user charges for public transportation on the basis of cost-avoidance considerations. The relative use of mass transportation versus private vehicular transportation is clearly affected by the respective prices of the two modes of transportation. Moreover, present technology does not permit an effective marginal-cost pricing of vehicular traffic. If, then, vehicular traffic is underpriced, excessive traffic-congestion costs may sensibly be avoided by underpricing the use of mass transportation.

The principle of counterbalancing pricing distortions is interesting in its own right. This particular application to public-service pricing is especially noteworthy, however, because it shows how the technological inability to generate efficient user charges on one public service implies the inadvisability of fully applying pricing to a related area in which such pricing is actually feasible.

Indirect benefits. Finally, there is the highly important class of government services in which an enforceable property right exists for the direct beneficiary but the by-product indirect benefits are indivisible and therefore unpriceable. Educational activities are cited as the classic example of this situation, but a host of other state and local governmental activities are also alleged to generate spillover benefits to indirect beneficiaries.

When spillover benefits exist to a significant extent, the imposition of full marginal-cost user pricing will lead to a suboptimal level of the activity in question. The proper subsidy to such an activity is the marginal value of the spillover benefits to society. Unfortunately, the value of those marginal spillover benefits is not easily quantifiable. Emotion and subjectivity doubtless play a very important role in limiting the levels of user charges on spillover-producing goods. In fact, a cynic might be tempted to argue that nonquantifiable indirect benefits are a catchall argument which can be used to rationalize almost any subsidized government service. Because such subjective attitudes are notoriously volatile, state-local policy in this area may alter dramatically, even unpredictably.

The Influence of Deductibility

When their influence on a taxpayer's *overall* tax liabilities is considered, most user-related charges have important disadvantages as means of state-local finance. With the exception of motor-fuel taxes, practically all user charges fail to qualify as deductible for purposes of the federal income tax. Payments to state and local governments through non-deductible charges reduce an individual's disposable income by the full amount of the charge. By contrast, the same dollar payment to a state or local government would produce an indirect federal tax reduction if made through one of the broad-based tax forms levied on income, sales, or property. Thus, for a taxpayer in a 25 per cent marginal income-tax bracket, the true net cost of one dollar in local property taxation is only seventy-five cents. If the local taxpayer resides in a state that levies income taxes, the advantage may not stop here. Many such states permit the deduction of local taxes under rules similar to the federal statutes. This deductibility provides a further reduction in net cost to the local taxpayer whose government is financed out of the broad-based forms of taxation.

Advantages vary with income. The advantages of a tax-deductible revenue-collection form versus those of a nondeductible form are, in general, correlated with income because the value of a marginal dollar's worth of tax deduction is determined by a person's marginal income-tax rate. Also, a disproportionate number of low-income families utilize the statutory standard deduction, in which case the magnitude of itemizable deductions does not affect their tax liabilities. If the net personal costs are properly understood, however, a very large proportion of state-local taxpayers should perceive important disadvantages in the imposition of user-related charges rather than broader tax forms. If the essential deductibility features of general taxes remain unchanged, their differential advantage over charges can actually be expected to increase in the future. This is so because even if statutory rate structures remain unchanged, the secular growth of personal income increases the marginal income-tax rates upon which the advantages of deductibility depend.

How fully the deductibility feature enters into the choice of state and local financing media is, of course, a moot question. Nevertheless, a little reflection suggests that fully rational appreciation of the deductibility feature would produce a very powerful bias in favor of taxes rather than charges, especially at the local-government level.

In the collective sense, choosing methods of financing on this basis is inefficient because citizens are merely shifting financial burdens away from themselves as lower-level taxpayers at the cost of increasing necessary tax rates imposed on them by higher-level governments. Still, from the standpoint of an individual state or local government, the net tax disadvantages of user charges are nonetheless very real.

Should charges be deductible? The federal tax treatment of state and local user charges appears to limit the attractiveness of these sources of revenue. It is tempting, therefore, to suggest that federal tax deductibility be extended to them. Unfortunately, the argument for this is ambiguous. One objection, of course, concerns the recognition that deductibility would entail a revenue loss at the federal level. However, this is not at all an important consideration compared with the less obvious impact of deductibility on the balance between the private and public sectors. If user charges are deductible, state and local governments are faced with an incentive to provide essentially private goods through the public sector. Whereas a price paid to a private producer reduces disposable income by the full amount of the price, a charge for the same service by a local government would reduce disposable income by less than the nominal price paid.

State and loval governments already operate many enterprises, and the desirability of this governmental involvement is debatable. On the one hand, deductibility of user charges would encourage the intrusion of governments into what are properly areas for private enterprise. On the other hand, nondeductibility does discourage the heavier application of user charges to areas in which they would be both feasible and appropriate. Hence, the balance of the arguments is not clear.

Additional Factors

With this information as a background, it is possible to make a final assessment of the potential growth of user charges by means of a process of elimination. The relative importance of various state and local service categories can be estimated by using present expenditures as a point of departure (see Table 6). In most of these areas, the further application of user pricing seems either contrary to strong public sentiment or not technologically feasible. Only a few major possibilities remain, and their prognosis is largely uncertain.

Social attitudes as constraints on pricing. In a number of areas of state-local expenditure, increased efforts to impose user charges would be inconsistent with prevailing public attitudes about the governmental function involved. This is, for instance, almost certainly the case with welfare, public housing, and a large proportion of health and hospital expenditures that are explicitly intended to produce income transfers. Welfare alone accounted for over 10 per cent of state-local direct expenditures in recent years and constitutes a completely off-limits item for user charges. All other categories nonetheless pale into insignificance compared with education, which accounts for slightly over 40 per cent of state-local direct expenditures and is growing in relative budgetary importance. Realistically, there seems little possibility of gaining public acceptance for anything beyond the most minimal user charges at the primary and secondary school levels. The future of user charges in higher education is more difficult to predict but of much greater probable importance.

Table 6. State and Local Direct Expenditures, by Major Category, 1969 (millions)

Type of Expenditure	State Expenditure	Per Cent[a]	Local Expenditure	Per Cent[a]
Total direct general expenditure	$43,244	100.0	$73,483	100.0
Education	12,304	28.5	34,934	47.5
Local schools	365	0.8	33,387	45.4
Higher education	10,004	23.1	1,547	2.1
Other	1,935	4.5	–	–
Highways	10,414	24.1	5,003	6.8
Welfare	6,464	14.9	5,646	7.7
Health and hospitals	4,257	9.8	4,262	5.8
Police and fire	585	1.4	5,109	7.0
Sewerage and sanitation	–	–	2,969	4.0
Natural resources, parks	2,035	4.7	2,162	2.9
Housing and urban renewal	15	0.3	1,887	2.6
All other	7,170	16.6	11,511	15.7

[a] Calculated

Source: U.S. Bureau of the Census, *Governmental Finances in 1968-69*, Table 18, pp. 34–39.

In recent years, the validity of the indirect-benefits argument at the university-education level has increasingly been called into question. Almost certainly, tuition fees are much lower than can be rationalized on the basis of social spillovers alone. A questioning finger has also been pointed at the redistributional aspects of subsidized higher education. Although there is as yet no evidence of a definite public attitude change on higher-education pricing, the possibility of this should not be completely discounted. In fact, this is the one area where user charges seem to have any realistic potential as major additional revenue sources for state governments.

A possible new area: effluent charges. One interesting possibility is not reflected in present-day statistics. As governments, on behalf of society, assert jurisdiction over property rights to certain features of environmental quality, a whole new category of user charges may arise in the form of effluent taxes. This type of charge would be particularly advantageous to governments because it most certainly implies a very high ratio of net revenues to charges; the charges will not in general be matched by significant, related expenditure items. Any estimate of the magnitude of revenues derivable from this source would be almost pure speculation.

Effluent charges depend on the development of a practical system of pollution measurement. Unfortunately, this technology is not nearly as advanced as the general public probably believes. Questions relating to the geographic diffusion of pollutants raise additional problems not only of measurement but also of governmental jurisdiction.[3] Over the longer term, some of these feasibility problems may be reduced. However, if one is an optimist about the long-term ability of technological development to increase the elasticity of substitution between pollution and other productive inputs, effluent charges may not have the revenue potential that current conditions seem to indicate. More simply, the prediction of pollution as a large tax base carries the gloomy implicit assumption that pollution will continue to occur at high levels even after charges and technology have been allowed to have their impact.

What is left? Other than higher education, the various forms of highway charges probably present the highest incremental revenue potential. This involves principally higher motor-fuel taxes, license fees,

---

[3] There are, moreover, no grounds for great optimism about the social efficiency of governments in setting the levels of effluent charges. For a formal analysis, see Charles J. Goetz, "Political Equilibrium vs. Economic Efficiency in Effluent Pricing," in *Economic Decisionmaking for Environmental Control,* ed. J. R. Conner and E. Loehman (Gainesville: University of Florida Press, 1973).

and perhaps dramatically increased parking charges. Recreation, parks, and allied activities constitute another functional area in which expansion of user-related charges should be both feasible and acceptable. The remaining areas of user-charge application, excluding functions where social attitudes against charges seem prohibitive, simply do not add up to very great quantitative significance. This does not mean that the user charges cannot serve a highly useful efficiency role in rationing out public services among individual consumers. In many cases, more efficient allocation of expenditures would indirectly ease the pressure on state and local revenues because a lower expenditure level would suffice to satisfy public demand.[4] On the other hand, contrary to some impressions, a realistic appraisal of user-related charges certainly does not seem to portend any really radical changes in the future of state-local finance.

APPENDIX
Complementary Private Resources in Lieu of Public Prices

In certain specialized cases, a restructuring of the public-expenditure technology may produce effects that are similar to user charges. In such cases, revenues are not generated, but expenditures are reduced by stimulating use of private rather than public resources. An example can be provided from police patrols, a function normally thought to be indivisible.

Police patrols and burglar-alarm systems are, to a considerable extent, substitute inputs. A police department might choose to reduce its patrol manpower and simultaneously activate a quick-response alarm trunk system. In order to benefit from such a system, consumers would be required to invest in one or more local alarms that could be connected to the police system. It is entirely possible that such a system

---

[4] It should be noted, however, that this common expectation implicitly assumes that society's politically expressed demand function for the public service in question is inelastic. Since a rationalization of expenditure amounts to a decline in the price of an "effectiveness unit" of the public good, a relatively elastic public demand might actually lead to higher expenditure levels and increased revenue pressure. (An "effectiveness unit" is measured in terms of the *value* of its output rather than in physical terms; e.g., for an educational system, the effectiveness units might be expressed as values of the human capital produced, while more orthodox measures might involve simply the number of students trained.)

might produce the same protection output at a lesser investment of resources (public plus private) than the patrol system. Moreover, the alarm system allows an individual to buy more or less protection at the price of a more or less costly local hookup.

Part Two: New Sources of Revenue

CONSUMPTION AND NET-WORTH TAXES

C. Harry Kahn

THE PLACE OF CONSUMPTION AND NET-WORTH TAXATION IN THE FEDERAL TAX STRUCTURE

I TAKE IT TO BE AXIOMATIC that all tax burdens are ultimately borne by people. The distribution of taxation effects among people according to some relevant criteria is therefore an important consideration entering into tax-policy decisions, although perhaps not the only one. But it is likewise true that between the two broad forms of taxation—that imposed on persons directly and that imposed indirectly on things (*ad rem*)—the personal form tends to be more complex and hence administratively more difficult and expensive. Thus, these two propositions unfortunately have opposing policy implications.

If the distribution of the tax burden among people according to certain policy criteria is of paramount importance, then the logically preferred unit of taxation is the person, or some meaningful grouping of persons such as the family, as opposed to nonpersonal units of taxation such as buildings, dollars of sales, or number of telephone calls. This is especially true if society's equity standards require so-called fine tuning of the tax-burden distribution by differences in personal circumstances. The greater the desire to take into account personal differences (e.g., family size, age, and state of health) in distributing the tax burden, the more imperative it becomes to impose taxes at the personal level. However, the cost in terms of possible accounting complexity must be placed against the desire to achieve fine tuning of the tax-burden distribution among people.

There are essentially three broad bases available for taxes with

133

large potential yield: income, wealth, and consumption. Each of these can be, and indeed has been at some time, tapped at either the personal or the *ad rem* level (see Table 1).

Examples of personal-level taxation are the personal income tax, the annual net-worth (wealth) taxes found in European countries, and the so-called spendings or expenditures tax. At the *ad rem* level, income can be taxed as factor payments, as in the case when a tax is imposed on employers' payrolls, business profits, and interest. Likewise, there is an *ad rem* counterpart to the net-worth tax in the property tax, and consumption expenditures are taxed *ad rem* through retail-sales and value-added taxes of the consumption type.

As shown in Tables 2 and 3 personal taxation in the United States has been restricted largely to an income base, whereas taxes on consumption and wealth are almost entirely *ad rem*. Even so, it should be noted that the total amount of *ad rem* income taxation ($60 billion in 1968–69) is larger than the amount of *ad rem* consumption or wealth taxation. However, of the total of $173 billion of income taxes collected in 1968–69, $96 billion, or 55 per cent, was on persons directly. Federal taxation is thus mostly on income, the larger part of which (although by no means all) is on persons directly. State-local taxation is mostly on consumption and wealth and overwhelmingly indirect, or *ad rem*. Of total U.S. taxes, $142 billion was *ad rem* in 1968–69, compared with $117 billion in personal taxes.

With personal taxation almost entirely in the form of the income tax, the question is whether the United States should broaden the area of personal taxation. There are two approaches to this question. First,

Table 1. Types of Broad-Based Taxes

Base	Personal Form	Indirect or Ad rem Form
Income	Personal income tax	Employer's payroll tax Corporate income tax Interest tax Value-added tax, income base
Wealth	Annual net-worth tax	Property tax
Consumption	Spendings or expenditures tax	Retail-sales tax Value-added tax, Consumption base

Table 2. Total U.S. Taxes, by Type of Tax Base and Level of Government, 1968–69 (billions of dollars)

Type of Tax	Federal			State-Local			All Governments		
	Personal	Ad rem	Total	Personal	Ad rem	Total	Personal	Ad rem	Total
Income									
Individuals	87.2		87.2	8.9		8.9	96.2		96.2
Corporations		36.7	36.7		3.2	3.2		39.9	39.9
Payroll[a]	16.8	16.9	33.7		3.0	3.0	16.8	19.9	36.7
Total	104.0	53.6	157.6	8.9	6.2	15.1	113.0	59.8	172.8
Consumption									
Retail sales					14.0	14.0		14.0	14.0
All other		18.6	18.6		18.9	18.9		37.5	37.5
Total		18.6	18.6		32.9	32.9		51.5	51.5
Wealth									
Property					30.7	30.7		30.7	30.7
Transfers	3.5		3.5	1.0		1.0	4.5		4.5
Total	3.5		3.5	1.0	30.7	31.7	4.5	30.7	35.2
Total	107.5	72.2	179.7	9.9	69.8	79.7	117.5	142.0	259.5

[a] The OASDI part of payroll tax was divided equally between employees (personal) and employers (*ad rem*). This division is essentially correct even if the ultimate incidence of the "employers' part" is mostly on employees. What matters is that the tax paid directly by the employer could, even if it currently does not, take account of personal differences in a way in which the tax on payrolls at the employers' level cannot. Even now the employee obtains a refund for overpayment on account of multiple wage sources during the year. But even this minor refinement is omitted at the employers' level.

Source: U.S. Bureau of the Census, *Governmental Finances in 1968–69*, Table 4.

Table 3. Per Cent Breakdown of Total Taxes, by Type of Tax Base and Level of Government, 1968–69

Type of Tax	Federal			State-Local			All Governments		
	Personal	Ad rem	Total	Personal	Ad rem	Total	Personal	Ad rem	Total
Income									
Individuals	81.1		48.5	89.9	4.6	11.2	81.0	28.1	37.0
Corporations		50.8	20.4		4.3	4.0		14.0	15.3
Payroll	15.6	23.4	18.8			3.7	14.3		14.2
Total	96.7	74.2	87.7	89.9	8.9	18.9	96.2	42.1	66.5
Consumption									
Retail Sales					20.0	17.6		9.9	5.4
All others		25.8	10.4		27.1	23.7		26.4	14.5
Total		25.8	10.4		47.1	41.3		36.3	19.9
Wealth									
Property	3.3		1.9	10.1	44.0	38.5	3.8	21.6	11.8
Transfers						1.3			1.7
Total	3.3		1.9	10.1	44.0	39.8	3.8	21.6	13.5
Total[a]	100.0	100.0	100.0	100.0	100.0	100.0	100.0	100.0	100.0

[a]Some numbers may not total, due to rounding.

Source: U.S. Bureau of the Census, Governmental Finances in 1968–69, Table 4.

are other bases of personal taxation (i.e., wealth and expenditures) desirable on their own grounds and for intrinsic reasons? Second, are other personal taxes desirable from the more pragmatic viewpoint of compensating for weaknesses in the existing personal income tax? Finally, there is the still-broader question of whether income taxation should be supplemented to a greater extent than is now the case by the taxation of wealth and consumption regardless of whether this takes the form of personal or *ad rem* taxation.

Consumption as a Diminution of Society's Wealth

The general taxation of consumption has historically had two intellectual roots. The first, usually associated with Thomas ·Hobbes[1] and more recently seconded by Nicholas Kaldor, raises the question of whether a person should not be taxed according to what he consumes rather than according to what he produces.[2] If what is called a person's income is taken as a measure of what he contributes to society and his consumption is taken as a measure of what he receives from society, taxation according to the former appears somewhat ludicrous. In the words of Hobbes: "What reason is there, that he which laboureth much, and sparing the fruits of his labour, consumeth little, should be more charged, than he that living idly getteth little, and spendeth all he gets: Seeing the one hath no more protection from the commonwealth than the other?"

In this view, a person's contributions to and withdrawals from society's pool of goods are a central consideration of tax policy because (1) it is considered better to add to, than to withdraw from, the pool and (2) the benefit from government services is considered more nearly related to the withdrawals than to the additions. If this is true, then consumption expenditures are an eminently reasonable basis for taxation. Proposition 1 becomes especially relevant if pressure on resources is considered a limitation on economic growth or on some other socially desired resource use such as education or space exploration. Proposition 2 is relevant only if one thinks the tax-burden distribution among

---

[1] See Thomas Hobbes, *Leviathan* (New York: Dutton, 1914), p. 184.

[2] Although Kaldor fully supports Hobbes' view in favor of consumption taxation, it should be stressed that he marshals at least three other major arguments besides the Hobbesian one; the latter cannot be considered Kaldor's major point.

people should have some relation to the distribution of benefits from government-provided services. Although Hobbes, in the above quotation, emphasizes both propositions, Kaldor, in his modern version of the Hobbesian view, advances only proposition 1, namely, that "it is only by spending, not by earning or saving, that an individual imposes a burden on the rest of the community in attaining his own ends."[3]

As is so often the case, one's ultimate attitude on consumption taxation must hinge on what objectives are given priority. In the views just presented, the possible conflict between the individual's spending and society's spending is emphasized. By implication, the individual's spending constitutes an index to "the sum of the benefits he receives from the community."[4]

In adopting as a basis for taxation what is usually designated as income, the aim is differentiation among people on the basis of their power to satisfy their wants. A person's power to satisfy his wants is of course measured by what *could* have been spent, not by what was actually spent, that is, actual spending plus personal savings. The payments corresponding to this sum may well have arisen from an individual's current contribution to output, although it is important to note that they need not have done so. If one's basic interest is in the distribution of spending power as the relevant measure of economic equality or inequality, the possibility that these differences in spending power correspond to different levels of contribution to output is not necessarily decisive. In taxing income, the aim is to tax not a person's contribution to the common pool but his power to draw on the common pool. The latter may, of course, depend on the former, but if it is the distribution of economic power (power to spend) that one wants to modify, then a measure of economic power may be preferable as the tax base.

It would thus appear to be a matter of what trade-off one wishes to assign at a particular time (and place) to the objective of saving (economic growth) and maximum economic output, on the one hand, versus income-distributional considerations, on the other. Kaldor does not concede the need for such a trade-off decision. Unlike Hobbes, who most probably had in mind an *ad rem* tax "upon those things

---

[3] See Nicholas Kaldor, *An Expenditure Tax* (London: Allen & Unwin, 1965), p. 53.
[4] Ibid.

which men consume,"[5] Kaldor argued for a tax graduated by size of personal expenditures. But, at best, such a tax is a blunt instrument with which to modify the income distribution because its efficacy depends on how predictable and uniform the relation between consumption expenditures and income is for given income levels. Only when one's interest in progression is not the modification of the income distribution but the redistribution of consumption expenditures with a view toward their greater equality is there no need for a trade-off between growth and egalitarian objectives. This view may be desirable at times when society is less concerned over the distribution of economic power than with the distribution of consumer goods.

Income Defined as Consumption

Whereas the Hobbesian view makes a distinction between income and consumption and simply expresses preference for the latter as a basis for taxation, the views associated with John Stuart Mill and Irving Fisher start from the proposition that persons should be taxed according to the size of their income but conclude by defining income as essentially equal to consumption. By regarding savings, as they are invested, as equal to the present value of a future income stream,[6] Mill argued that "unless . . . savings are exempted from income tax, the contributors are twice taxed on what they save, and only once on what they spend."[7]

Following the same line of reasoning, Fisher looked at income as the value of services flowing from capital (wealth) of all kinds (including human capital in order to simplify analysis).[8] The value of capital in turn is nothing but the summation of present values of future services (income) that may be expected. What, then, are savings in Fisher's terminology? Savings are additions to the capital stock; that is,

---

[5] This interpretation is also that of Edwin R. A. Seligman in *Essays in Taxation*, 2nd ed. (New York: Macmillan, 1897), p. 10.

[6] Thus, an investor whose rate of time preference is 10 per cent would be willing to pay in the present as much as $100 for a permanent annuity of $10 per year. The $100 is therefore simply the purchase price paid by the annuitant for the right to receive $10 per year.

[7] See John Stuart Mill, *Principles of Political Economy* (London: Longmans, Green, 1929), p. 813.

[8] See Irving Fisher and Herbert W. Fisher, *Constructive Income Taxation* (New York: Harper, 1942), p. 40.

savings constitute future income and therefore cannot be part of current income. Since income is here defined as net of any outlays necessary to maintain or add to the capital stock, it follows that income must equal goods and services used for consumption. Fisher's view is thus one that utilizes the fruit-and-tree analogy to define income. If one were to tax savings as well as the fruit of saving, the same thing would be taxed twice. In Fisher's words:[9]

> If we levy a tax of 1 per cent on an orange grove of 100 trees, we may (theoretically) do it simply by handing over, once for all, one tree to the government. This is equivalent to handing over annually the oranges which one tree bears. But to do both, to hand over one tree at first and then to hand over annually 1 per cent of the oranges borne by the ninety-nine trees remaining, is virtually to hand over two series of oranges and reduce the fruit of the orchard twice; for the only value of an orange tree lies in its yield of oranges.[10]

Although the tree-and-fruit analogy is helpful in clarifying the view of Mill, Fisher, and others,[11] all that it proves beyond doubt is that double taxation occurs when one's aim is to tax the fruit. No double taxation is proved if one's aim is to tax the *accretion* to an individual's power to satisfy his wants. If income is defined in terms of power to satisfy wants, then both the trees and the oranges constitute such power.

The Pragmatic View: Offsets to Present Shortcomings

Perhaps the most compelling, although not very "pure," argument in favor of a general consumption tax at the federal level is that it might compensate for some of the omissions and shortcomings of the present

---

[9] Ibid., chap. 8. Fisher's fruit-and-tree analogy should not be mistaken for the legal doctrine regarding separation of fruit from tree, which led to the distinction between stock dividends and cash dividends as unrealized and realized income.

[10] Fisher may have gotten carried away with the force of his analogy. Trees usually do have other uses aside from the fruit they bear. But if they did not, the analogy to saving and the yield of savings would not hold completely. For in Fisher's own way of reckoning, capital (the tree) would become income whenever the owner decided to consume a part or all of it.

[11] Among these "others" were Alfred Marshall, A. C. Pigou, and Luigi Einaudi.

tax structure as judged by some widely accepted rules. One widely accepted rule is that individuals in equal circumstances should pay equal amounts of tax (usually referred to as *horizontal equity*).[12] A relevant definition of "equal circumstances" is that income and family status are the same. Violation of the horizontal-equity rule would cause not only arbitrarily unequal treatment of equals but also some unintended change in the use of resources in favor of the less heavily taxed sources and uses of income. Horizontal equity is, however, not quite enough to assure neutrality with respect to resource use. If the omission from the tax base were the same percentage of every person's income, horizontal and vertical equity would be unaffected but resources might be diverted into the undertaxed area. Such unintended diversion is prevented by a further rule: The concept of income should be all-inclusive without regard to source or use.

Agreement on what is an appropriate concept of income against which to judge horizontal equity and neutrality with respect to resource use is not universal. But most economists would now interpret income for taxable purposes in the broadest sense as consisting of any increase over a period of time in a person's power to satisfy his wants. It must be equal for any period of time to consumption plus change in net worth. In principle, any source of accretion to a person's power to satisfy wants is includable: free time, appreciation in the value of property, earnings from work inside as well as outside the home, and so forth.[13]

Not only is income the almost universally adopted criterion by which the tax system's horizontal and vertical equity (redistribution) are judged but also nearly nine-tenths of federal tax revenue comes

---

[12] We are primarily concerned with horizontal equity here, for it is only the unintended unequal treatment of persons with equal incomes that cannot be remedied by appropriate adjustments in tax rates. If omissions were the same in amount at given income levels but varied between levels (vertically), adjustments in rates would suffice to obtain the desired tax-burden distribution among income groups.

[13] This is the well-known accretion concept of income usually attributed to Haig and Simons in the United States, but actually presented much earlier, as generously acknowledged by Simons, by Georg Schanz in Germany. See Georg Schanz, "Der Einkommensbegriff und die Einkommensteuergesetze," *Finanzarchiv* (1896); Robert M. Haig, "The Concept of Income—Economic and Legal Aspects" in his *The Federal Income Tax* (New York: Columbia University Press, 1921); Henry C. Simons, *Personal Income Taxation* (Chicago: University of Chicago Press, 1938).

from income taxation (Table 2). The question of what gaps in the federal tax structure might be closed by consumption taxation is thus for the most part a question relating to gaps in the income-tax structure. The latter, as shown in Table 2, consists of three main parts: the personal income tax, which accounts for nearly half of federal tax revenue; the corporation income tax, which accounts for one-fifth; and the payroll tax, which accounts for only slightly less than the corporate income tax.

The idea that reliance on diversity of taxes rather than a single "ideal" tax might produce optimum results has been advanced from time to time.[14] What major shortcomings in our present income-tax structure are more likely to be corrected by some form of consumption tax rather than by revisions in the income-tax structure itself? The following discussion examines this question in respect, first, to distortions caused by lack of neutrality of the income tax with regard to the choice between earnings and leisure, consumption and savings, and safety and risk taking; next, to undertaxation because of omissions from the income tax; and, finally, to overtaxation because of multiple inclusions.

Choice between leisure and earnings. Under a comprehensive accretion concept of income, the value of leisure is, in principle, includable in income. Failure to do so makes leisure more attractive (lowers its price) relative to income from work. Most or all of this price effect may be offset by an income effect: the attempt by individuals to recoup some of the reduction in money income caused by the tax through increased work effort. The two effects on amount of work are offsetting, and the net result is not predictable on theoretical grounds. However this may be, it is only the magnitude of the price effect that determines the resulting distortion in the income-leisure choice and the ensuing excess burden. Since this effect is operative, such a burden will result unless labor supply is wholly fixed.[15]

Imposition of a consumption tax will also impose such an excess

---

[14] Its most recent proponent is Carl S. Shoup, although perhaps for somewhat different reasons than those examined here. See his *Public Finance* (Chicago: Aldine, 1969), pp. 12–15, 465–481.

[15] For a brief summary of inconclusive empirical evidence, see Richard Goode, *The Individual Income Tax* (Washington, D.C.: The Brookings Institution, 1964), pp. 54–56.

burden, but there is reason to expect that the burden will be less. If the two taxes are compared on the assumption that tax rates are set so as to obtain equivalent yields from each, then, as a first approximation, the aggregate income effect on work may be assumed to be the same for each. The price effect, however, will tend to be less under the consumption tax. This is the case because income (which may be either consumed or saved) will be worth more under a consumption tax as it avoids the distortion in the rate of substitution of future for present consumption which occurs under the income tax. Hence we expect the income-leisure distortion to be less and the level of work effort to be higher under the consumption tax.

At the same time, the quantitative importance of this difference is very uncertain. This depends, first, on individual flexibility with respect to work effort and, second, on how important economic rewards are in determining amount of work. It is possible that those individuals who can be most flexible with respect to work input are also least sensitive to monetary rewards. For instance, independent professionals are among those least limited by institutional arrangements such as length of work-week. But interest in subject matter and professional recognition may also be major motivations in their work effort.

Choice between consumption and savings. The interest received by savers may be viewed as representing the trade-off between present and future consumption. At 5 per cent interest, and in the absence of any tax, a person who saves $100 trades $100 of present consumption for $105 of consumption one year hence.

Under an accretion concept of income, there is no question concerning the proper tax treatment. Both the amount saved and the interest received as a result of it constitute increases in an individual's power to spend. This, of course, also corresponds to present practice, and there is therefore no distortion (as there was in the leisure-work choice) in the sense of lack of strict adherence to an accretion concept of income.

Nevertheless, a problem exists on the score of neutrality between income uses. Ideally, and actually in most respects, the income tax is neutral concerning various forms of consumption. It does not change relative prices of goods and services at any given moment. However, it does change the relative price between consumption now (C_1) and consumption a year from now (C_2). In the above example, the ratio of substitution of future consumption for present consumption (C_2/C_1) is 1.05. The imposition of a 50 per cent income tax would leave $50 for present consumption or $51.25 one year from now. C_2/C_1 is now 1.025, that is, more favorable to consumption in the first period.

If approximately the same tax yield were to be obtained with a consumption tax of 100 per cent, the same individual could either consume $50 now and pay $50 in tax or save his $100 at 5 per cent interest until a year from now, when he would have $105, of which $52.50 could be spent for consumption and $52.50 would be payable in tax. But with the consumption tax, $C_2/C_1 = 52.50/50.00 = 1.05$, which is the same as in the absence of tax.

In this sense, the income tax discriminates against saving and in favor of current consumption. But it should be noted that the discrimination is not the result of an unwarranted inclusion of interest as a form of accretion in the sense in which the omission of leisure is unwarranted although unavoidable. The discrimination against saving cannot be remedied within the income-tax framework without creating other problems, such as those that would arise from the exemption of interest.

Choice between safety and risk taking. A graduated income tax discriminates against fluctuating incomes; a tax on consumption expenditures similarly discriminates against fluctuating expenditures if it is graduated and neither tax involves such discrimination practically not at all if it is imposed at a flat rate.[16] Consumption expenditures tend to be more evenly distributed over time than income realization, and their bunching is often related to causes other than fluctuations in income. The partial substitution of a consumption tax even if graduated, for the income tax would undoubtedly overcome the bias is the income tax against fluctuating compared with stable incomes. This is of course not merely for equity reasons but because of the likely association between venturesome enterprises and highly variable incomes.

Consumption taxation is one answer to the problem, but by no means the only one. As far as the tax problem is concerned, income

---

[16] Some differentiation arises even with a flat-rate consumption tax unless expenditures for durable goods (such as refrigerators) are averaged. Otherwise, purchase precedes consumption, and the taxpayer in effect pays tax in advance of use, thereby losing some interest.

variability may be divided (purely for policy rather than conceptual reasons) into two parts: variability resulting in losses and variability in positive income resulting in effective tax rates that are higher than rates on an equal amount of income distributed evenly over time. Both problems can be, and to a considerable extent now are, remedied within the income-tax framework itself. Business operating losses, to the extent that they are not offset against other current-year income of proprietors,[17] can be carried back three years and forward five years against other income, thus providing a partial averaging over a nine-year period. A rather imperfect averaging provision currently applies to sharp increases but, unfortunately, not to decreases in taxable income. Improved and more extensive averaging may not be far off.

The significance for investment in risky ventures is that both forms of averaging help to maintain the odds that existed on a before-tax basis. Assuming a 50 per cent proportional tax rate, a venture that has an even chance of producing a $2,000 gain or $1,000 loss would have its odds changed from 2.1 to 1.1 in the absence of loss offset. With perfect loss offset, the after-tax gain would be $1,000 and the after-tax loss $500, leaving the "reward" per unit of risk unchanged.[18]

One aspect of high income variability that has thus far not been satisfactorily solved in the income tax is capital gains and losses. By counting them as they are realized rather than as they occur, they are apt to become a highly bunched form of income because the gains (losses) have often accrued over many years preceding realization. In the absence of averaging, their inclusion in full along with other income would either create some serious equity problems or cause further postponement of realization. The present preferred treatment of capital

---

[17] For individuals, the major part of business losses is offset against income from other sources in the same year as they are incurred. See C. Harry Kahn, *Business and Professional Income Under the Personal Income Tax* (Princeton: Princeton University Press, 1964), p. 88.

[18] The complete theory underlying this statement was first presented in a major article by Evsey D. Domar and Richard A. Musgrave, "Proportional Income Taxation and Risk-Taking," *Quarterly Journal of Economics,* Vol. 58 (May 1944), pp. 388–422. While more decent discussion has shown that the net effects of a tax with full loss offset is more complex than the earlier study suggested, the importance of loss offset has not been questioned. See J.E. Stiglitz, "The Effects of Income, Wealth and Capital Gains Taxation on Risk Taking," *The Quarterly Journal of Economics* (May 1969); and Martin S. Feldstein, "The Effects of Taxation on Risk Taking," *Journal of Political Economy* (September 1969).

gains and the limited deductibility of capital losses are intended to
serve in place of averaging. Here, too, solutions within the income-tax
framework are very feasible.

Offset to income omissions. Would income-tax omissions be
filled in by a consumption tax? As is well known, the federal income
tax falls considerably short of being as comprehensive as an accretion
concept of income requires it to be. Some of the omissions are unintended and exist mainly because inclusion of the items in question in
taxable income would require difficult imputations of their money's
worth. Other omissions are intentional, at least in the sense that there
would be no important valuation problems associated with their inclusion. Items of major quantitative importance falling into the former
group are the imputed rental income on owner-occupied dwellings,
imputed interest on savings invested in life insurance, and imputed interest on money held in cash. In contrast with the omissions requiring
difficult imputations, some omissions are more or less intentionally
made. For example, in the case of the tax exemption of interest on
state and local government bonds and the realization accounting with
respect to capital gains and interest on U.S. government bonds, accounting difficulties are not the dominant reasons for current treatment.

All the omissions cited above fall under the heading of property
income. There are also several important omissions from work income
(wages, salaries, and labor earnings of unincorporated business and
professions). Again some exist purely because of the difficulty of im-
puting their money equivalent to individual taxpayers: the value of
goods and services produced and consumed in the home (including
the value of housewives' services) and the value of vacations, holidays,
and other free time paid for but not worked. Important items omitted
for reasons other than measurement difficulty are government transfer
payments (consisting largely of social security items) and employer
contributions to employee retirement and welfare plans.

The total value of the items cited is large. For several, no data
are available to obtain even an approximation. The major items for
which rough estimates can be made are shown on page 147 in juxtaposi-
tion to the estimated total of income (adjusted gross income or AGI) in
1968 conceptually comparable to that required on tax returns.[19]

---

[19] All the estimates, except total AGI (adjusted gross income) and net capital
gains accruals, are from Roger A. Herriot and Herman P. Miller, "The Taxes We

	(billions)
Imputed rent on owner-occupied nonfarm housing	$ 12
Imputed interest on bank accounts	11
Imputed interest on life insurance savings	10
Employer contributions to retirement and welfare funds	21
Net capital-gains accruals in excess of realized gains reported	123–276
Total adjusted gross income	$600

The figures for capital-gains accruals should be taken as suggestive of the order of magnitude involved rather than treated as estimates. They suggest that progressivity may be seriously affected by the existence of large capital appreciations that are never realized for tax purposes. Some economists see taxation of retained earnings through the corporate income tax as partially offsetting this problem. Retained earnings tend to lead to greater corporate equity, and this is likely to be reflected in share prices. However, the incidence of the corporation income tax is surrounded by so much uncertainty that it is hard to consider it a partial offset to the flawed treatment of capital gains.

To what extent can a tax on consumption expenditures, personal or *ad rem,* compensate for omissions in the income tax? There is, to begin with, little reason to assume that various forms of income in kind that are not now reckoned as income could be more readily included in the expenditure-tax base. The net rental value of owner-occupied homes or the value of home-produced goods and services is as difficult to impute in one case as in the other.

Pay," *The Conference Board Record,* Vol. 8, No. 5 (New York: The Conference Board, May 1971); total AGI is from Joseph A. Pechman, *Federal Tax Policy* (Washington, D.C.: The Brookings Institution, 1966), Appendix Table B-1; net capital gains accruals are estimated by assuming that realizations, before long-term capital gains deduction, were between 10 to 20 per cent of accruals. These percentages are approximately the lower and upper limits cited by Martin J. Bailey, "Capital Gains and Income Taxation," in Arnold C. Harberger and Martin J. Bailey, eds., *Taxation of Income from Capital* (Washington, D.C.: The Brookings Institution, 1969), pp. 17, 23. Total realized net capital gains reported for 1968 were $30.7 billion. This results in an estimated range of $154–307 billion for total accruals and a range of $123–276 for excess over realization. Data presented by Martin David for the period 1951–1958 gives a range of 10 to 40 per cent for realization relative to accruals; see his *Alternative Approaches to Capital Gains Taxation* (Washington, D.C.: The Brookings Institution, 1968), pp. 60–62.

But a consumption-expenditures tax may take indirect account of some of the income in question. Since capital gains, employer contributions to pension and welfare funds, and imputed interest and rent all represent accretions to spending power, will variations in *actual* spending not reflect these accretions in a way in which taxable income now fails to do?[20] It is most likely that part of capital-gains accruals and employer contributions on behalf of employees will result in increased consumption expenditures and thus will be captured in part by a consumption tax. A further question arises, however, concerning the extent to which increased consumption is possible without *realizing* capital gains in cases where such gains furnish the basis for increased spending power. The individuals concerned may, of course, reduce their other saving to zero, draw on other assets such as savings accounts, and borrow in order to avoid realization of gains and yet increase consumption.

The likelihood of entering into a consumption base is even greater for the transfer payments now omitted from taxable income. There is no obstacle to their expenditure for consumption, and for the most part, they are no doubt used in that way. However, since transfers are typically received by individuals with low current income, their inclusion in the income-tax base would assure that the income status of recipients is taken into account in determining tax liability; whereas only a personal-expenditure tax could do the same. Imputable interest and rent are not likely to show up in the same manner in a consumption tax because they are, in effect, consumption items and more likely to be reflected in higher savings.

From the foregoing analysis, it may be concluded that any consumption tax would to some unknown extent reach elements of income now largely omitted from the income tax. But these elements are income sources that could, if desired, be reached at least as well by appropriate changes in the income tax. Employer contributions on behalf of employees and transfer payments can without difficulty be made part of the income-tax base. The large capital-gains-and-loss accruals are slightly more difficult to reach. But the capital-gains

---

[20] This is essentially Kaldor's argument, particularly with respect to capital gains. See Nicholas Kaldor, op. cit., p. 47. However, Kaldor's reasoning assumes that the income tax is abandoned in favor of an expenditure tax. Appreciated assets can therefore readily be sold for the purpose of obtaining cash for consumption without incurring tax liability on the gain as such.

problem would go a long way toward solution if gains and losses were to be constructively realized at the taxpayer's death, counted in full, and subject to generous averaging to avoid the high rates resulting from bunching.

Curiously, those items most difficult to reach by an income tax are also equally difficult to reach with a consumption-expenditure tax: net rent from owner-occupied houses, imputable interest generated by cash balances in banks and cash that generates liquidity income, jewelry, and art objects. For these cases and others like them, a periodic net-worth tax like that which exists in some European countries might be appropriate.

Offset to multiple inclusions. Would multiple inclusion of sources be offset by a consumption tax? In contrast with undertaxation arising from failure to include some income sources, overtaxation may airse from multiple inclusion of some sources. Multiple inclusion arises because the income tax consists of a tax on employment income and a tax on corporate income in addition to the tax on personal income. In the case of the employment income tax, payrolls are subject to tax both as part of personal income and selectively to finance social security. At least the employer's part of the tax must be viewed as an excise on the use of labor with possible adverse effects on employment. In addition, both the employer's and employee's part are highly regressive because they are imposed at a flat rate on only the first $9,000 of an employee's payrolls (at the time of writing) and because property income is omitted from the base. The incidence of the tax, as estimated in two recent studies, is shown in Table 4. It should be noted that no attempt is made to include social security benefits along with the tax incidence, a correct procedure in our view.

The case of the corporation income tax is more complex, and simple conclusions are not possible. Mutliple inclusion clearly exists with respect to the dividend component of corporate income. It is taxed both as part of corporate income and as received by individuals. Retained corporate earnings may be subject to corporate income tax only, except where they result in appreciation of stockholders' equity and the capital gain is realized in the stockholder's lifetime.

The issue is further complicated by the fact that multiple inclusion, as described above, does not necessarily mean overtaxation. The latter might be true only if the burden of the corporate tax could be shown to be on stockholders. There is no consensus about the incidence of the corporation tax, a severe demerit for the tax in itself. Because scholars have argued, on the one side, that the tax appears to be fully passed forward in higher prices even in the short run[21] and, on the other, that the tax is, after some long-run adjustment, borne by the

Table 4. Estimated Incidence of U.S. Taxes on Income,
1965 and 1968

Income Class	Tax as per cent of			
	Personal Income	Corporate Income[a]	Payroll[b]	Total
1965				
Under $ 2,000	1.9	4.5	3.2	9.6
$ 2,000–$ 3,000	3.1	4.3	3.4	10.8
$ 3,000–$ 4,000	4.5	5.5	3.8	13.8
$ 4,000–$ 5,000	6.4	3.6	4.1	14.1
$ 5,000–$ 6,000	6.9	3.9	4.0	14.8
$ 6,000–$ 7,500	7.7	3.4	3.8	14.9
$ 7,500–$10,000	8.8	3.4	3.5	15.7
$10,000–$15,000	10.0	5.3	3.3	18.6
$15,000 and over	16.1	10.9	1.7	28.7
Total	8.3	4.6	3.5	16.4
1968				
Under $ 2,000	1.2	6.0	7.6	14.8
$ 2,000–$ 4,000	3.5	4.3	6.5	14.3
$ 4,000–$ 6,000	5.3	3.6	6.7	15.6
$ 6,000–$ 8,000	6.5	3.2	6.8	16.5
$ 8,000–$10,000	7.4	2.9	6.2	16.5
$10,000–$15,000	8.7	2.9	5.8	17.4
$15,000–$25,000	9.9	3.9	4.6	18.4
$25,000–$50,000	12.9	7.5	2.5	22.9
$50,000 and over	19.8	15.4	1.0	36.2
Total	9.5	4.7	5.1	19.3

[a] In the 1967 study, the corporate tax is assumed to be one-half shifted forward to consumers and one-half borne by stockholders. The corresponding fractions for 1968 are one-third and two-thirds.

[b] Three-quarters of the tax is assumed to be borne by wage earners and one-quarter by consumers.

Sources: Tax Foundation, *Tax Burdens and Benefits of Government Expenditures by Income Class, 1961 and 1965*, (1967) Table 7 (for 1965 figures); and Roger A. Herriot and Herman P. Miller, "The Taxes We Pay," *The Conference Board Record*, Vol. 8 (New York: The Conference Board, May 1971) for 1968 figures.

---

[21] See Marian Krzyzaniak and Richard A. Musgrave, *The Shifting of the Corporation Income Tax* (Baltimore: Johns Hopkins Press, 1963).

owners of capital,[22] the assumption underlying most recent incidence studies regarding the corporation income tax is that some arbitrary fraction is passed forward and the rest borne by stockholders. Table 4 shows incidence estimates for the corporation income tax. Both show a U-shaped curve for the ratio of tax to income when ascending to income scale. It is also evident from the table that the overall progressivity of the U.S. income tax is the result of the progressivity of the personal income tax; the corporation and payroll taxes are, for the most part, regressive elements.

Unlike the cases of undertaxation because of omissions, multiple inclusion is not partly offset by the adoption of a consumption tax. However, a consumption tax may be considered as part of a tax package to substitute for all or part of the payroll and corporate income tax. One such package would include abolition of the payroll tax with the resulting revenue loss made up through correspondingly higher personal income-tax rates. The corporation income tax would be integrated with the personal income tax through the so-called partnership method. Stockholders would be permitted to write up the cost basis of their stock by the pro rata shares of retained earnings imputed to them through the partnership method. By this device, retained corporate earnings would not be taxed under both the partnership method and, possibly, as capital gains. The revenue loss from substituting the partnership method for corporate tax would be made up through a consumption tax. Through appropriate exemptions such as food, consumption taxes have been found to be close to proportional to income and an additional element of progressivity could be introduced by an exemption. The overall effect of this package over a substantive part of the income range would be an increase rather than a decrease in progressivity.

A modification of this package with respect to corporate income tax would involve constructive realization of capital gains and losses in full at time of death or other transfer in place of the partnership method. Here, too, all retained corporate earnings would eventually be subject to tax. A periodic net-worth tax at a low rate would be adopted to compensate for the postponement of tax on retained corporate earnings when the latter are taxed as capital gains at time of transfer.

[22] See John G. Cragg, Arnold C. Harberger, and Peter Mieszkowski, "Empirical Evidence on the Incidence of the Corporation Income Tax," *Journal of Political Economy,* Vol. 75 (December 1967), pp. 811–821.

Net-Worth Taxation

In the preceding pages, there have been several allusions to the net-worth tax as part of a possible future tax-reform package. In the following brief discussion, the net-worth tax will be compared with other forms of wealth taxation now in use in the United States, and the extent to which net-worth taxation might fill certain gaps in the tax structure will be considered.

Differences between net-worth tax and other taxes on wealth. As was shown in Tables 2 and 3, at the federal level, wealth taxation contributes only 2 per cent of total tax revenue. At the state-local level, the property tax (an *ad rem* form of wealth taxation) accounts for nearly two-fifths of tax revenue.

The net-worth tax is a tax on a person's total assets minus his liabilities. It is usually an annual tax, but for administrative convenience, it could, of course, be collected less frequently. In contrast, the familiar general property tax, also annual, applies only to particular categories of property, without aggregation of all properties owned by a particular individual and without deduction of indebtedness. At the federal level, the tax on wealth is essentially a net-worth tax but is collected only at the time the owner parts with his estate through either death or prior gift. In any one year, the base of a wealth-transfer tax is therefore much smaller than the base for a tax on total personal wealth in existence at any moment of time. However, tax rates of annual net-worth taxes are of necessity much lower than the rates for wealth-transfer taxes. Unless the effect on the propensity to accumulate is to be disregarded, the annual tax rate on net worth is limited by the general level of yields on property. If the average yield were near 5 per cent, a 1 per cent tax on net worth would approximate a 20 per cent income tax on property income. Thus, most of the European countries that have annual net-worth taxes have tax rates between 0.5 and 1.0 per cent.[23] For 1968–69, the period covered in Table 2, a federal personal net-worth tax at 0.5 per cent might have yielded in the neighborhood of over $10 billion.

A comparison of the existing federal wealth-transfer tax system

---

[23] See Carl S. Shoup, *Public Finance* (Chicago: Aldine, 1969), p. 359.

with an annual net-worth tax is in order because the former could be strengthened in a number of ways as an alternative to adopting the latter. A major advantage of a net-worth tax is that it does not depend on the advent of a transfer to heirs or donees. The problems created by generation skipping through various trust devices are therefore avoided. However, an annual or biannual net-worth tax requires frequent and complex valuations of assets and perhaps many arbitrary valuation procedures in the interest of administrative workability. Both taxes may have some effect on saving propensities and the location of capital. Since an individual's net worth is the result of past saving, one way to minimize tax is by saving less. But this price effect may be offset partly or completely by a desire to maintain capital intact through increased saving. In the absence of empirical information, the only thing that can be concluded is that most taxation effects will be weaker for a wealth-transfer tax than for an annual wealth tax, since the former is remote in time and individuals may be more concerned with their own accumulation than with the position of their heirs.

Does the net-worth tax fill gaps left by income and consumption taxes? Net-worth taxation, annual or at time of transfer, will reach certtain accretions that neither income nor consumption taxes successfullly reach. This is especially true for wealth on which no explicit cash return is earned but which may be held in order to obtain various forms of non-money income. Prominent in this category are the imputed rent on owner-occupied residences, the imputed liquidity income derived from holding cash, and the pleasure and prestige from owning art objects, antiques, and jewelry.

Property having accretions that could be, but currently are not, reached through income taxation is in a somewhat different category. Cases in point are state and local securities and mineral properties, which would be reached by a net-worth tax but are currently taxed not at all or only lightly under the income tax. Accrued capital gains that are reached only with great delay or not at all by the income tax would be taxed promptly by the net-worth tax and with some delay by the wealth-transfer tax.

Although an annual net-worth tax has certain advantages, such as reaching accrued capital gains promptly and taxing owner-occupied residences, most of the cited advantages can also be obtained either through appropriate reforms in the income tax or through strengthening the system. Those pure advantages that remain seem too few and too small to justify the highly complex administrative machinery that would be required in order to achieve a well-functioning net-worth tax.

VALUE-ADDED TAX

Charles E. McLure, Jr.

ECONOMIC EFFECTS OF TAXING VALUE ADDED

ADOPTION OF A VALUE-ADDED TAX (VAT) has been the key feature of recent tax reforms in Europe. France has used VAT (although not in its present form) since 1954, and in the wake of the Neumark report on tax harmonization, the other six member nations of the European Common Market agreed to adopt such a tax eventually. Germany (in 1968), the Netherlands (in 1969), Luxembourg (in 1970), and Belgium (in 1971) have already initiated the tax, and Italy plans to do so (in 1973). In preparation for its entry into the European Community (EC), Britain will follow suit in 1973. In addition, among developed non-EC nations, Denmark (in 1967), Sweden (in 1969), and Norway (in 1970) now have a tax on value added.

This ascendancy of the value-added tax in Europe has contributed to a growing interest in its application in the United States, and a lively debate between proponents and opponents has emerged.[1] The proponents of a value-added tax expect considerable economic advantage to derive from its use, especially if it is substituted partly or wholly for the corporation income tax. They expect such a substitution to benefit the balance of payments because border-tax adjustments, which are not

---

[1] See, for example, Dan Throop Smith, "Value-Added Tax: The Case For," and Stanley S. Surrey, ". . . The Case Against," *Harvard Business Review* 48 (November-December, 1970): 77–94. The present chapter was completed before it was rumored that the Nixon administration was considering proposing the use of revenue from a federal tax on value added to replace part of the revenues from property taxes now used to finance education. There has been no consideration of that potential proposal in this analysis.

permitted under the corporation tax, are permitted under VAT. In its
domestic impact, VAT is expected to free the economy from distortions
resulting from present taxes. By permitting a relative shift from direct
to indirect taxation, with its more favorable treatment of saving, investment, and risk taking, VAT is expected to induce economic growth.
Finally, proponents argue that it would be advantageous to spread federal
taxes among a number of major bases, rather than to rely so heavily on
the income taxes. Diversification, they argue, will relieve the pressure for
base erosion of any one tax. Although all these points have been raised,
the prime support for an American tax on value added has been based
upon hoped-for balance-of-payments effects.

Opponents of the value-added tax note that it would almost certainly be regressive in its incidence, especially if substituted for part of
the individual or corporation income taxes. They argue (as do some
proponents) that substitution for the corporation tax should not be considered unless there is also assurance that retained earnings will be
included in the personal income tax, whether through reform of capital-
gains taxation or through integration of the personal and corporation
income taxes. Next, opponents question whether substitution of a value-
added tax would improve the U.S. balance of payments and whether this
is a reasonable policy objective, given the recent currency realignment.
The validity of the claim, they maintain, depends on unrealistic assumptions about the economy's response to a reduction in the corporation tax.

Moreover, they note that the prime reason for introduction of a
tax on value added in Europe does not apply in the United States. In
Europe, VAT was introduced as a substitute for a cascade-type turnover
tax, which is a clearly inferior form of taxation.[2] In the United States,
there is no such tax, and substitution for the corporation income tax is
quite a different matter. Moreover, the case for VAT as a self-enforcing
tax is considered weaker in the United States because the level of voluntary taxpayer compliance is higher here to begin with. Opponents con-
tend that central reliance on income taxation at the federal level is called
for on equity grounds and that tax reform should continue to stress
improved income taxation. A major shift to indirect taxation is thus

---

[2] A cascade-type turnover tax is applied to gross sales at each stage in the
production process, without allowance for taxes paid on productive inputs. It
discriminates in favor of vertically integrated production processes, and accurate
border-tax adjustments (see "International Economic Effects") are impossible.

opposed. But if such a shift were to be made, they hold that a national retail-sales tax would be preferable to a tax on value added.

This chapter will examine the economic arguments for and against the value-added tax, including its distributive implications, its effects on the domestic economy, and its effects on the balance of payments. Throughout, a distinction will be drawn between introduction of VAT as an additional revenue source and its substitution for various other taxes.

The details of administering a value-added tax are not analyzed in detail in this chapter, although the definition of the tax base and its calculation are described briefly in the next section. Moreover, this chapter does not consider in detail the question of whether increased indirect taxation, if it is to occur, should take the form of a value-added tax or a retail-sales tax.[3] Nor are the difficulties encountered in achieving the associated tax reforms that ideally would accompany adoption of a value-added tax considered here.

The Tax Base and Its Calculation

The most general case for a value-added tax is that a broad-based, flat-rate tax should be introduced into the system. Assuming that this is to be done, the major policy question is whether this tax should apply to total income or to consumption only. In either case, there is a second question: Should the tax be imposed as a single-stage tax or as an incremental, multiple-stage tax.[4] If the income base is selected, the choice is between an income tax and a VAT of the income type. If the consumption base is selected, the choice is between a retail-sales tax and a value-added tax of the consumption type. Then there is the problem of how the value-added tax is to be calculated (i.e., by the addition, the subtraction, or the credit method).

Posing the first two questions in this fashion shows that it may be misleading to speak of a tax on value added as a tax levied on a base

---

[3] See the chapters by Carl S. Shoup and John F. Due.

[4] The case of a multiple-stage tax using total sales rather than incremental value added is not discussed in this chapter. Such a tax, referred to as a *turnover tax,* is clearly inferior because it discriminates between products depending upon the number of stages involved in their production and marketing and, for a given number of stages, upon whether or not value is added early or late in the production process.

distinct from all others. More accurately, taxing value added is a method of collecting a flat-rate tax levied on income or consumption. Rather than collecting a tax on income directly from recipients of factor incomes, as is done under the traditional income tax, it is possible to collect the tax on increments to the value of products at each stage in the production and distribution process, so that finally, the sum of factor incomes is taxed. Similarly, rather than levying a tax on all retail sales to final consumers, it is possible to collect an equivalent tax as the products move through the production process. In either case, it is more meaningful to speak of the aggregate tax base as being income or consumption rather than as being value added.

Calculating tax liabilities.[5] Under a value-added tax, as the name indicates, a firm pays tax only on its contribution to the value of a product. Thus, its taxable value added equals total sales less its purchases of inputs. Or value added can be computed as the sum of payments to factors (wages and salaries, interest, and rents) plus profits. (This does not take into account net investment and the treatment of capital goods, which are discussed later in this chapter.) In the aggregate, the tax base of the economy is both the sum of sales to final consumers and the sum of all factor incomes and profits.

An example should clarify this. Suppose that there are three firms, each of which is involved in a different stage in the production process. Industry B buys intermediate goods from industry A and sells its output to industry C, which in turn sells to ultimate consumers. Each firm hires factors and earns profits in the amounts noted in Table 1. For each firm, value added can be calculated by either of the two methods just described; for the economy as a whole, value added is $500.

The tax liability of the various firms can be calculated directly by applying the tax rate (say 10 per cent) to value added calculated either by adding together factor payments and profits (the addition method) or by subtracting purchased and therefore previously taxed inputs from total sales (the subtraction method). In either case, the liability of the three industries would be $10, $20, and $20, respectively.

In actuality, a third method, the credit method, is the most popular means of calculating tax liabilities. Under this approach, a firm's gross

---

[5] For a more complete description of the types of value-added taxes, the methods of calculating tax liabilities, and the advantages and disadvantages of each, see Carl S. Shoup, *Public Finance* (Chicago: Aldine, 1969), pp. 250–64.

tax liability is determined by applying the tax rate to its total sales. The firm is then allowed credit for value-added tax paid on all its inputs, which will have been reflected in higher prices for them.[6] As shown in Table 1, for this simple example, the credit method produces the same results as the addition and subtraction methods. Because it is the most likely candidate for adoption in the United States, primarily this method of computing the tax is considered in the remainder of this chapter.[7]

Table 1. Example of Value Added and Value-Added Tax (dollars)

| | Industry | | | Overall Economy |
	A	B	C	
1. Sales				
a. Intermediate goods	100	300	–	400
b. Consumer goods	–	–	500	500
2. Purchased inputs	–	100	300	400
3. Factor payments and net profits	100	200	200	500
4. Value added (line 3 or line 1 – line 2)	100	200	200	500
5. Tax on gross sales (10% of line 1)	10	30	50	90
6. Credit for taxes paid (10% of line 2)	–	10	30	40
7. Net tax liabilities (line 5 – line 6 or 10% of line 4)	10	20	20	50

---

[6] This description follows Shoup, *Public Finance*. It may be more useful to distinguish between the addition method on the one hand and two variants of the deduction method on the other. The addition method takes as the tax base the sum of factor payments and profits and thus is useful only for the income-type value-added tax (discussed in the section "Income versus consumption base"). According to the subtraction method (the first of the deduction variants), the tax base is determined by deducting purchased inputs from sales. According to the credit method (the second deduction variant), the tax on purchased inputs is deducted from the tax on sales to determine the net tax liability. Although either of these methods could be used to implement an income-type value-added tax, calculation of liabilities under the consumption-type value-added tax is more straightforward, especially for the credit method (as noted in "Income versus consumption base"), because no distinction need be made between capital and intermediate goods.

[7] All the taxes now levied on value added in Europe employ the credit method of calculating tax liabilities. Credits can exceed gross tax liabilities if sales are largely for export, if investment bears a large relation to taxable sales, or if

Income versus consumption base. The choice of base upon which to impose the value-added tax will determine the distribution of its burden and its economic effects. The most important issue involves the treatment of capital goods. If each firm is allowed immediate credit for all taxes paid on capital goods as well as for those paid on intermediate inputs, then only sales to final consumers are taxed, and the tax is a consumption-type VAT. If, on the other hand, credits for taxes on capital goods are allowed to be taken only over the life of the asset as it depreciates, the tax base in the aggregate is national income, and the tax is an income-type VAT. See Appendix A for an example (similar to Table 1) that illustrates the application of the tax in each of these two cases.

In discussing a potential value-added tax for the United States, it seems advisable, for several reasons, to restrict consideration in this chapter to the consumption type. First, as a practical matter of tax administration, the consumption type is far simpler to apply. Under it (assuming the credit method of implementation), credit would be allowed for taxes paid on *all* purchases by business firms, that is, for purchases of both intermediate and capital goods. On the other hand, under the income type, credit would be limited to taxes on intermediate products and on the portion of the value of capital goods represented by depreciation.[8] Implementation of the income-type VAT would make it necessary, therefore, to distinguish between intermediate and capital goods and to apply depreciation schedules for the latter, as under the income taxes. These administrative difficulties would be avoided entirely under the consumption type of value-added tax.

Second, some of the economic advantages claimed for VAT depend upon its being the consumption type. In particular, potential inducements

---

sales are exempt or taxed at reduced rates. In principle, cash refunds should be immediately available in any case in which credit exceeds gross tax liability. In practice, this is true only if the excess credit arises from export sales. The extreme case occurs in France, where, under a "buffer rule," a firm investing heavily does not receive refunds. Rather, it must accumulate credits and carry them forward against the time when they can be offset against liabilities. For a description of this and other aspects of the value-added taxes in Europe, see National Economic Development Office, *Value Added Tax* (London: Her Majesty's Stationery Office, 1971), especially chapter 4.

8 Under the subtraction method, purchases of capital goods would be deducted immediately in calculating the base for a consumption-type value-added tax; whereas only depreciation would be subtracted for the income type. As noted above, the addition method lends itself only to implementation of the income-type value-added tax.

to growth are greater under the consumption type because it exempts capital goods from taxation; that is, it permits immediate depreciation of capital assets. There would be less difference between the two types with regard to balance-of-payment effects, but the consumption-type VAT would do at least as well as the income type.

Third, if a tax is to be levied on income, there is little reason for collecting it through a newly created value-added tax rather than through the existing personal income tax, which can be tailored to individual circumstances and made progressive. In the case of a broad-based consumption tax, there is no similar alternative because the present system does not include a personal-expenditure tax. To be sure, the income base is proportional, whereas the consumption base tends to be regressive. This may be one argument in favor of an income base. However, this aspect of the consumption-type VAT might be compensated for by choosing the appropriate mix of tax substitutions (as outlined below).

Finally, since the European countries employ the consumption-type VAT, pressures to adopt a similar approach (if the United States should choose to impose a tax on value added) would be enormous. For all these reasons, references to a value-added tax in the remainder of this chapter should be understood to mean the consumption type, except where explicit mention is made of the income type.

Tax base and yield. In its pure form, the value-added tax would apply at equal rates to all consumption spending. However, as a practical matter, it is likely that exemptions would be afforded to certain products and activities. Several potential categories of exemptions are considered in this section.

Equity aspects of base limitation. Replacing part of the corporation income tax with a tax on value added may be considered unduly regressive if the latter is applied equally to all categories of consumption. Thus, exemptions from VAT may be proposed for certain items of expenditure that figure prominently in the budgets of low-income families and for other items presumed to have unusual social value. Food for home consumption, household utilities, and medical expenses are among the obvious candidates.

Exemption of these or other final products results in preferential tax treatment and can be expected to distort consumer choices in their favor. These distortions must be weighed against the potential benefits in terms of equity to be gained from the exemption. The case for such exemptions thus depends upon which tax is to be replaced by VAT. The combinations leaving a less regressive (or more progressive) net effect (see "Distributional Aspects") would reduce the necessity of these exemptions and thus, would seem preferable to more regressive policies for this reason as well as in terms of equity.

Administrative considerations. Housing is one of the most difficult items to handle under a value-added tax. Rental housing in and of itself poses no conceptual problem. Rents would be taxed, and immediate credit would be allowed for all taxes paid on investment in residential structures for rental purposes. However, inclusion of rental receipts in the tax base would create a considerable administrative problem in that a substantial number of rental payments pass between individuals. Many recipients of small rental incomes might have no other sales taxable under VAT.

The tax treatment of owner-occupied housing is even more troublesome. Ideally, imputed rents would be taxed, and credit would be allowed for taxes paid on owner-occupied residential structures as well as on those intended for rental. But taxing imputed rents would be no easier under the value-added tax than it is under the personal income tax. Thus, administering VAT in a pure consumption manner would almost certainly be impossible.

A second-best approach to the taxation of housing under VAT might be to tax rentals as just described and to tax owner-occupied houses at the time of construction, that is, to treat them essentially as con-sumer goods for tax purposes. Owner-occupied housing would be treated somewhat unfavorably in comparison with other items in the household budget, and the tax would discriminate in favor of present homeowners. However, this might be the most feasible means of including housing in the tax base.

It is doubtful that all housing could be included in the tax base on equal terms. If owner-occupied housing could not be taxed equitably, it probably would not be taxed at all. In that case, it would appear undesir-able to levy the tax on rental housing. To do so would be to accentuate the preferential treatment of homeowners that is now provided by the personal income tax. Moreover, it is not clear that housing should be included in the VAT base even if it were possible to do so. Local property taxes in most states now result in a tax burden on residential property equal to a sales tax of around 20 to 25 per cent on housing expenditures.[9] This can be expected not only to distort consumer choices away from housing but also to produce a highly regressive pattern of tax incidence. This being the case, exempting all housing from the value-added tax would redress some of the imbalance in the current tax treatment of this important budget item and would avoid a further increase in regressivity. The exemption of housing reduces the potential tax base by $91 billion (at 1970 levels of income).[10]

Even if it were decided that the base of the value-added tax would have only limited exemptions, administrative realities would dictate that exemptions be allowed for certain other items included in consumption in the national-income accounts. Food provided for government and commercial employees, food produced and consumed on farms, and standard clothing issued to military personnel would almost certainly be excluded from the tax. Domestic service, services furnished without payment by financial intermediaries, and the expense of handling life insurance would probably be exempted also, as would bridge, tunnel, ferry, and road tolls, and transportation on street and electric railway and local buses. Admissions to legitimate theaters, opera, and entertainment of nonprofit institutions; the activities of clubs and fraternal organizations; expenditures on private education and research; and expenditures on religious and welfare activities would most likely be excluded as a matter of public policy, as well as for administrative convenience. Finally, foreign travel by U.S. residents and expenditures abroad by U.S. government personnel would clearly be omitted from the tax base. In total, these more or less inevitable exemptions (other than housing) would reduce the tax base by about $65 billion (at 1970 income levels).[11]

---

[9] See Dick Netzer, *Economics of the Property Tax* (Washington, D.C.: Brookings Institution, 1966), pp. 29–31, 106.

[10] The $91.2 billion of housing consumption indicated in Table 2 includes $62.4 billion imputed to owner-occupied nonfarm dwellings and the rental value of farmhouses.

[11] For either political or administrative reasons, it may be desirable (or inevitable) to exempt certain sectors such as agriculture and small businesses from statutory liability for the value-added tax. Except to the extent that exempted producers sell directly to ultimate consumers, exemptions of this kind should pose no problem of lost revenue. Under the credit method of calculating tax liabilities, exemptions at earlier stages would be "washed out" in subsequent transactions (in the absence of an explicit provision to have them carried through to the final product). In the example in Table 1, if no tax were collected from industry B on its sales to industry C, the latter would have no previous tax paid

If a value-added tax yields less than $5 billion, it is probably not worth establishing the administrative machinery and imposing the compliance costs necessary to collect it. As shown in Table 2, the base for a consumption-type VAT, most broadly defined, would be about $615 billion (at 1970 levels of income). In actuality, a base of about $465 billion, because of exemptions required by administrative necessity, is more realistic. Moreover, exemptions that are probable as a matter of public policy can be expected to reduce the tax base to no more than $290 billion. Thus, a 2 per cent tax would probably be worth collecting, a 3 per cent tax would yield from $9 to $14 billion, and a 5 per cent VAT would yield from $14 to $23 billion, the exact amount depending upon the liberality of the exemptions granted. It can be expected that by 1975, personal-consumption expenditures will have grown to something like $845 billion.[12] If so, the tax base would be about $640 billion and $395 billion under the two sets of assumptions about exemptions. Thus, by the mid-1970s, a 3 per cent tax would yield from $12 to $19 billion; and a 5 per cent tax, from $20 to $32 billion.

In summary, the size of the tax base of a tax on value added depends crucially upon whether such things as housing, food, medical services, household utilities, and financial and legal services are covered by the tax. Liberal exemptions for these items (plus the more or less administratively inevitable exemptions) would have reduced the potential tax base in 1970 from the $615 billion of personal-consumption expenditures to about $290 billion, or roughly 53 per cent. Quite stringent limitations on exemptions would have resulted in a 1970 tax base of perhaps $465 billion, or 75 per cent of consumption expenditures. These

---

to claim as a credit and therefore would be responsible for the entire $50 of gross tax liability. The more serious problem, as emphasized by Shoup, would seem to be the possibility of overtaxation due to breaking of the chain of tax credits. In terms of Table 1, industry B would pay $10 tax on its purchases from industry A but, being outside the value-added tax system, would receive no credit or refund. Because these problems are considered in detail in the chapters by Carl S. Shoup and John F. Due in this volume, they are not discussed in the remainder of this chapter.

[12] These estimates assume a rate of growth of personal-consumption expenditures of 6.5 per cent per year from their 1970 level. This implies a rate of inflation of 2.2 per cent per year if the Council of Economic Advisers' projection of a 4.3 per cent real rate of growth is realized; see its *Annual Report* for 1971, chapter 3. Although these estimates may prove to be inadequate as forecasts, they are indicative of the magnitudes involved.

alternatives are described in detail in Table 2. The crucial difference is, of course, the treatment of food, medical expenses, and household utilities. In both cases, it is assumed that housing is omitted from the tax base. Inclusion of housing would add from \$30 to \$50 billion, depending upon whether the tax was levied on total residential construction or on cash rental plus construction of owner-occupied housing only.

Table 2. Estimated Base of Consumption-Type Value-added Tax, with Limited and with Liberal Exemption, at 1970 Levels of Consumption (billions)

	Personal-Consumption Expenditures	Estimated Tax Base	
		Limited Exemptions	Liberal Exemptions
Food and tobacco	\$142.9	\$140.1[a]	\$ 39.6[b]
Clothing, accessories, and jewelry	62.3	62.1[c]	62.1[c]
Personal care	10.1	10.1	10.1
Housing	91.2	–	–
Household operation	85.6	80.9[d]	57.2[e]
Medical-care expenses	47.3	47.3	–
Personal business	35.5	12.3[f]	6.3[g]
Transportation	77.9	75.8[h]	75.8[h]
Recreation	39.0	36.1[i]	36.1[i]
Private education and research	10.4	–	–
Religious and welfare activities	8.8	–	–
Foreign travel and other, net	4.8	–	–
Total personal consumption	\$615.8	\$464.7	\$287.2
Percentage of personal consumption	100.0%	75.5%	46.6%

[a]Excludes only food furnished to government and commercial employees and food produced and consumed on farms.

[b]Includes only purchased meals and beverages and tobacco products.

[c]Excludes only standard clothing issued to military personnel.

[d]Excludes only domestic services.

[e]Excludes domestic services and household utilities.

[f]Excludes services furnished without payment by financial intermediaries except life insurance companies and expenses of handling life insurance.

[g]Excludes items in f and legal services and funeral and burial expenses.

[h]Excludes bridge, tunnel, ferry, and road tolls, and street and electric railway and local bus.

[i]Excludes admissions to legitimate theaters, opera, and entertainments of non-profit institutions; clubs and fraternal organizations, except insurance; and pari-mutuel net receipts.

Source: U.S. Department of Commerce, *Survey of Current Business* (July 1971), p. 24.

Value-added tax or retail-sales tax. Thus far in this section, only the possibility of adding a value-added tax to the federal fiscal arsenal has been examined. But it is worthwhile to ask whether a broad-based consumption tax might not better be implemented simply by imposing a federal retail-sales tax than by going to the value-added tax, which is almost completely new to the United States.[13] The two taxes would, after all, have virtually the same base and would probably have almost identical economic effects.

The familiarity of the retail tax and the greater ease of horizontal and vertical intergovernmental fiscal coordination under it are among its chief advantages.[14] Among the advantages of VAT, relative to the retail-sales tax, are the superior treatment of services, capital, and intermediate goods and the self-enforcing features of VAT, although the importance of the latter in the United States is questionable. Neither tax handles the problems of taxing housing, domestic services, and financial intermediaries very well. On balance, it is thus not clear which way the scale tips. But the discussion of the value-added tax should not proceed without consideration of the possibility of using its economic equivalent, the retail-sales tax, instead.

Distributional Aspects

In examining the distributional implications of VAT proposals, it is necessary to consider this tax as an alternative to other revenue sources. If VAT is to be introduced to provide additional revenue, it should be compared with alternative sources of obtaining such revenue; and if VAT is to be used to replace other revenue sources, it is necessary to specify just which sources are to be replaced. Estimates of the distributional effects of the value-added tax in both contexts are given in Table 3. The results

---

[13] This assumes that expenditure taxation is not a viable alternative. For a detailed examination of that question from an administrative point of view, see the chapter by Richard E. Slitor. Moreover, it assumes that an income-type value-added tax might be more directly (if not exactly) implemented through a simple addition of several points to the rates of the personal income tax.

[14] For a more detailed examination of the relative advantages of the value-added tax and the retail-sales tax *if* a broad-based federal tax is to be levied on consumption, see the chapters by Carl S. Shoup and John F. Due. For a more complete examination of the implications of the choice for state and local governments and the relations between them and the federal government, see Charles E. McLure, Jr., "TVA and Fiscal Federalism," in the *Proceedings* of the 1971 annual conference of the National Tax Association.

Table 3. Distributional Effects of Various Taxes and Tax Substitutions[a] (Increase or Decrease in Tax Liability as Percentage of Family Income)

Tax Change	Income Group									
	Lowest	2d	3d	4th	5th	6th	7th	8th	Highest	Total
Additional revenue of $5 billion from										
1. Value-added tax	0.9	0.8	0.7	0.7	0.6	0.6	0.6	0.5	0.4	0.6
2. Personal income tax	0.1	0.2	0.3	0.5	0.5	0.5	0.6	0.7	1.1	0.6
3. Corporation income tax	0.2	0.3	0.6	0.3	0.4	0.3	0.3	0.8	2.4	0.6
Value-added tax of $15 billion, of which $10 billion is replacement for (revenue lost in)										
4. Personal income tax	+2.6	+1.8	+1.5	+1.1	+0.9	+0.7	+0.4	+0.1	-1.2	+0.6
5. Corporation income tax (not shifted)	+2.4	+1.6	+0.9	+1.5	+1.2	+1.2	+1.2	-0.1	-3.7	+0.6
6. Partial integration of income taxes	+1.8	+0.8	-0.4	+1.1	+0.7	+1.0	+0.8	-0.6	+0.8	+0.6
7. Payroll taxes	+2.5	+1.6	+1.0	+0.6	+0.5	+0.4	+0.4	+0.4	+0.1	+0.6
8. Income-tax reform	-48.4	-14.0	-8.8	-3.5	+0.1	+4.6	+6.7	+6.5	+1.7	+0.6
Selected effects under alternative incidence assumptions for corporation tax										
50 per cent shifting										
9. For line 3	0.6	0.5	0.7	0.5	0.5	0.4	0.4	0.7	1.4	0.6
10. For line 5	+1.7	+1.2	+0.8	+1.1	+0.9	+0.8	+0.8	+0.2	-1.6	+0.6
11. For line 6	+0.1	-0.4	-0.6	0.0	0.0	+0.1	+0.1	+0.3	+6.4	+0.6
100 per cent shifting										
12. For line 3	0.9	0.8	0.7	0.7	0.6	0.6	0.6	0.5	0.4	0.6
13. For line 5	+0.9	+0.8	+0.7	+0.7	+0.6	+0.6	+0.6	+0.5	+0.4	+0.6
14. For line 6	-1.7	-1.6	-0.9	-1.1	-0.8	-0.8	-0.6	+1.2	+12.0	+0.6

[a] See Appendix B for sources of data, methods of estimation, and qualifications.

shown in the table lean heavily on certain assumptions regarding the incidence of the various taxes and therefore are speculative in nature, but they are indicative of patterns of tax incidence and are the best that can be done in this context. Moreover, these results (which pertain to the *differences* in the incidence of alternative taxes) are less precarious than frequently used estimates of the absolute incidence of the various taxes compared here.

Net addition to revenue from alternative sources. Lines 1 to 3 of Table 3 show the results of raising an additional $5 billion by alternative means. The value-added tax results in a regressive burden distribution throughout the income scale, whereas the personal income tax results in a progressive distribution. The corporation income tax is progressive at the upper end of the scale.[15]

The assumptions underlying these results may be noted here briefly. The regressive pattern for VAT reflects the assumption that its burden is distributed in line with consumption. Since the tax might contain exemptions beneficial to lower-income groups, the regressivity of VAT is probably somewhat overstated. The incidence of the personal income tax is assumed to be on the taxpayer. It should be noted in this context, however, that no account was taken of recent changes in the tax law that eliminate large numbers of low-income families from income-tax liability. Thus, at the bottom of the income scale, an increase in income-tax rates would have less effect than is suggested by Table 3. Finally, the results for the corporation income tax are based on the assumption that this tax is not shifted, so that the burden is distributed in line with dividend income.

Alternative assumptions regarding the incidence of the corporation tax are reflected in lines 9 and 14. As indicated, the corporation income tax becomes less progressive if it is assumed to be shifted partly to the consumer, and it becomes regressive if full shifting is assumed. In the case of full shifting, the overall burden distribution is essentially the same as under the value-added tax. Although the matter cannot be resolved here, these alternatives have been included in the tables because of the considerable controversy about the shifting of the corporation tax.

---

[15] The slight "hump" in the pattern of incidence for the corporation income tax in the third income group reflects the importance of dividends in that income bracket. It should be noted at this point that the estimates presented here are based upon tax law as of late 1970.

Nevertheless, most economists would conclude that the burden distribution would be more progressive (or less regressive) if increased revenue came from the corporation tax than if it came from the value-added tax.

Net addition combined with replacement of revenue. What would be the distributional impact of a $15-billion value-added tax, $10 billion of which would be used to replace revenue from various existing taxes or to compensate for revenue lost in tax reform? The results are shown in lines 4 to 8 of Table 3. The alternative tax reductions are as follows:

Line 4 A 10.8 per cent across-the-board reduction in the rates of personal income tax

Line 5 A 25.5 per cent reduction in the rates of the corporation income tax

Line 6 A partial integration of the personal and corporation income taxes[16]

Line 7 A 21.5 per cent reduction in the rate of payroll taxes

Line 8 A more far-reaching plan of tax reform and relief to low-income families through a negative income tax that would lose $10 billion on balance[17]

The results shown in lines 4 to 8 give the *net* change in tax liability of each income group resulting from the combined effects of VAT and other changes, expressed as a percentage of income. Note that substitution for the personal income tax (line 4) is regressive. Substitution for the corporation tax, assuming no shifting (line 5), is regressive, especially at the extreme ends of the income scale. If combined with integration of the personal and corporation taxes (line 6), the VAT package be-

---

[16] This involves eliminating roughly 70 per cent of the corporation income tax and taxing individuals under the personal income tax on the basis of their proportionate share of retained earnings as well as dividends. See Appendix B for details.

[17] The relief of low-income families is roughly consistent with the approach in the 1970 statement on national policy by the Research and Policy Committee of the Committee for Economic Development, *Improving the Public Welfare System*. The effective rates in the top income brackets are generally consistent with the findings of a recent Brookings Institution study of the effect of implementing in the United States the comprehensive proposals for tax reform made by the Carter Commission in Canada. These proposals, described in greater detail in Appendix B, would result in a definition of income for tax purposes much nearer the economists' concept of income than is contained in existing tax law.

comes roughly proportional. Substitution for the payroll tax (line 7) turns out to be regressive for the lower end of the income scale. Since payroll tax coverage on low-income groups is not universal, replacing that tax with a value-added tax would increase tax burdens on low-income groups.[18] Combination of VAT with income-tax reform, including a negative income tax (line 8), would result in a sharp reduction in tax liabilities (or net transfers) at the lower end of the scale, thus giving rise to a highly progressive package.

Some of these results are repeated in lines 9 to 14 under alternative assumptions regarding the shifting of the corporation income tax. A fully shifted corporation income tax (line 12) would have about the same incidence as an equal-yield VAT (line 1). Thus, imposition of a $15-billion value-added tax accompanied by a $10-billion corporate-tax reduction (line 13) would have the same net effect as imposing a $5-billion value-added tax. Integration of the corporate and personal income taxes would be especially progressive if the corporation income tax was shifted (line 14). Besides the newly imposed VAT, a tax borne at progressive rates on personal shares in corporate profits would be substituted for a tax on consumption. Of course, the results for 50 per cent shifting (lines 9 to 11) are intermediate between those for zero shifting and complete shifting.

In conclusion, this brief investigation of distributive effects points to two important conclusions. First, if the value-added tax is considered as a source of additional revenue, the resulting burden distribution is more regressive or less progressive than would be the case with reliance on the more traditional revenue sources such as the personal or the corporation income tax. Second, if the value-added tax is considered as part of a package including tax substitutions, the results are largely dependent upon what substitutions are to be made, varying from a highly regressive to a highly progressive burden distribution. It should also be noted that the substitutions shown in Table 3 are only samples. Thus, other patterns of income- or payroll-tax reduction might be considered. In the case of an income-tax reduction, an equal point reduction in all bracket rates might be considered rather than a proportional across-the-board cut in liabilities; in the case of a payroll-tax reduction, introduction of exemp-

---

[18] In arriving at this conclusion, it is assumed that the payroll tax burden is borne entirely by the wage earner. To the extent that the tax is shifted to the consumer, the regressivity of line 7 is reduced at the lower end of the scale.

tions might be considered rather than a reduction in rates. Finally, the comparison might be extended to other possible revenue sources such as a progressive expenditure tax. What matters in this case, as in other contexts of tax reform, is the *net* effect of the *entire* reform package to be undertaken, rather than the effect of any particular measure considered by itself.

Domestic Economic Effects

In addition to its distributional impact, introduction of a tax on value added could have important effects on the domestic economy and the international economic relations of the United States. These would, of course, depend upon which tax was replaced in part by the value-added tax. This section compares VAT with alternative sources of revenue in terms of economic neutrality, effects upon economic growth, and potential contribution to economic stability. Effects upon the balance of payments are discussed under "International Economic Effects."

Neutrality. Market prices are usually accepted as fairly accurate indicators of what consumers want and how best to produce it. They register consumer preferences among goods and services, they indicate the cheapest combinations of factors to use in producing a given output, and (through the return to capital) they regulate the amount of output to be devoted to saving and investment rather than to consumption. Thus, one goal of tax policy is neutrality: the avoidance of unintended distortions of market prices.

Neutrality is one of the chief advantages of the tax on value added. In theory, it applies uniformly to all legal forms of organization and to all industries not exempted by law. Thus, it does not distort the consumer's choice between products or the producer's decisions concerning production techniques or modes of business organization. In fact, however, VAT is not likely to be levied in its pure form. Some exemptions are likely to be enacted as a matter of equity and administrative necessity.[19] In practice, the value-added tax is likely to be substantially less neutral than it is in theory. Nevertheless, it is probably reasonable to think of VAT as a basically neutral tax.

---

[19] Exemptions provided as a matter of social policy cannot consistently be said to involve unintentional distortion of market prices.

A group of subtler issues involves the choice between the income and consumption varieties of VAT. The consumption-type tax in effect exempts capital goods from taxation, whereas under the income-type tax, credit is allowed for taxes paid on capital goods only as the assets depreciate (as noted earlier in this chapter). Thus, producers of capital goods, firms in capital-intensive industries, and recipients of capital income can be expected to prefer the consumption variety over the income variety. On the other hand, producers of consumer goods, firms in labor-intensive industries, and recipients of noncapital income can be expected to prefer the income variety. Moreover, they may claim that allowing immediate credit for taxes paid on capital goods is nonneutral because it can be expected to result in a somewhat higher saving rate, and therefore more capital-intensive production, than would prevail under the income-type tax.

These preferences for the two varieties of VAT are not difficult to understand and appreciate. The real question is which form is neutral with respect to economic decisions. This can be answered most meaningfully for perfect flat-rate taxes on income and consumption.

Economic theorists believe that only the consumption type is completely neutral.[20] It does not distort the choice of whether to consume now or later because it applies at equal rates to consumption at either point in time (in the absence of statutory rate changes). On the other hand, the income type discriminates against saving and future consumption because it includes saving in the tax base. Thus, neutrality requires taxation of consumer goods but not of capital goods, even though this is more favorable to capital accumulation and capital-intensive production than is income taxation. Yet the nonneutrality involved in taxing income rather than consumption is by itself not decisive, as evidenced by heavy U.S. reliance on the personal income tax. Rather, this chapter focuses on the consumption-type VAT, rather than the income type, because it is administratively simpler and because, being used in Europe, it is more likely to be adopted in the United States.

Since the consumption-type VAT that is the center of attention in this chapter is essentially neutral, its introduction as an additional source of revenue would involve no distortions. How it would compare with alternative sources of additional revenue can be seen by considering it as a partial substitute for various other taxes. It may be worthwhile, how-

---

[20] Even the consumption-type tax distorts the choice between labor and leisure. This qualification is, for the most part, not taken into consideration in this chapter.

ever, to note at the outset that these conclusions hold only if the value-added tax is truly neutral, not shot through with exemptions.

Value-added tax versus corporation income tax. Whereas the choice between income and consumption bases may not make much difference in terms of neutrality, the same cannot be said of the choice between the value-added tax and the corporation income tax. The corporation income tax is distinctly partial and therefore nonneutral. It discriminates between firms organized as corporations and those organized as partnerships and proprietorships, and within the corporate sector, it discriminates between high- and low-margin firms and between financing from equity capital and from borrowed funds. Because margins, the latitude in adopting noncorporate organization, and the use of equity capital differ between industries, the tax also discriminates between products of the corporate and noncorporate sectors and in favor of industries characterized by low margins and by high debt-equity ratios. Furthermore, because certain industries are favored by so-called tax preferences, even the tax treatment of similarly organized and financed firms differs between industries. Moreover, within the corporate sector, the tax creates a tendency for labor to be substituted for capital, so that production in the corporate sector may be abnormally labor-intensive and, conversely, production in the noncorporate sector may be overly capital-intensive.

That VAT is a neutral tax (assuming the absence of significantly distorting exemptions) does not imply that substituting it for part of the corporation tax would have no effect upon patterns of consumption, production, and resource use. The interindustry distribution of tax liabilities would be altered because of the elimination of the various nonneutralities of the corporation income tax, and it can be expected that the envisaged tax substitution would result in the reallocation of resources toward those industries that presently are more heavily taxed than average. This shift of resources would, in fact, be one of the chief advantages to be expected from employing a fully neutral VAT; the distortions induced by the corporation income tax would be eliminated in part.[21]

But among the expected shifts would be an artificially increased preference for the corporate form of organization. Simply replacing part

---

[21] It should be noted that this distortion could also be eliminated by imposing a general tax on profits in place of the corporation income tax. Discrimination against saving would, however, be accentuated by such a policy.

of the corporation tax with a value-added tax would not restore neutrality with respect to choice of forms of business organization. Retained earnings would become a substantial tax haven because corporate profits would be taxed only if distributed, and, therefore, the existing distortion against investment in the corporate sector would be reversed. Full neutrality would be achieved only if the corporate and personal income taxes were integrated by allocating corporate profits to households and taxing them under the personal income tax. The corporation tax, if it existed at all, would be no more than a device for withholding taxes on the corporate profits attributable to individuals. Double taxation of dividends would be eliminated, but without letting retained earnings go untaxed, as they would if the corporation tax were reduced without integration. Form of business organization, debt-equity ratios, product mix, and capital-labor ratios would no longer be distorted by the existence of a separate corporation income tax. Thus, on efficiency grounds, integrating the two income taxes is far superior to simply reducing the corporation tax as part of a proposal to introduce a value-added tax.

Value-added tax versus individual income and payroll taxes. The personal income and payroll taxes involve relatively little economic distortion.[22] Tax preferences under the personal income tax favor certain economic activities relative to others. But aside from this, both the personal tax and the payroll tax, because they are essentially universal in their coverage, do not discriminate between industries. Combining VAT with a thoroughgoing reform of the tax structure would be superior on neutrality grounds to reduction of either income tax and even to integration because it would eliminate (or at least reduce) existing tax preferences.

In summary, on efficiency grounds, the value-added tax is preferable to the corporation income tax, the personal income tax, and the payroll tax if it has no significant exemptions. The extent to which even an ideal VAT would be less distorting than the payroll tax is probably slight. If the value-added tax is accompanied by integration, its superiority over the corporation income tax in terms of efficiency is enormous, particularly if the tax preferences under the corporation tax

---

[22] Perhaps the greatest distortion involves the choice between leisure and labor in the highest tax-rate brackets. The maximum tax on earned income enacted in the Tax Reform Act of 1969 helps to mitigate this distortion.

are not carried over in the form of exemptions under the value-added tax. Finally, the superiority of VAT over personal taxation is intermediate, involving primarily the elimination of differential treatment of various economic activities stemming from existing tax preferences and the exemption of savings from the tax. Of course, if the value-added tax contained substantial exemptions, it would probably be inferior to the income and payroll taxes and might not even be preferable to the corporation income tax on efficiency grounds.

Integration of the two income taxes and imposition of a general tax on value added would be superior to reduction of the corporation income tax but would not affect the distortions that a thorough tax reform would correct. Whereas substitution of the neutral VAT for the nearly neutral payroll and personal income taxes would have little effect on production, consumption, and resource use, combining VAT with corporate-tax reduction, income-tax integration, or broader income-tax reform would probably induce massive economic adjustments.[23]

Economic growth. One reason advanced for replacing part of the corporation income tax with a value-added tax is the positive effect such a replacement would have on the rate of economic growth. It is argued that the rate of saving would be higher under VAT and that there would be more risk taking and investment. In support of substituting a value-added tax for the corporation income tax, it is noted that the countries of Europe which have experienced rapid economic growth in the postwar period rely relatively more heavily upon indirect taxes, including value-added taxes, than the United States does.

Saving. It is likely that a shift to a tax on value-added would be conducive to a higher rate of saving. On the assumption that public policy will be such that severe excess capacity and unemployment are avoided, this can be interpreted as leading to increased investment. The crucial question is the amount by which saving would increase if $10 billion raised through a value-added tax were substituted for various other taxes.

Substitution of VAT for the corporation income tax would probably have little impact on the rate of saving if the latter tax is shifted to consumers. But if the corporation tax is not shifted, the increase in the rate

---

[23] See Appendix B for a more complete description of the thoroughgoing tax reform envisaged.

of saving could be quite dramatic. Reduction of the corporation tax would increase after-tax corporate profits, which would in turn be reflected in higher retained earnings and/or dividends. Since, on the average, corporations retain about five-sixths of increases in net profits, a $10-billion reduction in the corporation income tax would increase retained earnings by about $8⅓ billion. When saving out of dividends is included, the total increase in saving resulting from a tax cut of this kind would be on the order of $8.5 billion.[24]

On the other hand, if the personal income tax were cut by $10 billion, saving would probably increase by about 6 per cent of that amount, or about $600 million. Imposition of VAT would probably reduce saving by somewhat less than 6 per cent of the tax, so that on balance, substitution of a $10-billion VAT for that much of the personal income tax would result in some addition to saving, although the impact would not be large. The saving response to substituting the value-added tax for the payroll tax would probably be even smaller.

The most favorable impact on saving would easily come from substituting the value-added tax for the corporation income tax. Such a tax policy might raise total private saving by close to $8 billion; whereas substituting VAT for the personal income or payroll taxes would have little net impact on saving. Raising $5 billion of new revenue would, of course, reduce private saving, probably by about one-quarter billion dollars. The quantitative effect of combining VAT with tax integration is difficult to foretell (if the corporation tax is not shifted) because it is far from clear how dividend policies would be affected.[25] The impact of a complete tax reform is even more difficult to estimate, but presumably it would be less favorable to saving than integration alone because of the elimination of tax preferences on capital income and the initiation of negative-income-tax payments to low-income families.

---

[24] A value-added tax yielding $10 billion in 1972 would yield about $12 billion in 1975, given a rate of increase of the tax base of about 6.5 per cent. Thus, corporate-tax reduction of $10 billion in 1972 would result in an increase of about $10 billion in saving by 1975.

[25] The reduction of the corporation tax involved in integration would free perhaps $25 to $30 billion for retention or distribution. Using the average figure of five-sixths, this would translate into $20 to $25 billion of retained earnings. But in addition to the small reduction in personal saving resulting from increased personal taxes and the value-added tax, there would be a sizable offset because of the pressures to distribute earnings, since retained earnings would no longer be favored by the tax law and stockholders would have to pay personal income taxes on their shares of corporate profits.

In the context of this discussion of the effect of tax policy on the rate of saving, perhaps it should be noted that private saving, which is influenced by the *form* of taxation, is only one part of the total saving of an economy. The surplus of the government sector, which, given the level of government spending, is a matter of the *level* of taxation, is the other important (if often negative) component of total saving. It may be possible to give somewhat less emphasis than is usual to the effects of structural tax policy on the level of private saving, provided the level of surplus is amenable to control.[26]

Investment. Increased saving is, of course, of no advantage unless matched by increased investment, since by itself it would only add to unemployment, rather than to economic growth. Thus, it is necessary to ask how alternative taxes affect investment. It is often asserted that the corporation income tax, as a tax on profits, discourages risk taking because it is paid by efficient, successful, and profitable firms, not by their less efficient and unprofitable competitors. The value-added tax, on the other hand, as a tax on all consumption (or income), would be more or less neutral with regard to risk taking. According to this line of reasoning, it may be concluded that the substitution of VAT for the corporation tax would induce more risk taking in the economy.

But the problem is more complex than it appears at first sight. By the same token that the corporation income tax (if not shifted) makes the government a silent partner in profitable ventures, it also results in governmental sharing of the losses from unprofitable ventures so long as loss-offset provisions (that is, carry-back and carry-forward of losses) are adequate. The net effect of these two aspects is not obvious.

The effect of income taxation upon risk taking has recently been the subject of several highly sophisticated analyses employing the theory of portfolio choice.[27] But at present, no definitive statements can be made

---

[26] However, if firms are insistent on financing investment from internal funds, it may not be sufficient to generate saving through a budget surplus. It may be necessary to focus on policies, including tax policies, that will increase the flow of internal funds.

[27] See, for example, Joseph Stiglitz, "The Effects of Income, Wealth, and Capital Gains Taxation on Risk Taking," *Quarterly Journal of Economics,* May 1969, pp. 263–83. This is a generalization of the classic articles on the subject by Evsey D. Domar and R. A. Musgrave, "Proportional Income Taxation and Risk-taking," *Quarterly Journal of Economics,* May 1944, pp. 387–422, and by James Tobin, "Liquidity Preference as Behavior Toward Risk," *Review of Economic Studies,* February 1958, pp. 65–87.

concerning whether or not income taxation increases risk taking. Risk taking may actually be greater under the unshifted corporation income tax than under VAT. Of course, if the corporation income tax is shifted, substituting VAT for it should have little effect on risk taking.

A line of reasoning similar to that discussed for an unshifted corporation income tax applies (although less strongly) to substituting the value-added tax for part of the personal income tax. It seems unlikely, finally, that substituting a value-added tax for part of the payroll taxes would significantly affect risk taking.

Saving and investment combined. It should be borne in mind that this analysis relates to a given pool of investment funds. If budget policy can be used to achieve national goals for total saving, the analysis of risk taking from a given pool of funds seems reasonable. However, given this country's mixed record in consistently using budget policy in this way, it is instructive to consider the argument independent of the effect of budget policy.

As already indicated, the flows of private saving may depend crucially upon tax policy. Thus, although the corporation income tax may be more conducive to risk taking than the value-added tax for a given pool of funds, the pool may be substantially larger under the value-added tax than it would be under the corporation tax. Therefore it seems likely that more investment would occur under the VAT than under the corporation income tax. On the other hand, probably not much effect on saving and investment would result from either of the other simple tax substitutions.

Stabilization aspects. One of the key considerations in the evaluation of proposals to substitute a tax on value added for some part of various other taxes is the effect such a policy would have upon the success of efforts to stabilize the economy. The potential effects fall into two categories: those involved in the transition to VAT and those involved in its continued operation.

Transitional impact on prices. If the changeover to VAT were to result in product prices rising by the amount of the tax, it might lead to further wage and price escalation and create a most unwelcome addition and prolongation of the current inflationary woes. Moreover, most, if not all, of the hoped-for gains on balance-of-payments grounds (discussed in the section "International Economic Effects") would be greatly reduced or would vanish. Unfortunately, the answer to the question cannot be found in the recent European experience in introducing value-added taxes. There, introduction of VAT did not significantly affect price levels, but—and this is crucial—VAT was generally introduced as a replacement for turnover or retail-sales taxes. In the United States, this would not be the case, and the results would therefore differ.

In the absence of empirical evidence, it is necessary to consider what may be expected on theoretical grounds. As is usually the case, many answers can be obtained, depending on the behavioral assumptions that are made. Since this chapter advances suggestions of policy and does not attempt to present a complete theoretical analysis, all possible cases need not be considered here. The discussion proceeds on the basis of two assumptions: that money wages are downward rigid and that government is committed to a high-employment policy. The realism of the first assumption is hardly debatable.[28] The second assumption also seems reasonable, at least for the longer run.

To begin with the simplest case, suppose that VAT is substituted for a corresponding amount of personal income tax. Reduction of the income tax removes a tax wedge between personal and disposable income; introduction of VAT introduces a wedge between gross and net receipts of firms. What will the outcome be? Removal of the income-tax wedge will leave money-wage rates (and hence unit-labor costs) unchanged but will increase disposable income. Since elimination of the income tax does not affect unit-labor costs, it does not affect prices. Insertion of the VAT wedge cannot push down wage rates. Hence, it must either be absorbed in reduced profits or be reflected in higher prices. Chances are that the higher prices will be the case. In short, substitution of a value-added tax for part of the personal income tax is likely to raise prices by more or less the amount of tax.

It might be argued that the government need not tolerate this. If the same high-employment output is to be taken off the market at higher prices, monetary-fiscal policies must underwrite a higher level of demand. This the government may refuse to do. But if it does (i.e., if it refuses to permit the higher level of demand to be generated), the result most likely

---

[28] The results would differ in a world of completely flexible prices. In such a world, the effect of tax changes on the price level would be solely a matter of monetary policy, and monetary policy could be adjusted to maintain price-level stability while maintaining real income at the full-employment level.

will be reduced employment rather than prevention of the price rise. The more likely outcome, therefore, is that the government will permit prices to rise.[29]

If VAT were substituted for the corporation income tax, the result would depend upon the response of prices to the removal of the corporation tax. If the corporation tax is not shifted (in the sense of being reflected in higher product prices), its removal would not affect prices. The argument and conclusions, therefore, are similar to those for substitution for the personal income tax. If, however, an increase in the corporation tax raises prices, its reduction may in turn lower them. In this case, the European experience of substitution of VAT for the turnover tax would be applicable, and substitution of VAT for the shifted corporation tax could be expected to leave the general price level unchanged. One consumption tax would simply be substituted for another.

Note, however, that this outcome depends not only on the assumption that the corporation tax was shifted in the first place but also on the further assumption that it would be unshifted when reduced. Since the corporation tax falls heavily on highly concentrated industries with administered pricing, it is doubtful on theoretical grounds that unshifting would occur, and empirical studies that support the shifting conclusion are less certain with regard to unshifting. Moreover, even if reverse shifting occurs, some upward pressure on the general price level may remain. Substitution of VAT for the corporation tax would call for changes in relative prices that, given the tendency for prices to be downward rigid, might occur only in the context of a rising price level.

Are the conclusions described above the same if a value-added tax is introduced not as a substitute for other taxes but to finance additional expenditures? In a high-employment economy, an increase in government expenditures would be consistent with price stability only if accompanied by a corresponding restriction in private demand. Obviously, finance by VAT would be less inflationary than finance by credit expansion. Even though it is assumed that VAT would be likely to raise prices by the amount of the tax wedge, this would be a once-and-for-all increase and much less inflationary than the effects generated by credit expansion. At the same time, income-tax financing of the expenditure increase would be even more effective in forestalling price increase be-

---

[29] Substitution of the value-added tax for the payroll tax is essentially similar to the income-tax case and is therefore not dealt with separately.

cause it would not involve introduction of a tax wedge between factor costs and prices.

The same reasoning applies if VAT were introduced or raised in order to check an excessively high level of demand. Here it would be fallacious to argue that a tax which raises prices (by being an addition to costs) cannot be used to check inflation. Of course it can. The increase in prices caused by insertion of the tax wedge is a one-time increase, whereas the depressing effect on aggregate demand resulting from the withdrawal of purchasing power is a more powerful and continuing check to expansion. But as before, it may be concluded that checking inflation via income taxation will be more effective because the initial price-increasing effect is avoided.

In all, it seems highly likely that introduction of a tax on value added will raise prices by about the amount of the tax. Taken by itself, this is a one-shot effect, but it may well be magnified by wage escalation. How serious a matter this is will be left for the reader's judgment.

Cyclical stability.[30] As economic conditions change, tax bases (income, profits, consumption, and so forth) and tax receipts change with them. The induced variations in tax receipts tend to act as an automatic stabilizer by damping fluctuations in economic activity.[31] Moreover, tax rates can be varied in a conscious effort to offset economic fluctuations; that is, they can be raised to counteract tendencies toward overheating of the economy and reduced to mitigate recessionary tendencies.

The efficacy of various taxes as fiscal stabilizers depends upon the response of tax liabilities to changes in economic conditions and the impact a given change in liabilities has upon private spending. The former involves both the automatic response of tax liabilities to economic conditions and the ease and likelihood of making discretionary changes in tax rates as economic conditions warrant.

Because corporation profits are extremely volatile over the cycle, revenues from the corporate income tax exhibit considerably more built-in flexibility than is likely to characterize a tax on value added. But its

---

[30] The relative impact of the value-added tax and other taxes as countercyclical tools is examined in the chapter by William H. Branson and is discussed here only briefly.

[31] In the discussion leading up to the 1964 tax cut, increasing attention was paid to the "fiscal drag" created by automatic stabilizers operating in a growth context. The stabilizers tend to hold back desired economic growth, as well as undesirable overexuberance of aggregate demand.

greater responsiveness to economic conditions is not sufficient to render the unshifted corporation income tax a more effective automatic stabilizer than the value-added tax. Reductions in corporate-tax liabilities occurring during a downswing may not flow automatically into corporate investment. Because of the cyclical assymetry in the response of investment to the net rate of return on capital and the flow of internal funds, it is likely that VAT would be more stabilizing for recessionary periods but that the corporate income tax would be more stabilizing for expansionary periods.

If the corporation income tax (including cyclical variations in it) is shifted to consumers, then for a given amount of revenue, it and VAT would have about the same impact on private spending. Because the built-in flexibility of receipts is less under VAT than under the corporation income tax, the latter would be the better automatic stabilizer.

Whether the value-added tax or the personal income tax would be the better automatic stabilizer is unclear. Taxable income exhibits greater cyclical variations than consumption does. But being more progressive than the potential tax on value added, the personal income tax is likely to reduce saving more (and thus spending less) per dollar of revenue. On balance, there may be little to choose between the two on the basis of contribution to built-in stability. On the other hand, the payroll tax may be marginally better as a built-in stabilizer than the value-added tax.

There is clearly little that can be said about the likely contribution of various taxes to automatic stability, although, on balance, VAT seems to rate somewhat lower than any of the direct taxes being considered. Thus, it seems that in any decision of whether or not to impose a value-added tax, considerations of built-in stability need be given only minimal consideration.

In respect to discretionary fiscal policy, little has been written about the feasibility of altering VAT rates in response to changes in economic conditions in order to stabilize the economy. This lack of discussion suggests that discretionary changes in the rate of the value-added tax could be a useful tool of fiscal policy. However, several aspects of this question require examination.

There seems little to choose between the value-added tax and the income taxes as tools of discretionary fiscal policy in terms of ease of implementation. Once enacted, the 1968 income-tax surcharge became effective quickly and with little administrative difficulty. There is no reason to believe an increase in the rate of VAT would be any harder to implement.

A temporary increase in the value-added tax could be expected to exert a greater dampening effect upon the economy than a temporary increase in either income tax. First, the income taxes would be more likely than the value-added tax to be paid out of savings rather than consumption. Second, some expenditures might be postponed until VAT rates returned to their normal levels. On the other hand, temporary increases in personal income taxes might have little direct and immediate impact on spending if households draw on savings to maintain customary outlays. Experience with the 1968 surcharge suggests this to be the case.

The other side of this coin, however, is that expectations of a countercyclical increase in the VAT rate could induce anticipatory buying that would have perverse macroeconomic effects, whereas an increase in income taxation would not. Thus, it would be crucial that the president have discretionary authority to alter VAT rates within prescribed limits. Although the long delay preceding enactment of the tax surcharge in 1968 certainly made controlling inflation more difficult, it did not actively worsen the situation. A long discussion of whether or not to raise the VAT rate almost certainly would do so because, unlike an increase in the income tax, such an increase could not be made retroactive to the date of presidential request.

It can be concluded that as automatic stabilizers or as tools of discretionary fiscal policy, the various taxes examined appear to be about equally useful. Income-tax receipts, especially from the corporation tax, are more volatile cyclically than the value-added tax, but they also have less impact on private spending per dollar of revenue. Discretionary changes can be made in all the taxes for countercyclical purposes, at least in principle.

Summary of domestic effects. Substituting the value-added tax for part of either the personal income tax or the payroll taxes would reduce distortions of market prices, but only marginally. The real gains in economic efficiency would come from combining VAT with integration of the two income taxes or a program of complete income-tax reform. Either of these combinations would, however, require massive economic adjustments, as would a simple substitution of VAT for part of the corporation income tax. Substitution for the corporation tax would not, however, result in neutral taxation because it would create a substantial tax shelter for retained earnings unless accompanied at least by a tighter tax treatment of capital gains.

By far the greatest impact on saving (about $8 billion for a $10-billion tax change) would occur if the value-added tax were substituted for part of the corporation income tax. Substituting a tax on value added for personal income or payroll taxes would affect saving only marginally. The effects on saving of combining VAT with income-tax integration or reform are too uncertain to predict with confidence. However, integration would probably increase saving considerably, although less than corporate-tax reduction would, and reform would probably increase saving somewhat less than that.

Substituting VAT for part of the corporation income tax would probably increase investment, but combining it with tax integration or reform would probably reduce risk taking. Substitution for the payroll taxes would have little effect on risk taking, and substitution for the income tax would probably be an intermediate case.

Introduction of a tax on value added would probably raise prices by the amount of the tax, especially if wages are rigid downward and a high-employment policy is pursued. On the basis of contribution to cyclical stability, there seems to be little to choose between the value-added tax and the various taxes it might replace. VAT receipts would vary less over the cycle, but they would have a greater impact on private spending per dollar of revenue. As tools of discretionary fiscal policy, all the taxes seem more or less equally usable.

International Economic Effects[32]

Among the most publicized features of value-added taxation are the border-tax adjustments (BTA) allowed on international trade. Exports are exempt from the tax and any value-added tax already paid on productive inputs used in manufacturing them is rebated. Similarly, imports are subjected to a tax designed to equalize tax treatment of them

---

[32] Virtually the entire discussion of the international aspects of substituting a value-added tax for the corporation income tax has been in the context of improving the U.S. balance of payments, rather than in terms of reducing distortions. Thus, the recent devaluation of the dollar should render this discussion passé, although in reality it probably will not.

relative to domestically produced goods. These tax adjustments made at the border under VAT have no counterpart under the corporation income tax and therefore may appear to give firms in nations employing VAT a competitive advantage over American firms. In fact, these tax adjustments made at the border are sometimes simply called *border taxes* or are thought of as outright export subsidies.

Moreover, it is often claimed that because border-tax adjustments are allowed for value-added taxes but not for various types of direct taxes, a switch from direct taxes to value-added taxes would help the U.S. balance of payments by improving the competitive position of domestic industries relative to imports and of U.S. exports in world markets. A second argument is that quite aside from the effect on the balance of trade, such a switch would create in the United States a more attractive climate for investment. This, it is argued, would stimulate the flow of foreign capital into the United States and retard the outflow of investment funds from the United States, thereby improving the capital account in the balance of payments. This section will examine the validity of each of these arguments.

Balance of trade. To begin with, it may be useful to consider the proper role of border-tax adjustments. If a country wishes to tax all consumption occurring within its borders, it must tax consumption of goods produced abroad as well as goods produced domestically. Under VAT, this requires that imports be taxed; otherwise, they would be favored relative to domestically produced goods and services.[33] Under a retail-sales tax, no BTA is needed because this tax applies to all sales to consumers, regardless of where products are produced. Moreover, since only consumption is to be taxed, exports should occur tax-free. Under VAT, this requires rebate of, or exemption from, all taxes paid on exports, whereas under a retail-sales tax, no such adjustment is needed at the border because no tax would have yet been paid. These border-tax adjustments thus differ sharply from distorting import duties and export subsidies. They are essential to provide that all domestic consumption— but only that—is taxed. In other words, they are needed to assure that products entering international trade are taxed in the nation in which

---

[33] Strictly speaking, only imports by ultimate consumers need actually be taxed at importation. Taxes on intermediate goods would be made up at the first taxable transaction because no credit would be available for the taxes not paid. The same is true, if less obvious, for capital goods.

they are consumed, and only there. Thus, introduction of a value-added tax with border-tax adjustments would create no more competitive advantage for the nation employing it than a retail-sales tax would.

The traditional argument based on this reasoning is that imposing a value-added tax as a source of additional revenue or substituting it for any of the direct taxes would have no effect on the balance of trade. The tax on value added would raise the prices of domestically produced goods, but rebates of taxes paid on production for export and compensating import duties would cancel this effect for exports and would place American and foreign goods on equal footing in domestic markets. On the other hand, removal of the direct taxes would have no effect on prices, which are traditionally assumed not to be shifted. Thus, trade would not be significantly affected whether VAT is imposed as a new source of revenue, as a partial substitute for one of the direct taxes, or as part of a package including tax integration or reform.

The conclusion would be different, however, if the value-added tax is not reflected fully in higher product prices. In the extreme case, prices would not rise, so that substitution of VAT for the corporation tax would have the effect of raising import prices and lowering export prices by the amount of the tax.[34] Similarly, substituting a shifted VAT for a shifted corporation tax could improve the balance of trade, provided the shifted corporation tax was reflected in lower prices when removed. The general price level would be unchanged, but border-tax adjustments would raise import prices and lower export prices by the amount of the tax. Finally,

---

[34] The $10-billion value-added tax required to replace the revenue lost in reduction of the corporation tax would require a tax rate of about 3 per cent. Import prices would rise and export prices would fall by that amount. This would have the following effects upon the dollar value of the trade balance resulting from changes in imports and exports (data based upon two recent estimates of response to price changes):

	Adams	Houthakker
	(millions of dollars)	
Imports	+ 1,250	+ 950
Exports	− 430	+ 250
Trade balance (imports + exports)	+ 820	+ 1,200

These estimates are based upon 1969 data for international trade flows and elasticity estimates contained in F. G. Adams, H. Eguchi, and F. Meyer-zu-Schloctern, *An Econometric Analysis of International Trade* (Paris: OECD, 1969); and in H. S. Houthakker and S. P. Magee, "Income and Price Elasticities in World Trade," *Review of Economics and Statistics* 51 (May 1969); 111–25. If the portion of the value-added tax intended to provide new revenue also did not raise prices, these effects would be proportionately larger.

substituting a value-added tax that was not reflected in higher prices for a corporation income tax that was unshifted when removed would have even more favorable effects on the balance of trade. Border-tax adjustments would be given in the context of a lower general price level.

Whether VAT would be fully reflected in higher product prices depends (as noted in the discussion under "Stabilization aspects") upon the monetary and fiscal policy that accompanies it. Given the downward rigidity of prices and a commitment to a policy of high employment, the value-added tax would probably raise prices by about the amount of the tax.[35] On the other hand, removal of any of the direct taxes would probably have little effect on prices. It thus seems likely that the outcome would be very nearly what classical theory predicts: Imposition of a tax on value added, whether as an addition to revenue or as a substitute, would probably have only a minimal effect on the balance of trade.[36]

A final argument that is sometimes heard is that substitution of a value-added tax for part of the corporation income tax would make American producers more "competitive" in world markets by stimulating investment and increasing productivity. This, of course, depends upon the corporation tax not being shifted. How important this consideration is will be left an open question. If export sales are a relatively unprofitable residual (as is sometimes claimed), this, too, may be a fairly weak argument for a value-added tax on balance-of-payments grounds.

Capital account. Even if the substitution of VAT for other taxes would have little (or an unknown) effect upon the balance of trade, it can be argued to have a favorable impact on the capital account. This argument is most relevant to the substitution of the value-added tax for the corporation income tax, which is the only tax change considered here. As in almost every case, the effect of the proposed tax change depends crucially on the incidence of the corporation income tax. If the corpora-

---

[35] See "Stabilization aspects" for the detailed discussion of this point. It may be argued that a more restrictive policy would prevent the value-added tax from being reflected in higher prices and having little favorable impact on the balance of trade. But following such a policy is in no way contingent upon imposing a value-added tax and should be considered on its own merits.

[36] Most of the discussion of balance-of-payments effects of substituting a value-added tax for the corporation income tax assumes—implicitly, if not explicitly—that exchange rates are fixed. Currency realignments and differential rates of inflation in various countries open this entire line of reasoning to question.

tion income tax is really only an inefficient way of collecting a sales tax because it is shifted forward, then substituting a value-added tax for part of it probably would have little effect upon the relative attractiveness of the United States to investors. On the other hand, if the corporation income tax is not shifted, replacing part of it with a value-added tax could raise the net rate of return in the United States and attract capital from abroad or prevent outflow of U.S. capital potentially going to finance investment abroad. The magnitude of such effects cannot be predicted with great accuracy. They depend upon relative tax rates here and abroad and the specific provisions of double-taxation treaties, not to mention the responsiveness of capital to international differences in the return to capital.

Moreover, what is involved here is essentially a process of stock adjustment. Once existing capital had been reallocated internationally in the light of relative rates of return, further benefit from the tax change would be small and might be outweighed by repatriation of earnings. Although the time required for complete stock adjustment is not short and the amount of capital potentially involved is large, little can be known with confidence about even the magnitude of the effects of substituting a value-added tax for an unshifted corporation income tax. Ignorance of the incidence of the corporation tax further compounds the uncertainty of these effects.

It seems unlikely that imposing a value-added tax would have a significant effect on the current account. Chances are that VAT would be reflected in higher prices and would, in turn, be offset by the border-tax adjustments, thus leaving the net position of traded goods unchanged. On the other hand, reduction of the corporation tax is unlikely to reduce prices, so that the relative position of domestically produced goods would not be improved thereby. Finally, effects upon the capital account, although presumably favorable in the short run, are not likely to be important in the long run.

Framework for Tax Policy

The value-added tax has been examined in this chapter primarily as a substitute for several taxes now in use. The comparison has been based upon distributional implications and likely economic effects, that is, effects upon economic efficiency, growth, stability, and the balance of payments. As could be expected, the results of the comparisons do not point unambiguously toward one uniquely best tax policy. Thus, the various likely effects, including the many that necessarily are uncertain, must be weighed in framing tax policy. This section suggests a framework for weighing the various effects.

Tax policy affects the rate of private saving and the rate of investment. But so do other public policies. Moreover, private saving can be augmented by public saving in the form of a government surplus; and ideally, full employment can be maintained through the proper mix of monetary and fiscal policies. Thus, although structural tax policy may be a useful tool in assuring a satisfactory rate of saving, investment, and growth, it may not be a necessary one if the other available tools are wisely used.

Similarly, it is convenient to have taxes that contribute to automatic stability and that can be changed easily and effectively for countercyclical purposes, but it may not be necessary to require that each tax meet this requirement, so long as there are adequate countercyclical weapons in the economic armory. The same comment applies with regard to the effects of tax policy on the balance of payments. These effects must be considered, but they need not be the deciding factor in determining tax policy, as indicated by the recent devaluation of the dollar.

On the other hand, it is impossible to neglect the effects of the tax system upon economic efficiency and equity. If the tax system distorts economic decisions, no other imaginable public policy can restore neutrality. Similarly, there may be many ways to assure that, on the average, the distribution of real income is equitable. But most are cumbersome substitutes for a well-designed tax system. Moreover, what exists on the average is of little comfort to the individual household that is treated inequitably.

This discussion suggests that relatively more attention should be focused on the equity and the neutrality of the value-added tax and of the various taxes it might replace than on the effects the taxes would have upon economic growth, stability, and the balance of payments. This is not to denigrate the importance of such considerations, as should be clear from the sections devoted to these points. It does suggest, however, that in formulating tax policy, attention should focus on those goals that only tax policy can effect.

This suggests, in turn, that any VAT should be imposed with as few exemptions as possible because exemptions distort resource allocation and because low-income relief can be better provided directly through refundable credits against the income tax or a negative income tax than through exemptions for particular items. Since the gain in neutrality would probably be marginal, substitution of even a general VAT for part of the personal income tax would be acceptable only if it were thought desirable to reduce the overall progressivity of the tax system. On the other hand, substitution for a shifted corporation income tax would clearly be desirable because although the two would have approximately the same incidence, the latter is distinctly nonneutral. Substitution for an unshifted corporation tax would greatly reduce the progressivity of the American tax system, and although it would eliminate most of the distortions now caused by the corporation tax, it would create a substantial tax haven in retained earnings. Only if the corporate and personal income taxes were integrated or capital-gains taxation tightened could such an effect be avoided. Thorough tax reform, including initiation of a negative income tax, would restore neutrality and increase progressivity substantially. Of course, a value-added tax imposed with important exemptions would be less neutral than the personal income tax, with or without integration or reform, and might be no less distorting than the corporation income tax. On the other hand, it would presumably be less regressive than the truly general VAT.

Finally, it is worth recalling that within very broad limits, any statement about a value-added tax also holds for a retail-sales tax with the same exemptions. The choice between these two broad-based consumption taxes can therefore be made largely on administrative grounds.

Summary

Tax base. An American tax on value added would probably be of the consumption type and would probably be collected via the credit method. Under this approach, a firm would incur tax liability on its sales but receive credit for taxes paid on its purchases, including capital goods. Depending on the exemptions allowed, the tax base would be about $290 to $465 billion of 1970 consumption of $615.8 billion. Housing, domestic services, and payments for certain financial services, plus several other minor items, would probably be exempted for administrative reasons.

As a matter of public policy, exemptions might also be allowed for food, medical services, household utilities, and so forth.

Alternative revenue sources. It is assumed that a $15-billion tax on value added would serve as a replacement for $10 billion of existing tax revenue and as a source of $5 billion of new revenue. In this chapter, the comparisons are made in terms of distributional impact and effects upon economic neutrality, growth, stability, and the balance of payments. The assumed $10-billion reductions in existing taxes include across-the-board rate reductions for the personal income tax, the corporation income tax, and the payroll taxes. Moreover, integration of the two income taxes and a program of tax reform, including a negative income tax, are considered. These are not, however, intended to constitute an exhaustive list of tax changes that might accompany imposition of a value-added tax; they are presented here only for illustration and as a basis of discussion.

Distributional impact. The value-added tax is considerably more regressive than either of the income taxes, provided the corporation income tax is not shifted. For this reason, it is sometimes argued that VAT would be acceptable only if accompanied by a complete income-tax reform, including initiation of a negative income tax or at least integration of the two income taxes. Of course, if the corporation income tax is shifted to consumers, substitution of the value-added tax would have little effect on the distribution of tax burdens.

Neutrality. A value-added tax levied with few exemptions would not distort economic decisions. On the other hand, the corporation income tax is a distinctly nonneutral tax. It distorts choices between forms of legal organization, methods of financing, products, and factors of production. Thus, combining a general VAT with integration of the two income taxes or income-tax reform would represent an enormous gain in neutrality. The superiority of the value-added tax over the personal income and payroll taxes with regard to neutrality is considerably less because these two taxes are themselves more or less neutral. Substituting VAT for part of the corporation income tax would eliminate the distortions the corporation tax creates, but at the cost of creating a tax shelter for retained earnings. Finally, if the value-added tax were not truly general, but contained substantial exemptions, it would be less neutral than the personal income tax (with or without integration or reform) and the payroll tax and might be no less distorting than the corporation income tax.

Growth. Effects upon the rate of economic growth would be felt in two areas: saving and investment.

Saving. Combining a $10-billion VAT with any of the tax reductions being considered would probably increase saving. But because of the impact on retained earnings, the increase would be about $8 billion greater if VAT were substituted for the corporation income tax than if it were substituted for the personal income or payroll taxes. Combining a value-added tax with tax integration or tax reform would have less easily predictable, but presumably intermediate, effects.

Investment. Investment might be reduced if the value-added tax were substituted for the corporation income tax because the government would share less in losses as well as in profits. The impact on investment of substituting VAT for the personal income and payroll taxes would probably be small. Integration and tax reform would have such far-reaching effects on the economy that it is impossible to know how risk taking would be affected under them.

Stabilization. In its initial effect, a value-added tax would probably be fully reflected in higher prices, whether it was imposed as a substitute for existing taxes or as a source of additional revenue. Because automatic stability depends upon the per-dollar impact on private spending as well as the cyclical variability of tax revenues, it is impossible to predict whether the corporation income tax is a better automatic stabilizer than the value-added tax. Similar conclusions apply to the other alternative revenue sources. The merits of the various tax policies do not differ greatly from the viewpoint of discretionary fiscal policy, although the value-added tax might be a useful additional instrument.

Balance of payments. Because VAT would probably raise prices by the amount of the tax but the accompanying tax reductions would not affect prices, imposing VAT would be unlikely to improve the balance of trade. It would do so only if VAT were not fully reflected in higher prices

or if the corporation tax were originally shifted to consumers and unshifted when removed. The effects on the capital account, although presumed to be favorable, cannot be predicted with confidence.

Framework for tax policy. Other policies exist to further the goals
of economic growth, stability, and balance of payments. But no policy
can undo distortions created by a nonneutral tax system, and no policy
can rival the potential contribution of tax policy to equity in income
distribution. Thus, attention in the discussion of the value-added tax
should focus on these two aspects of the problem. Finally, it should be
remembered that virtually all the economic effects of a value-added tax
are likely to be shared by a retail-sales tax. Therefore, even if it is decided
that the federal government should impose a broad-based consumption
tax, it does not follow that VAT is indicated. Administrative considerations and the familiarity of the retail approach may suggest that the sales
tax is the preferable route toward taxation of consumption, although the
choice is far from clear.

APPENDIX A
Income and Consumption Types of Value-Added Tax

An example similar to that given in Table 1 can be used to clarify
the distinction between the consumption and income varieties of value-
added tax. In Table 1, no distinction was drawn between intermediate
goods and capital goods, and no mention was made of net investment or
depreciation. Now suppose that, in a given year, part of the sales of industry B to industry C involve capital goods and that all three industries
use capital (either existing or newly acquired) that depreciates during
the year. Table A-1 describes the transactions between the firms, each
firm's capital stock and net investment, the depreciation claimed by each
firm, each firm's factor payments and net profits, and the value added by
each firm. The last column shows the relevant totals for the economy as a
whole. It can be seen that for the entire economy, the income base
($350) is equal to consumption base ($300) plus net investment ($50).

Table A-2 describes the calculation of tax liabilities under the credit method.[37] Each firm incurs a tentative tax liability (line ID of Table A-2) equal to 10 per cent of its total sales (line I of Table A-1). Against that liability, the firm is allowed credit for taxes paid on purchased inputs. Under the consumption-type VAT, taxes on purchases of capital goods (line IIA2 of Table A-2) as well as those on purchases of intermediate goods (line IIA1) are immediately creditable. Thus, total taxes paid would be $30 (line IIIA of Table A-2), which is 10 per cent of the economy's total consumption spending of $300 (line IC of Table A-1).[38]

Table A-1. Three-Stage Calculation of Value Added (dollars)

	Industry			Overall Economy
	A	B	C	
I. Sales	100	300	300	700
A. Intermediate goods	100	200	–	300
B. Capital goods	–	100	–	100
C. Consumer goods	–	–	300	300
II. Purchased inputs				
A. Intermediate goods	–	100	200	300
B. Capital goods	–	–	100	100
III. Depreciation	10	20	20	50
A. Old assets (10% of line VIIA)	10	20	10	40
B. New assets (10% of line IIB)	–	–	10	10
IV. Factor payments and net profits	90	180	80	350
V. Value added				
A. Consumption base (line I – line IIA – line IIB)	100	200	0	300
B. Income base (line IV or line I – line IIA – line III)	90	180	80	350
VI. Net investment (line IIB – line III)	–10	–20	80	50
VII. Capital stock				
A. Beginning	100	200	100	400
B. Ending (line VIIA + line VI or line VIIA + line IIB – line III)	90	180	180	450

---

[37] Calculations under the addition and subtraction methods are described briefly later in Appendix A.

[38] It should be noted that in this example, industry C has no net tax liability because its purchases of intermediate and capital goods equal its total sales.

Under the income-type VAT, taxes on intermediate goods are treated in the same way as they are under the consumption type, but credit can be taken for taxes paid on purchases of capital goods only as the assets depreciate. Thus, if capital goods have an expected life of ten years (and no salvage value), only 10 per cent of the taxes paid on new investment can be taken as a credit in each of the ten years (assuming straight-line depreciation). In addition, each industry is allowed credit for taxes paid on its preexisting capital stock to the extent of depreciation.[39] The total credit for taxes on capital goods derived from the pattern of depreciation assumed in lines IIIA and IIIB of Table A-1 is given in line IIB2 of Table A-2, and the net tax liability under the income-type VAT is indicated in line IIIB. Total tax collections of $35 represent 10 per cent of national income of $350 (line IV of Table A-1). The $5 by which tax liabilities under the income-type VAT exceed those under the consumption type represents the tax charged on the $50 of net investment (line VI of Table A-1) for which credit is allowed only over

Table A-2. Calculation of 10 Per Cent Value-Added Tax in Three-Stage Example, Using Income and Consumption Bases (dollars)

	Industry			Overall Economy
	A	*B*	*C*	
I. Tax on gross sales				
A. Intermediate goods	10	20	0	30
B. Capital goods	0	10	0	10
C. Consumer goods	0	0	30	30
D. Total	10	30	30	70
II. Credit for taxes paid				
A. Consumption base				
1. Intermediate goods	0	10	20	30
2. Capital goods	0	0	10	10
3. Total	0	10	30	40
B. Income base				
1. Intermediate goods	0	10	20	30
2. Capital goods	1	2	2	5
3. Total	1	12	22	35
III. Net tax liability				
A. Consumption base				
(ID – IIA3)	10	20	0	30
B. Income base (ID – IIB3)	9	18	8	35

---

[39] This assumes that the value-added-tax system has been in operation and ignores the transitional problems that accompany adoption of such a system.

the life of the asset. Of course, if net investment in the economy were zero, the two tax bases would yield the same revenue because in such a case income equals consumption.

Because it requires adding net profits to other factor payments, the addition method is appropriate for implementation of the income-type VAT but not for the consumption type. Under this method of calculating liabilities, the tax rate of 10 per cent would be applied directly to the total of factor payments and net profits of each firm (line IV of Table A-1). The result would be the same as the result for the income-type VAT levied using the credit method (line IIIB of Table A-2). Under the subtraction method, the tax rate would be applied to the difference between sales and the portion of purchased inputs allowable as deductions (line VA of Table A-1 for the consumption type, line VB for the income type). Again, the results are the same as the results when the credit method is used (lines IIIA and IIIB of Table A-2, respectively, for the consumption- and income-type taxes).

APPENDIX B
Derivation of Incidence Estimates

The estimates of the incidence of existing taxes and of a value-added tax used in the section "Distributional Aspects" are based on a 1967 study by the Tax Foundation, *Tax Burdens and Benefits of Government Expenditures by Income Class, 1961 and 1965*. George A. Bishop, director of Federal Affairs Research, was primarily responsible for the study. In that study, Bishop used data from the Bureau of Labor Statistics survey of family income and consumption for 1960–61 to estimate the distribution of 1961 national income among families grouped by income brackets and to allocate the then-existing taxes among the income groups. In this way, he produced estimates of the incidence of the various taxes in terms of the percentage of income they represent at each income level.

Bishop's estimates for 1965 were based on the working assumptions that the distribution of before-tax income among families was roughly the same as it was in 1961 and that each kind of tax was also distributed among the income groups in roughly the same proportions as in 1961. These assumptions are both clearly inaccurate. Although the first may do no great violence to reality, the second is much more troublesome because of changes in tax laws between 1961 and 1965. The most important of these were contained in the Revenue Act of 1964, which reduced the individual income taxes of low-income families relatively more than those of high-income families. Bishop, of course, recognized these shortcomings and did not emphasize the estimates for 1965.

The approach followed in estimating tax incidence for 1969 for use in this chapter is essentially parallel to that used by Bishop in deriving his estimates of tax incidence for 1965. Income and (with several exceptions, which are noted below) each kind of tax were allocated among income groups in the same percentages as Bishop derived for 1961. The bases for his allocations were as follows:

Tax	Basis for Allocation(s)
Individual income	Personal taxes
Corporate income	Alternative methods on different assumptions of incidence
	Total current consumption
	Half total current consumption and half dividend income
Excises, customs, and sales	
Alcoholic beverages	Alcoholic-beverage expenditures
Tobacco	Tobacco expenditures
Telephone and telegraph	Telephone and telegraph expenditures
Automobile purchase	Automobile-purchase expenditures
Automobile operation	Automobile-operation expenditures
Other	Total current consumption
Estate and gift	Completely to the $15,000-and-over income class
Social insurance	
Personal contributions	Social security, railroad and government retirement contributions
Employer contributions	Total current consumption

In this chapter, the following modifications were made in these allocations:

1. Both employee and employer contributions to social security were allocated in total to employees, rather than in part to

consumers. Economic theory suggests that this is the most likely outcome.

2. A third allocation of the corporate-profits tax—by dividends alone—was included.

3. The total amount of indirect taxes was allocated as in Bishop's study, rather than on the basis of detailed analysis of the incidence of individual indirect taxes.

4. The potential tax on value added was allocated among income groups on the basis of total current consumption.

These assumptions resulted in the percentage distribution among income groups presented in Table B-1. The number of families in each income bracket is included as a guidepost to the distribution of income and taxes.

The use of Bishop's estimates for 1961 as the basis for estimates of the incidence of taxes existing now is even more troublesome than Bishop's own use of the estimates in 1965. The Revenue Act of 1969 went even further than the 1964 act in reducing the individual income taxes of low-income groups, and its reform measures increased taxes of some upper-income families through the elimination or reduction of tax preferences. Any comparison of substituting the value-added tax for the personal income tax based on the calculations described above can thus be expected to understate the extent to which the poor would be burdened by the change and the extent to which high-income groups would benefit.

In order to determine the distributional effects of integrating the corporation and personal income taxes, it was necessary to calculate the personal income taxes that would be payable on each income group's share of corporate profits if profits were taxed under the assumption that they were earned in a partnership. This involves calculating the marginal tax rate paid within each income group, on the average. Using data from the 1961 *Statistics of Income,* such calculations were made, although in a fairly rough way. Except in the highest income bracket, almost all taxable income was subjected to only the 20 per cent marginal rate or to the 22 and 26 per cent marginal rates. For these income brackets, the important question was the distribution of dividends between taxable and nontaxable returns. For the highest income bracket, virtually all dividend income would have been reported on taxable returns, on which the weighted average of the marginal tax rates appears

Table B–1. Bases for Allocation of Taxes by Income Brackets (percentage distribution)

Basis for Allocation	Income Group									
	Lowest	2d	3d	4th	5th	6th	7th	8th	Highest	Total
Number of families	14.21	10.99	11.45	12.61	12.69	15.19	13.71	7.16	1.99	100.00
Income	2.89	4.53	6.67	9.71	12.11	18.21	21.25	15.53	9.10	100.00
Personal taxes	0.65	1.71	3.66	7.58	10.09	17.06	22.61	18.82	17.82	100.00
Dividends	0.91	2.51	7.26	4.19	7.42	8.06	10.77	21.99	36.83	100.00
Consumption	4.62	5.84	8.12	10.87	13.04	18.24	20.09	13.51	5.63	100.00
Social security contributions	0.79	3.13	6.31	11.80	14.79	21.28	22.89	15.38	3.58	100.00
Excises, other	3.40	5.07	8.25	11.25	13.45	19.01	20.68	13.94	4.91	100.00

Source: Tax Foundation, Inc., *Tax Burdens and Benefits of Government Expenditures by Income Class, 1961 and 1965* (New York: Tax Foundation, Inc., 1967), pp. 47, 48, 52.

to have been about 42.5 per cent. The data on average marginal tax rates paid on taxable income in each income bracket and the percentage of dividend income reported on taxable returns in each income bracket can be combined as follows:

Income Group	Weighted Average of Marginal Tax Rates on Taxable Returns	Approximate Percentage of Dividend Income on Taxable Returns	Estimated Average Marginal Tax Rate on Dividend Income
Lowest	20.0	10	2
2d	20.0	40	8
3d	20.0	60	12
4th	20.0	85	17
5th	20.0	90*	18
6th	21.0	95*	20
7th	22.0	95*	21
8th	24.0	97*	23
Highest	42.5	99*	42

* Not calculable from data available; extrapolated from pattern for lower-income brackets.

Applying these marginal rates to 1969 corporation profits allocated among income groups in proportion to dividends results in an addition to personal-income-tax revenue of about $25 billion. Eliminating the corporation income tax would reduce revenue by $39.2 billion (at 1969 levels of income). Thus, in order to fit within the constraints of a net loss of $10 billion, integration could only be 70 per cent complete, and the estimated effects were adjusted accordingly. However, there is reason to believe that if the marginal tax rates were calculated as just described, they would understate the true rates. If corporate profits were allocated to individuals, many nontaxable returns would become taxable and many taxable returns would be put into higher marginal-rate brackets. No attempt was made to correct for this, nor for the effect integration would have on capital gains and the taxes on them.

The calculations of the effects of thorough tax reform and introduction of a negative income tax are presented primarily for purposes of illustration and comparison with the simpler forms of tax reduction described in this chapter. Because alternative schemes for tax reform and/or the relief of poverty could result in quite different figures, the calculations are not based upon detailed analysis.

It is assumed that in the lowest income bracket, payments under a negative income tax would average 50 per cent of a family's income from its own sources. For example, a family with income of $1,600 would receive $800, bringing its total income to $2,400. This assumption appears to be consistent with the approach to alleviating poverty spelled out in the 1970 statement on national policy by the Research and Policy Committee of the Committee for Economic Development, *Improving the Public Welfare System*. But because families with very low incomes could receive payments equal to several times their income from their own sources, the estimation of the percentage of own income that such payments would represent is extremely difficult.

Because the CED proposal would include childless couples and working single persons as well as families with children in a plan similar to President Nixon's Family Assistance Plan, it would be more expensive than the Administration program. But exactly how much more expensive involves calculations beyond the scope of this chapter. Offsets due to reduced welfare payments and savings on the food-stamp program are also not included in this discussion. It is simply assumed that the negative income tax and the tax reforms discussed here result in a $10-billion net loss of revenue. To the extent of the offsets, rates in upper-income brackets could be lower than suggested.

The effective tax rates in the upper-income brackets are generally consistent with those that Joseph A. Pechman and Benjamin A. Okner have recently estimated would result from implementing in the United States the comprehensive proposals the Carter Commission made for tax reform in Canada.[40] Among these proposals are integrating the corporation income tax, the personal income tax, and the gift and estate taxes; including in taxable income social security benefits and unemployment compensation, retirement income (including contributions not previously taxed), state and local bond interest, unrealized capital gains, and so forth; limiting personal deductions to expenses of earning income, medical expenses, charitable contributions, and contributions to retirement plans; substituting tax credits for personal exemptions; and five-year block averaging. No allowance was made in this chapter for the

---

[40] See their "Simulation of the Carter Commission Tax Proposals for the United States," *National Tax Journal* 22 (March 1969): 2–23.

Table B-2. Differential Incidence of $15-billion Value-added Tax as Replacement for and Addition to Federal Taxes Existing in 1969 (Percentage of Family Income)[a]

Tax Change	Income Group									
	Lowest	2d	3d	4th	5th	6th	7th	8th	Highest	Total
Additional Revenue										
$10-billion value-added tax	1.9	1.5	1.4	1.3	1.3	1.2	1.1	1.0	0.7	1.2
$5-billion value-added tax	0.9	0.8	0.7	0.7	0.6	0.6	0.6	0.5	0.4	0.6
Alternative Tax Reductions of $10 Billion										
Individual income tax										
Effect of tax reduction	-0.2	-0.4	-0.6	-0.9	-1.0	-1.1	-1.3	-1.4	-2.3	-1.2
Net effect of tax substitution	+1.6	+1.1	+0.8	+0.4	+0.3	+0.1	-0.1	-0.4	-1.6	0
Net effect, including added revenue	+2.6	+1.8	+1.5	+1.1	+0.9	+0.7	+0.4	+0.1	-1.2	+0.6
Social security taxes										
Effect of tax reduction	-0.3	-0.6	-1.1	-1.4	-1.4	-1.4	-1.3	-1.2	-0.5	-1.2
Net effect of tax substitution	+1.5	+0.9	+0.3	-0.1	-0.2	-0.2	-0.2	-0.1	-0.3	0
Net effect, including added revenue	+2.5	+1.6	+1.0	+0.6	+0.5	+0.4	+0.4	+0.4	+0.1	+0.6
Corporation income tax										
Allocated by dividends										
Effect of tax reduction	-0.4	-0.6	-1.3	-0.5	-0.7	-0.5	-0.6	-1.7	-4.7	-1.2
Net effect of tax substitution	+1.5	+0.9	+0.1	+0.8	+0.6	+0.7	+0.5	-0.6	-4.0	0
Net effect, including added revenue	+2.4	+1.6	+0.9	+1.5	+1.2	+1.2	+1.2	-0.1	-3.7	+0.6
Allocated half by dividends and half by consumption										
Effect of tax reduction	-1.1	-1.1	-1.4	-0.9	-1.0	-0.8	-0.9	-1.3	-2.7	-1.2
Net effect of tax substitution	+0.7	+0.4	+0.1	+0.4	+0.3	+0.3	+0.3	-0.3	-2.0	0
Net effect, including added revenue	+1.7	+1.2	+0.8	+1.1	+0.9	+0.8	+0.8	+0.2	-1.6	+0.6
Allocated by consumption										
Effect of tax reduction: equal in magnitude to effect of adopting $10-billion VAT, but opposite in sign										
Net effect of tax substitution: none										
Net effect, including added revenue: that of $5-billion VAT alone										

Integration of personal and corporation income taxes

Allocated by dividends										
Effect of integration	-1.0	-1.5	-2.6	-0.9	-1.2	-0.8	-0.8	-2.1	-0.3	-1.2
Net effect of substitution	+0.9	0.0	-1.2	+0.5	+0.1	+0.4	+0.3	-1.1	+0.4	0
Net effect, including added revenue	+1.8	+0.8	-0.4	+1.1	+0.7	+1.0	+0.8	-0.6	+0.8	+0.6
Allocated half by dividends and half by consumption										
Effect of integration	-2.7	-2.7	-2.8	-2.0	-1.9	-1.7	-1.6	-1.3	+5.3	-1.2
Net effect of substitution	-0.9	-1.2	-1.4	-0.7	-0.6	-0.5	-0.4	-0.2	+6.0	0
Net effect, including added revenue	+0.1	-0.4	-0.6	0.0	0.0	+0.1	+0.1	+0.3	+6.4	+0.6
Allocated by consumption										
Effect of integration	-4.4	-3.9	-3.0	-3.1	-2.7	-2.6	-2.3	-0.4	+10.9	-1.2
Net effect of substitution	-2.6	-2.4	-1.6	-1.8	-1.4	-1.4	-1.2	-0.7	+11.6	0
Net effect, including added revenue	-1.7	-1.6	-0.9	-1.1	-0.8	-0.8	-0.6	+1.2	+12.0	+0.6
Tax reform (including negative income tax)										
Allocated by dividends										
Effect of reform	-52.6	-16.4	-10.9	-6.5	-1.8	+2.7	+5.1	+5.2	+0.8	-1.2
Net effect of substitution	-49.8	-14.8	-9.5	-4.2	-0.5	+4.0	+6.2	+6.1	+1.4	0
Net effect, including added revenue	-48.4	-14.0	-8.8	-3.5	+0.1	+4.6	+6.7	+6.5	+1.7	+0.6
Allocated half by dividends and half by consumption										
Effect of reform	-55.4	-18.1	-11.2	-7.0	-0.9	+1.4	+4.1	+6.4	+8.4	-1.2
Net effect of substitution	-52.8	-16.5	-9.8	-5.7	+0.4	+2.7	+5.2	+7.3	+9.2	0
Net effect, including added revenue	-51.4	-15.7	-9.1	-5.0	+1.0	+3.3	+5.7	+7.7	+9.5	+0.6
Allocated by consumption										
Effect of reform	-58.5	-19.8	-11.4	-8.6	+0.2	+0.2	+3.1	+7.7	+16.5	-1.2
Net effect of substitution	-55.7	-18.2	-10.0	-7.3	+1.5	+1.5	+4.2	+8.6	+17.1	0
Net effect, including added revenue	-54.3	-17.4	-9.3	-6.6	+2.1	+2.1	+4.7	+9.0	+17.4	+0.6

[a] Columns and rows may not equal totals because of rounding.

elimination of the taxation of profits attributable to foundations, for-
eigners, and so on, under the corporation income tax.

The effective tax rates hypothesized are somewhat higher in the upper-income level than in either the Carter Commission report or the
Pechman-Okner study because of the necessity of financing through the
reformed personal income tax all but $10 billion of the costs associated
with the hypothesized poverty program in the lower-income brackets.
Effective rates over the middle-income range are slightly different from
the Pechman-Okner pattern because of the need for a smooth transition
between negative and positive income taxes.

As a result of the large changes in disposable income represented
by the poverty program, the consumption-tax burden in the lowest income bracket was raised by 50 per cent. In all other cases, the second-
order effects on burdens of consumption taxes resulting from tax-induced
changes in real income were not taken into consideration.

The effects of imposing a $5-billion VAT and of substituting $10-
billion VAT for each of the taxes under consideration are shown in Table
B-2 and are summarized in Table 3.

John F. Due

THE CASE FOR THE USE OF THE RETAIL FORM OF SALES TAX IN PREFERENCE TO THE VALUE-ADDED TAX

THIS CHAPTER IS CONCERNED solely with the question of the relative merits of the retail-sales tax, as compared with a value-added tax, if a sales tax were to be introduced by the federal government. It is assumed that the value-added tax would take the tax-deduction form, whereby the firm deducts tax paid on its purchases against tax due on its sales in order to ascertain its actual tax liability. This is the type of value-added tax used in France and other European Community (EC) countries and in Latin America. It is also assumed that, as far as possible, the coverage of the two forms of tax is the same.

From the standpoint of economic effects, the value-added tax and the retail-sales tax are essentially identical if complete forward shifting of both taxes is assumed. If the coverage is the same, a given tax rate will produce the same amount of revenue from the two levies because the sum of retail sales is equal to the sums of values added in the production process. Both levies are equally neutral with respect to the choice of methods of production and the organization of production and distribution, and both will produce the same pattern of distributional effects. The differences between them, and thus the relative merits of each, therefore center on compliance and administrative aspects, on the question of whether the coverage of the two can be equally well established in conformity with the objectives, and on the applicability of the assumption of full forward shifting to each tax.

The Administrative Advantages of the Retail-Sales Tax

The most important advantages of the retail-sales tax over the value-added tax center on administrative considerations.

First, the retail tax is a much simpler levy in concept, in compliance, and in administration. The tax is simple for any businessman to understand; the value-added tax appears complicated, at least to operators of smaller businesses. A more serious consideration is that the value-added tax requires that the firm keep a detailed record of tax paid on purchases as well as the figures of taxable sales; whereas the retail-sales tax requires only records of sales. For the smaller firm, the difference may be significant in terms of bookkeeper man-hours. At the same time, auditing by the government is somewhat more complex because a check must be made on tax paid on purchases as well as on tax due on sales. Firms have a strong incentive to overstate tax paid on purchases in order to reduce their own tax liability.

Second, the value-added tax involves a somewhat larger number of taxpayers. Under both taxes, retailers are taxpayers. Under the retail tax, wholesalers and manufacturers not making retail sales are not directly involved in the operation of the tax as long as all their taxable purchases from suppliers are made on a tax-paid basis. As the sales tax operates in some states, registration of all wholesalers and manufacturers is required so that they will have registration numbers for purposes of making tax-free purchases. But if they make no retail sales, they are generally placed on an inactive list and are not mailed periodic returns, or else they are required to file only on an annual basis. An increasing number of states are no longer registering these firms if they make no retail sales, allowing them to buy tax-free under certificate indicating that they are purchasing for tax-free purposes, without a registration number. Under a value-added tax, however, all manufacturing and wholesale firms, whether they produce finished goods or materials and parts, become active taxpaying firms. The number added is not a large fraction of the total (probably not over 10 per cent), but the firms are generally complex ones, requiring substantial auditing time. This conclusion is based on the assumption of equal tax coverage.

Third, the retail tax offers the great advantage of familiarity. Because the tax is now in use in forty-five states (in some instances for nearly forty years), all types of businesses are familiar with its operation. This is only a temporary advantage, but it would not be insignificant in the period of transition. These forty-five states have over 98 per cent of the population of the country. A number of them (including several of the largest: New York, California, Texas, and Illinois) also have local supplements or separately collected local sales taxes. If a federal sales tax were imposed at the retail level, substantial coordination of operation of the two taxes would be possible. The records required would be the same for the two taxes, and the tax-return forms would be similar. In fact, both taxes could be collected on the basis of a single tax return (as is common now with the state-local levies); and joint auditing, or at least reliance by one level of government on the audits of the other (as is now true with the corporate income tax) would be possible. The value-added tax would require two separate sets of sales-tax records and two types of tax returns (although theoretically they could still be included on the same form). Auditing would be different. A federal retail-sales tax would encourage greater uniformity among the state sales taxes; a value-added tax would have no such effect. The opposite argument is sometimes made: that the use of the retail tax by the states makes it necessary for the federal government to use a different form of sales tax. But this view has no merit. In the end, the value-added tax is carried forward into retail prices; and from the standpoint of the consumers (and taxpayers), it is no different from a retail-sales tax.

Attainment of Optimal Tax Structures

As noted, the economic effects of the two taxes are the same if the coverage is the same. But attainment of a given coverage is not necessarily equally easy. The value-added tax is, on the whole, less adaptable to exemptions than the retail-sales tax is. Exemptions cause trouble with any sales tax, but state experience has shown that a few clearly defined classes of goods (such as food, medicine, and hospital services) can be excluded without serious difficulty. Such exemptions are frequently regarded as essential in the interests of equity. The inherent character of the value-added tax makes exemptions more difficult to implement. The exemption of any class of goods would probably extend to production and distribution channels. This would involve far more firms in the segregation of exempt and taxable sales than a retail tax does. Furthermore, there may be questions about the ultimate use of a partly finished good. For example: Will it become a part of food? There are also questions of deductibility of tax on goods purchased for use in producing tax-free goods. If the exemption is applied only at the retail level, it would result in large refunds to stores handling primarily exempt products; there would be substantial waste motion as tax is collected on earlier stages and then handed back at the retail level.

Exemption from the registration requirement for certain classes of firms (such as farmers) would break down the tax-deduction cycle; these firms would not be able to obtain credit for tax paid on purchases of goods for business purposes. Therefore, means would have to be found to establish outright exemption of sales to these firms.

The Shifting Assumption

The assumption that both taxes are fully and exactly shifted forward is also open to question. The relevant issue for this chapter is whether one of the taxes is more likely to shift fully. The retail tax must shift only once (if the tax is confined to consumption goods); the value-added tax must be shifted a number of times in the production and distribution channels. Despite the requirement of separate quotation of tax that is necessary for the tax-deduction feature, it is not unreasonable to assume that the larger the number of times the tax must be reflected in price readjustments, the greater the likelihood that shifting will not be exact. If producers goods, including capital equipment, are completely exempt, a question may be raised about the amounts of the value-added tax the firms will attempt to shift. One competitor buys extensive capital equipment in the period; the credit for tax paid on his purchases is so great that he owes no tax at all. Will he still add the nominal tax to the selling prices of his goods? He may, of course, but he may not; there is no certainty that he will. If he does not, the efforts of other firms to shift the tax may fail.

Rate Adjustments and Fiscal Policy

The effects of anticipated rates changes are less with a retail-sales tax than with other types of sales taxes. These effects occur only at the consumer level, and evidence based on experience in Great Britain and other countries suggests that consumers are much less likely than merchants to stock up in anticipation of tax increases and to hold off buying in expectation of decreases. The value-added tax, therefore, would almost certainly have more disturbing effects. If the tax or an increase in the tax were anticipated, firms would hold off buying goods until after the increase in order to get a larger deduction; whereas consumers would increase their purchases in anticipation of higher prices, just as they would with the retail tax. The net effect would be one of greater disturbance in the smooth timing of production and distribution activity. The problems related to the change in tax rates with a value-added tax, therefore, make it less suitable as an instrument of fiscal policy (a major role charted for it by some economists.)[1]

Exclusion of Producers Goods and Taxation of Services

A major argument for the value-added tax relates to taxation of producers goods. To the extent that producers goods are taxed and there is no rebate of this tax element in the prices of finished goods at export, American producers are placed at some competitive disadvantage in world markets and some distortion of economic activity will occur. The defenders of the value-added tax maintain that exclusion of producers goods is easier with this type of tax than with the retail-sales tax.[2] With the usual value-added tax, although the firm pays tax on everything it buys, it can deduct the tax on all such purchases made for business purposes (with minor exceptions) from the tax due on its sales, with a rebate of the full amount of tax on export sales. It is argued that controlling this deduction is easier than controlling exemption of sales of producers goods under a retail-sales tax. Under the value-added tax, it is necessary to check only the purchasing firm (the one using the taxed goods); whereas under the retail-sales tax, both the purchasing firm and its suppliers must be checked. Belief that producers goods can be excluded more easily under the value-added tax than

---

[1] One proponent of this point of view is Arnold C. Harberger. See his "Let's Try a Value-Added Tax," *Challenge* 15 (November-December 1966), pp. 16–23.

[2] A strong presentation of this point of view is provided by Ann Friedlaender, "Indirect Taxes and Relative Prices," *Quarterly Journal of Economics* 81 (February 1967), pp. 125–39.

under the retail tax apparently influenced both Denmark and Sweden to select the value-added form.[3]

The validity of the argument is difficult to assess. Certainly both taxes require a check on purchases of producers goods in order to ensure that the goods are used for business rather than for personal purposes, a particularly serious problem with small, noncorporate businesses. The type of check that is required is essentially the same in both instances. The only difference—under the usual retail tax, the initial check begins with the vendor, whereas under the value-added tax, it begins directly with the purchasing firm—is of questionable significance. Furthermore, this system of exemption is not a necessary feature of the retail-sales tax. All registered firms could be allowed to buy all goods tax-free, and their accounts could be audited to determine the validity of the exempt purchases, in exactly the same fashion as with a value-added tax. Many states follow this procedure, using direct-pay permits for certain types of industry; and it could be applied to all firms.

A value-added tax would almost certainly not apply to farmers and might not be applied to other businesses, particularly professions and other service establishments. Such firms would not be able to obtain credit for tax paid on purchases because they would not be filing value-added tax returns. Under the value-added tax, exemption of sales to these firms would almost of necessity take the same form used under the retail tax, with the consequence of a dual system relating to producers goods: one for registered purchasers, one for nonregistered purchasers. For nonregistered purchasers, the problems of the two taxes would be identical.

In summary to the argument for exclusion of producers goods: the value-added tax appears to have no significant advantage over an appropriately designed retail-sales tax. Producers goods can be exempted under either tax, if desired, with much the same problems. Ann Friedlaender has also used a slightly different argument: that governments are more likely to exempt producers goods under a value-added tax than under a retail tax.[4] The European Community countries do exempt

---

[3] See Carl S. Shoup, "Experience with the Value-Added Tax in Denmark, and Prospects in Sweden," *Finanzarchiv* 28 (March 1969), pp. 236–52; see also Martin Norr and Nils G. Hornhammar, "The Value-Added Tax in Sweden," *Columbia Law Review* 70 (March 1970), pp. 379–422.

[4] See her "Indirect Taxes and Relative Prices: Reply," *Quarterly Journal of Economics* 82 (May 1968), pp. 344–46.

almost all producers goods from the value-added taxes. But the new value-added taxes in Latin America do not; there, restrictions are comparable to those of the retail taxes. It is likewise true that most states severely restrict the exemption of producers goods, but this is a matter of accident or policy largely unrelated to the form of the tax. By contrast, West Virginia excludes most business purchases from its retail tax, and Ohio excludes many. Neither state appears to have more difficulty with the tax than other states.

Another argument advanced for the value-added tax is the likelihood of obtaining broader coverage, particularly of services. It is true that the broader the coverage, the more effective the tax; but whether this would prove to have a significant impact in broadening the base is doubtful. The same pressures for exemption that exist under a retail-sales tax would exist under a value-added tax.

Enforcement, Retailer Attitudes, and Concealment

Other arguments made for the value-added tax relate to enforcement, retailer attitudes, and concealment of tax.

It is claimed that the value-added tax is easier to enforce than the retail tax because of the cross-audit feature. Tax reported as paid by one firm is shown as a credit against tax by another firm. It is therefore possible, particularly with the use of computers, to cross-check, to see whether tax reported by firm B as a deduction on purchases from firm A was actually paid by firm A. The check is of course not automatic; effort is required. In exactly the same fashion, because there is obviously a close correlation between a firm's sales and its purchases, the retail-sales-tax audit involves checking against the sales figures of a firm's supplier whenever there is doubt about the sales reported by the firm. This is a routine procedure in the administration of a state sales tax.

The claim is also made for the value-added tax that evasion is reduced because a larger portion of the tax is collected from relatively large-scale manufacturers and wholesalers. This is an important consideration in many countries because they are characterized by small-scale retailers whose records are inadequate and who are prone to evade tax; but it is not a significant consideration in the United States because of the nature of retailing and the high percentage of the retail-sales taxes that comes from a relatively small number of large firms. There is perhaps some net advantage to the value-added tax, but it does not appear to be great.

The impact of the value-added tax is spread out over the entire production and distribution system, instead of being concentrated entirely on retailers. As noted, this may result in a slight reduction in evasion. The argument is also made that divided impact reduces the resistance of retailers to the tax because they owe tax only on their margins, instead of on their total sales. Whether retailers see this as an advantage is not clear; there is some disadvantage to the retailer, in that he must advance the forward-shifted portion of the tax at an earlier date than he would otherwise need to do. Some retailers also believe that their tasks in handling exempt transactions in producers goods would be simplified because resale or other exemption certificates would not be necessary; the retailer would collect the tax, and the customer would take the credit for the tax against his own tax liability. Whether this represents any net compliance gain to firms as a whole is doubtful.

The argument that consumers will resist the value-added tax less strongly than the retail-sales tax has no validity; the burden on the consumer will presumably be the same with each tax.

The argument is sometimes advanced that the value-added tax would offer the advantage of concealment of the tax from the final consumer, with the requirement for separate quotation applying only to preretail sales. There are three objections to this argument. First, strong objection can be advanced as a matter of principle against the concealment of a tax in the price. Governmental expenditure and tax levels and structures are more likely to reflect the preferences of society if people know, as far as possible, the amounts of taxes they are paying. Second, separate quotation in the typical market facilitates exact shifting of the tax by increasing uniformity of policy. Third, there is no inherent difference between the two taxes on the issue of separate quotation of tax. The law could require that the value-added tax be quoted separately on the final sale, just as laws could require that the retail tax be included in the price and not stated separately.

In summary, the value-added tax offers very little in the way of advantage to compensate for its greater complexity of tasks for both vendors and government, its greater difficulty in handling exemptions, and its greater tendency to cause distortions in buying when rate changes are anticipated. It is by no means clear that there is any advantage as far as exclusion of producers goods from tax is concerned, and if there is not, there is no advantage from the standpoint of exports. The fact that a substantial portion of the tax is collected at preretail levels probably does not reduce evasion, but evasion is not likely to be great in the United States anyway. The cross-audit feature may be of some advantage, but it is of limited importance because similar techniques are used with the retail tax. Much of the lure of the value-added tax reflects its novelty; to many, it appears to be something new, which of course it is not. The bandwagon effect lures others. The feeling is "other countries are using it, so we must do so as well." Some exponents feel that it has more political appeal than a sales tax. These are not significant arguments in favor of the tax. The retail-sales tax is a simpler, more familiar levy that will accomplish the desired objectives more easily.

Carl S. Shoup

FACTORS BEARING ON AN ASSUMED CHOICE BETWEEN A FEDERAL RETAIL-SALES TAX AND A FEDERAL VALUE-ADDED TAX

ALTHOUGH I DO NOT FORESEE any need to introduce a general sales tax at the federal level in the United States,[1] I shall analyze in this chapter the factors bearing on the choice between a retail-sales tax (RST) and a consumption-type value-added tax (VAT-C), under an assumption that one or the other is to be imposed. (For convenience, the abbreviation VAT-C is shortened to VAT, with the understanding that all references in this chapter are to the consumption-type VAT.)

In pure theory, the choice would be made by the flip of a coin because the two taxes have an identical aggregate tax base—namely, consumption expenditure—with imports taxable and exports exempt. The retail-sales tax achieves this result (in pure theory) by taxing all sales to consumers and only such sales. The value-added tax achieves the same result by (1) not taxing value added that reflects the production of capital goods or the accumulation of inventory until depreciation of the capital good or depletion of the inventory gives rise to a consumption good and by (2) rebating previous-stage tax on exports and

---

[1] The possible exception would be a tax included as part of a wide-ranging reform that would reduce income-tax rates greatly and rationalize the income-tax structure. It would be a package deal that included not only a value-added tax but also a net-worth tax and a progressive-rate tax on household expenditures. See Carl S. Shoup, "Tax Reform," in *Theorie und Praxis des finanzpolitischen Interventionismus* ed. Heinz Haller et al. (Tübingen: Mohr, 1970), pp. 245–52.

taxing imports. Under the method employed by all the European value-added taxes, the tax due from each firm is computed as follows: When the firm bills a customer, it collects from him, along with its own sales proceeds, a tax on the sale at the VAT rate. The aggregate of the tax amounts thus collected by the firm from all its customers on all its sales for the quarter (or other taxable period) is computed. Against this aggregate tax on its sales, the firm credits the aggregate of the value-added tax shown on the invoices for all the purchases (including purchases of capital goods) that it has made from other firms in the same period. It pays the difference to the government treasury. There is no inventory accounting, no depreciation accounting, no computation of profits.

A few highly oversimplified examples may help explain how this procedure results in collecting the same amount that would be obtained under a retail-sales tax. The VAT rate used here is 10 per cent, except that exports are taxed at a nil (zero) rate. The assumption that a firm can produce its output solely by its own labor force is introduced in order to have a complete-economy reckoning, that is, in order to have no loose ends to the example.

Example 1. Firm A, employing only labor (buying nothing from other firms), pays wages of $1,000 and creates a capital good that it sells to firm B for $1,000 plus charge for the value-added tax. Since the VAT rate is 10 per cent, firm A bills firm B for $1,100, including tax. Firm A also actually pays a value-added tax of $100 because it has made no taxed purchases from other firms during this period and therefore has no tax credits to offset against the value-added tax on its sales.

Suppose that firm B does nothing in this taxable period except make the purchase. The value-added tax on firm B's zero sales is zero, and from this zero tax, firm B can deduct the tax shown on the invoice for its purchase from firm A: $100. Firm B therefore reports a tax of minus $100 and obtains this amount of cash from the government treasury. Thus, the tax paid to the treasury by firm A is passed on as a tax credit to firm B. Retail sales in this period: zero, hence zero RST. Total VAT is also zero.

Example 2. Firm A, using only labor, constructs a machine (a scale for weighing people, for example) that supplies services to consumers automatically, wearing out in the process of doing so. The machine is produced in period 1 at a cost of $1,000 and wears out completely (for simplicity in this example) in period 2 while bringing in gross revenues in period 2 of $1,100. Firm A's VAT in period 1: sales, zero; purchases from other firms, zero; VAT, zero. Firm A's VAT in period 2: sales, $1,100; tax on sales, $110; purchases from other firms, zero; hence, no credit against the $110 tax. Firm A pays $110 VAT in period 2. Under a retail-sales tax, the same amount would be paid because retail sales before tax equal $1,100. Depreciation in period 2 is $1,000, and profit is $100; but neither of these amounts needs to be computed for VAT.

Example 3. Firm B buys raw materials from firm A (made by firm A using only labor). For these, it pays firm A $2,000 plus $200 VAT, or $2,200. Firm B employs $1,000 of labor itself and experiences $500 depreciation on some capital goods it purchased in an earlier period. It draws down its inventory by $700. As a result of all this, firm B is able to sell $6,000 worth of its product, before VAT, of which $1,000 worth is sold to foreign firms (i.e., is exported) and $5,000 worth, before VAT, is sold to domestic consumers. Since a nil rate of VAT applies to export sales, firm B collects from its vendees a total of only $500 VAT. Its total sales including VAT come to $6,500: $5,500 to domestic consumers, $1,000 for export. Against this $500 VAT billed to its domestic vendees, firm B credits the $200 VAT shown on the invoice for its purchase from firm A. Firm B therefore pays to the treasury $300 VAT.

Meanwhile, firm A is paying $200 VAT. Total VAT from both firms: $500. Under a retail-sales tax, the total tax would also be $500, all collected from firm B.

This example shows that it is not necessary to apportion firm B's costs in any way between those applicable to the exempt (nil rate) export sales and those applicable to its taxable domestic sales. Here, the costs in question are raw-materials costs. Also, as always under the value-added tax, no reckoning of depreciation or profit is needed.

Example 4. Firm A produces raw material with labor costing $1,000 and sells it to firm B for $1,100 plus $110 VAT, or $1,210 total. Firm A's profit is therefore $100. In this example, firm B is exempt from VAT; it is completely outside the VAT system because it is a small firm, and all small firms are exempted.

Firm B adds $200 of its own labor to the raw materials and sells the resulting finished goods to a retailer, firm C, for $1,400, which represents a loss of $10.

Firm C adds retail labor of $400 and resells the product to consumers for $1,900 before tax plus $190 VAT, for a total of $2,090. Profit for firm C is $100.

The total net profit for all three firms is $190.

Firm B files no VAT return and obtains no credit or other benefit from the $110 VAT shown on the invoice for its purchase from firm A. It cannot apply for a refund because it is outside the VAT system.

Firm C, which collects $190 VAT from its consumer-customers, also pays $190 VAT to the treasury because the invoice for its purchase from exempt firm B of course shows no VAT paid by firm B.

Total VAT is therefore $300: firm A, $110; firm B, zero; firm C, $190. But $300 is 15.8 per cent of the retail value ex-tax, $1,900; whereas total VAT should be only 10 per cent, or $190. Excess VAT of $110 has been collected because firm B's exemption has broken the tax-credit chain.

If a competitor of firm B's, large firm BB, is inside the VAT system, it can deal with firms A and C on terms that leave them as well off as when dealing with firm B. Yet firm BB can turn a profit of $100; whereas firm B loses $10. The large, taxable firm BB, selling to firm C for $1,400 before VAT, will collect $1,540 from firm C, of which $140 is VAT. From this $140, firm BB subtracts the $110 on its purchase from firm A and pays $30 VAT to the treasury. Firm C, although it pays more over to firm BB than it did to firm B, is no worse off; firm C's VAT is now only $50, that is, the $190 computed on its sales, less the $140 VAT shown on the invoice for its purchase from firm BB.

Total VAT, with firm BB in the system, is $190, consisting of $110 from firm A (as before), $30 from firm BB, and $50 from firm C. Total VAT is thus $110 less than when the small, exempt firm B was buying and selling, and total profits for the three firms together are correspondingly $110 more (i.e., $300 rather than only $190). Sales, including VAT, are: from firm A to firm BB, $1,210; from firm BB to firm C, $1,540; from firm C to consumers, $2,090. The additional $110 in profit all goes to firm BB, as compared with firm B, converting a $10 loss into a $100 profit. Firms A and C obtain $100 profit, just as they did when firm B was buying and selling.

The small firm B can be protected by granting it a nil rate (zero rate) rather than an exemption, thus keeping it in the system. It must file a VAT return. Tax on its sales will be zero (at the nil rate), from which it subtracts the $110 VAT on the invoice for its purchase from firm A. This minus net tax of $110 entitles firm B to cash from the treasury equal to this amount. Total VAT is now $190: firm A, $110; firm B, minus $110; firm C, $190. Sales, including charges for VAT, are: firm A, $1,210; firm B, $1,400; firm C, $2,090. Profits after labor costs, purchase costs, and positive or negative VAT, are: firm A, $100; firm B, $100 (sales, $1,400; cash from treasury, $110; labor cost, $200; material cost, $1,210); firm C, $100.

Thus, it is the rate imposed at the very last stage, the retail stage, that determines the VAT rate for the economy as a whole, as long as there is no break in the tax-credit chain.[2] The tax rate on firm B is zero, yet on the economy as a whole, it is 10 per cent.

These examples will serve to clarify the advantages, disadvantages, and stand-offs for a consumption-type value-added tax as a federal tax in the United States at the present time, compared with an equal-yield retail-sales tax.[3]

Advantages of the Value-Added Tax

The retailer would be called upon to handle less tax money than he would under a retail-sales tax. He already has a considerable responsibility in this respect in the great majority of states because of the state and local retail-sales taxes. It might be thought unfair to ask retailers to take on full responsibility for a federal tax, too.

If a retailer evades a retail-sales tax completely, all the tax revenue due on his sales is lost. Under the value-added tax, only the tax on retail-value added is lost because the evading retailer does not get credit for VAT paid by wholesalers, manufacturers, and others at earlier stages. This argument may not be important quantitatively because the most typical type of evasion by retailers may be simply understatement of sales on a VAT return, rather than failure to file a return at all. Under-

---

[2] See Carl S. Shoup, *Public Finance* (Chicago: Aldine, 1969), p. 259.

[3] See the evaluation chart comparing nine types of general sales taxes, with respect to eleven criteria, in John F. Due, *Indirect Taxation in Developing Economies* (Baltimore: Johns Hopkins Press, 1970), pp. 186–87.

statement of sales, while claiming full tax credit on purchases, creates a revenue loss equal to the VAT rate times the amount of understatement of sales, just as the RST does.

The states might feel less aggrieved than they would if the federal government "invaded" their field of retail-sales taxation. The distinction is in part semantic, but not wholly so. A state that might otherwise raise the rate of or introduce a retail-sales tax might hesitate to do so if the federal government were placing full responsibility for collecting the new federal tax on retailers instead of spreading that responsibility by means of a value-added tax. To be sure, this would make no difference to the consumer if the value-added tax were stated separately from the price ex-tax. To the consumer, the value-added tax then looks like a tax on retail purchases, but at the VAT rate.

All retail-sales taxes, here and abroad, have always included in their definition of taxable sales the sales of some types of producer goods. This practice runs contrary to the general goal of a retail-sales tax. It causes an unequal burden among different types of consumer goods. It taxes more heavily those consumer goods that are composed mostly of, or produced mostly through the use of, the particular kinds of producer goods that are subject to the retail-sales tax. Exports, although in principle exempt, carry a hidden tax load insofar as they have been produced with the aid of taxed producer goods. Imports, especially of finished goods, are taxed more lightly than competing domestic products that have been made partly through use of taxed producer goods.

One reason why the principle of the consumers' retail-sales tax is thus disregarded in practice is that certain kinds of producer goods, e.g., typewriters, are also quite suitable for use as consumer goods. If the retail-sales-tax law exempted typewriters sold to business firms, as it should in principle, while taxing them when sold to consumers, some actual consumer-buyers would defraud the treasury by claiming that they were buying the typewriters for use by their firms. The seller of the typewriter cannot reasonably be asked to police his vendees; he must take their word for the use they intend to make of the typewriter. To uncover this type of evasion, the tax authorities must audit, connectedly, two firms, the vendor and the vendee (in this case checking the vendee's physical inventory). Under the value-added tax, all sales are taxable, whether made to other business firms or to households and whether the good is a consumer good or a producer good. It is up to the buyer to get a tax credit for the tax shown on the invoices of his purchases. To do so, in the case of the typewriter, he must make a false statement to the tax administration on his VAT return; he must claim credit for value-added tax on a purchase of a typewriter that he attests is being used in the business, although in fact he is using it as a consumer good in his home. It is psychologically more difficult for most taxpayers to file a false return than to make a false statement to a vendor. That this or some similar line of reasoning is valid is supported by the facts that the value-added taxes now in force do exempt virtually all producer goods by the inherent operation of the tax (save when the tax-credit chain is broken), as described in the examples in the preceding section, and that no retail-sales tax has ever exempted all producer goods.

Sweden's recent abandonment of its retail-sales tax in favor of a value-added tax was grounded chiefly on this one point.[4] So, too, was Denmark's recent replacement of its wholesale-sales tax with a value-added tax (all the value-added taxes in Europe are of the consumption type). Both Sweden and Denmark were concerned about the amount of sales tax that was getting into exports indirectly through the taxation of certain producer goods that went in part into exported products either physically or by being used up or worn out in the process of manufacturing the products. Similarly, finished-goods imports, taxed only at the statutory rate, were undertaxed relative to import-competing goods that had been made in part through the use of producer goods that had been caught in the retail-sales-tax or wholesale-sales-tax net.

Taxation of producer goods under the retail-sales tax is more extensive than the example of the administrative problems relating to the sale of the typewriter would suggest.[5] For a federal retail-sales tax, however, it may perhaps be assumed that no very extensive taxation of producer goods would be necessary or accepted.

---

[4] See Carl S. Shoup, "Experience with the Value-Added Tax in Denmark, and Prospects in Sweden," *Finanzarchiv* 28 (March 1969): 248–49 (Sweden) and 237–39 (Denmark). The Danish value-added-tax rate, initially 10 per cent on July 3, 1967, was raised to 12½ per cent by April 1, 1968, then to 15 per cent on June 29, 1970; see *Tax News Service* 1 (July 31, 1970):31. Norway introduced a value-added tax as of January 1, 1970 at a rate of 20 per cent to replace its retail-sales tax; see *Tax News Service* 1 (January 31, 1970): 5; and *European Taxation* 9 (1969): 170. The Swedish tax rate, initially 10 per cent, was raised to 14 per cent effective January 1, 1971; see *Tax News Service* 1 (March 15, 1970):12.

[5] See Due, *Indirect Taxation in Developing Economies*, pp. 102–3, 139–44.

If the U.S. balance of payments should someday go into an uncomfortably large surplus position (as in the early postwar years), a value-added tax could be employed to reduce the surplus. This could be accomplished by extending the tax to exports and exempting imports or (as Germany did for a few months prior to its last revaluation of the mark) by putting a few points of tax, but not the full rate, on exports and by reducing the rate on imports similarly. A retail-sales tax cannot be used in this way.[6]

The federal government should be unhampered in its use of its general sales tax as a stabilization instrument. An increase in the rate of a federal retail-sales tax would probably evoke protests from the states (as previously noted); an increase in the rate of a federal value-added tax might not.

If administrative considerations dictate that all very small retailers be left outside the tax, the resulting decrease in tax base will be greater under the retail-sales tax than under the value-added tax, hence a higher tax rate will be needed under the retail-sales tax to yield the same revenue. Under the retail-sales tax, exemption of all very small retailers will remove from the tax base the full amount of their sales; under the value-added tax, only the value added by these firms would disappear (see the second advantage discussed in this section).

Services are somewhat easier to tax under the value-added tax while insuring that the tax is a nonduplicative, comprehensive levy on services rendered to consumers or embodied in tangible goods sold to consumers. Under the retail-sales tax, each sale of service must be designated either as one to consumers or as one to firms. Under the value-added tax, all sales of a taxable service are taxed. If the sale is to a business firm, the tax-credit mechanism allows for this fact at the next stage.[7]

---

[6] "An origin-principle retail sales tax is a contradiction in terms with respect to exports, and poses insuperable administrative problems for imports." Shoup, *Public Finance,* p. 243.

[7] Due, *Indirect Taxation in Developing Economies,* p. 136. The problem noted by Professor Due with respect to the taxation of, say, freight transport—namely, that "some of the services may be provided to nontaxpaying business users—farmers, for example" (p. 148)—is not peculiar to services; it exists for any taxed input (see Example 4 in this chapter).

The only national governments now levying a retail-sales tax are those of Costa Rica, Honduras, and Rhodesia; whereas the comprehensive value-added tax has been adopted in many countries, always at the national level (except that Brazil's states levy a comprehensive VAT). RST rates do not exceed 6 per cent in the United States or 10 per cent elsewhere (except in Yugoslavia).[8] VAT rates in Europe are commonly between 10 per cent and 20 per cent. These facts suggest that at least some of the advantages of the value-added tax over the retail-sales tax that are discussed in this section have been influential in the choice of the value-added tax, in allowing higher rates.

Disadvantages of the Value-Added Tax

A much larger number of firms, including those in the sectors of wholesaling, manufacturing, farming, and raw-materials production, would have to file returns and be policed under the value-added tax than under the retail-sales tax. Only a few of these firms would be included under the RST system: those that engaged in sales to consumers or in sales of taxed producer goods to business firms.

This same disadvantage could not be overcome by keeping all small firms in the wholesaling, manufacturing, and other preretail stages outside the value-added-tax system. There would then be too many breaks in the tax-credit chain. Those small nonretail firms must be kept in the system, perhaps at a nil rate, which will give rise to tax refunds. Farmers, however, might be completely exempted with respect to sales to one another (as in Denmark) without impairing the VAT system greatly. Or (as in Holland) complete exemption might be coupled with a credit allowed to business firms that purchase from them at some percentage of purchases deemed to equal the average lost tax credits.

The taxed firms would be called upon to handle a completely unfamiliar type of tax. The value-added tax has been in force abroad for some five years at the most—Brazil (states) and Denmark were the first countries to adopt a comprehensive value-added tax in 1967.

---

[8] Due, *Indirect Taxation in Developing Economies*, p. 104.

Exemption of exports is accomplished with less paper work and less movement of funds under the retail-sales tax than under the value-added tax. The reason is that no retail-sales tax is collected until a domestic sale occurs at what the RST system considers a retail level (but see the fourth advantage discussed in the preceding section).

There may be a slight tendency toward pyramiding of the value-added tax, that is, imposing a standard markup percentage on price of purchases including tax, thus giving rise to a profit on the tax. But under the tax-credit, separate-statement method, pyramiding seems unlikely under the value-added tax.[9]

Any one firm has somewhat more paper work under the value-added tax than under the retail-sales tax because it must account for each purchase if it is to obtain its full tax credit.

Standoffs Between Value-Added and Retail-Sales Tax

Neither tax, as a federal tax, could be levied as a mere supplement to state taxation, to be collected perhaps by the states. No state levies a value-added tax. In the case of the retail-sales tax, no two states employ the same definition of a taxable sale.

For the same reasons, neither tax could be one against which the federal government would allow taxable firms to credit state or local value-added tax or retail-sales tax. If RST credit were granted, it would presumably be only for a retail-sales tax on a tax base identical to that employed by the federal government. The pressure would then be on the states and localities to redefine their tax bases accordingly. Such a redefinition through a federal RST, if coupled with a credit, might seem welcome to those economists, myself included, who regard present state-local RST definitions with disfavor. But from the broader view of federal-state-local relations, the appropriateness of such pressure is doubtful.

The question of how to treat housing is about equally troublesome under both taxes. In principle, both taxes should strike consumer ex-

---

[9] Due, *Indirect Taxation in Developing Economies,* pp. 112, 130.

penditures for dwelling space; but in both cases, the homeowner poses a virtually insuperable problem because for decades the stock of housing will still consist largely of housing built before the federal retail-sales tax or value-added tax was introduced. The only way to reach such housing is to impute a gross rental and require the homeowner to file a return and pay VAT or RST on this rental. Housing built after the VAT or RST was introduced could be taxed fairly easily: the sale of the house to the homeowner could be treated as an ordinary taxable sale (VAT) or as a retail sale (RST). But it would seem unfair to tax only those living in such houses. If housing, then, is to be exempt under either tax, through tax rebate to the homeowner or contractor under the value-added tax or through outright exemption of sellers of new dwelling space under the retail-sales tax, the value-added tax has perhaps one slight advantage: It can indirectly tailor the exemption to benefit a low-income home buyer by computing his rebate as so much per square foot of floor space or other physical measure.[10]

Either tax can give rise to a credit against income tax. The credit, now in use in six states in this country, is primarily intended to afford relief to low-income households. A cash refund is given to households too poor to be paying enough income tax to absorb the credit.[11]

Differences in tax rates designed to treat luxuries and necessaries differently from other goods, including exemption or a nil rate for certain basic necessaries, are about equally difficult to implement under the retail-sales tax and value-added tax. Of course, under the value-added tax, firms whose tax credits on all their purchases exceed the tax on their taxable sales will have to obtain cash refunds from the treasury.[12]

---

[10] This method is used in Denmark. See Shoup, "Experience with the Value-Added Tax in Denmark, and Prospects in Sweden," p. 244.

[11] Due, *Indirect Taxation in Developing Economies,* p. 103.

[12] Professor Due (*Indirect Taxation in Developing Economies,* p. 147) concludes that the value-added tax is more troublesome than the retail-sales tax, with respect to exempted goods. But if the nil rate is applied only on sales to consumers, not on sales to wholesalers or firms at earlier stages, the problems seem to be the same as with the retail-sales tax (except for the refund feature noted above). In any event, the tax-credit feature of the European value-added taxes is one that facilitates exemption of a particular final good, not a feature that makes such exemption more difficult. See Due, *Indirect Taxation in Developing Economies,* p. 152.

Financial intermediaries in services rendered to consumers are equally difficult to tax properly under both taxes. The free or under-priced service of banking facilities rendered to households is financed in part by interest the bank earns on its depositors' moneys. The banks' services to households are therefore understated (as long as the banks are in the system, such understatement on services to firms does not matter because it merely means more value-added taxes at the next stage). Insurance companies and similar firms raise comparable problems.

Used goods sold by the consumer to a dealer and resold by him seem equally troublesome under the retail-sales tax and the value-added tax. Exemption is preferable in order to avoid double taxation, but it leads to administrative difficulties. Since a tax credit can scarcely be made available, the value-added tax applies to the full sales price charged by the dealer; and so, of course, does the retail-sales tax.[13]

When the advantages and disadvantages of the value-added tax relative to the retail-sales tax are weighed, which tax comes out ahead? The fact that a few more advantages are listed here for the value-added tax is certainly not decisive. No doubt each economist has a somewhat different set of weights to apply. My own view is that the value-added tax is preferable to the retail-sales tax at the federal level in the United States at the present time if such a tax is considered necessary—an hypothesis which, as I stated at the outset, I do not accept.

---

[13] Professor Due states that this question is particularly troublesome with the value-added tax (p. 156), but it would seem equally so with the retail-sales tax.

EXPENDITURES TAX

Richard E. Slitor

ADMINISTRATIVE ASPECTS OF EXPENDITURES TAXATION

AN EXPENDITURES TAX, or spendings tax, as it is often called, is a direct personal tax. It entails essentially the same structural features as the income tax: exemptions, deductions, progressive rates, taxpayer returns, and withholding and current-payment requirements. The important difference is that its base is not income as such but personal expenditures for consumption. In simplest terms, for the positive saver, personal spending equals income minus savings; for the net dissaver, personal spending equals income plus dissavings. The base is therefore larger than income where dissaving occurs and smaller than income where net savings are made by the individual.

Consideration of a spendings tax is appropriate in connection with a thoroughgoing review of the potentialities and alternatives available in undertaking a major structural recasting of the revenue system. This is especially true at the present time because attention is being given to various forms of a broad-based tax on consumption, with particular reference to the value-added tax (VAT) of the consumption type.

A number of questions arise in such a study. For example: Would a combination of expenditures and income taxes provide a better approach to personal taxation than the present reliance upon income tax alone? In light of the present increased interest in adding a tax on consumption (such as a consumption-type VAT), what are the comparative advantages (and disadvantages) of approaching the taxation of consumption via the personal-expenditures route?

Traditionally, discussions of expenditures taxation have viewed this tax either as a supplement to or as a replacement of the personal income tax. Historically, its major proponents have viewed it as the ideal form of income tax, primarily for various reasons relating to its capacity to relieve savings. In the present context, however, it seems evident that a realistic framework of discussion must treat a possible expenditures-tax initiative as supplementary to, rather than as totally replacing, the conventional income tax.

The "supplementary" approach, although realistic, means that certain difficulties of the personal income tax (such as the capital-gains problem and the integration of personal and corporate income taxes with respect to retained earnings) would remain. Some of these difficulties, many observers believe, might be brought nearer to resolution, at least within the conceptual framework of the new approach, with total replacement of the income tax by an expenditures tax.

In the present context, the spendings tax also needs to be examined in terms of its feasibility as a long-term addition to the tax structure. Transitional problems that could be ironed out over time may loom large in terms of temporary adoption of a spendings tax. On the other hand, fiscal and economic emergency conditions may give rise to pressing demands and to the weighing of various drastic fiscal alternatives. Such a situation may justify assuming administrative difficulties of a spendings tax that under more normal peacetime conditions would be considered unacceptable. (The Appendix to this chapter presents a brief description of the U.S. Treasury Department proposal for a spendings tax during the World War II period and of the administrative problems as seen at that time.)

The introduction of an expenditures tax in lieu of a value-added tax, other forms of gross income or sales taxation, or a personal-income-tax increase through rate or structural adjustments would raise many issues of equity (both horizontal and vertical) as well as questions of economic impact (on saving, investment, incentives, and so forth). These are dealt with elsewhere in this volume and are not considered here. Although this separation of major areas of relevant considerations may appear to make for a specialized and one-sided analysis, it is essential almost at the outset in considering such a novel tax (on which pessimistic views concerning its practicability have often been expressed) to have some basis for determining whether it is administratively feasible. It is this range of aspects, therefore, that is the primary concern of this chapter.

Theory Versus Practicability

It is generally recognized that the spendings tax is more difficult to formulate and administer effectively than other forms of taxation aimed at taxing consumption rather than savings, such as a system of commodity excises, value-added taxes, or general-sales taxes. The simpler taxes, however, are not capable of the refined design of the progressive rates and personal-exemption structure associated with expenditures taxation. This chapter is not primarily concerned with refined comparative analysis of the administrative problems and costs of expenditures taxation versus more or less comparable alternatives. Rather, this chapter seeks to identify the major problems in the spendings-tax field and to question whether, on balance, it can be considered a feasible tax-policy option. This discussion views the spendings tax in terms of a permanent adjunct to the tax system and proceeds on the realistic assumption that even with a spendings tax, a major role would be retained for the personal income tax.

Theoretical proponents of the spendings tax, at least those who preceded Irving Fisher, were pessimistic about its practicability. John Stuart Mill, the famous English economist and philosopher, endorsed the exemption of savings under the income tax, using phraseology that reflected skepticism about whether this ideal could be practically realized. Full exploration of the merits of the spendings tax was delayed for decades by the conviction that because of the administrative difficulties of the tax, it was largely an academic exercise.

A. C. Pigou, both in his classic work on public finance[1] and in his testimony before the Colwyn Committee[2] on the spendings-tax idea, was apparently impressed with the impossibility of preventing dishonest taxpayers from making a practice of saving in one year, thus

---

[1] *A Study in Public Finance,* 3rd ed. (London: Macmillan & Co., 1947).

[2] Great Britain. Committee on National Debt and Taxation, *Report,* Cmd. 2800 (London: His Majesty's Stationery Office, 1927). Lord Colwyn was chairman of this Committee.

escaping taxation, and secretly selling out and spending their savings in the next year.

John Maynard Keynes, in his testimony before the Colwyn Committee, dismissed the expenditures tax in one sentence, saying that although the tax is perhaps theoretically sound, it is practically impossible.

Irving Fisher assisted the development of the spendings tax by formulating the computation of spendings on the basis of income minus savings or plus dissavings.

More recently, Nicholas Kaldor, presumably in the light of the administrative resources and techniques perfected under the income tax, concluded that, at least in Britain, nothing in the basic conception would present insuperable problems from the administrative standpoint or necessitate a departure from the customary high standards of tax administration.[3] However, he felt it was not possible to think of replacing the present income-tax system with an expenditures-tax system at one stroke. In his view, the only practical approach is one that would make a cautious beginning by introducing the expenditures tax side by side with the existing income tax and applying it to a limited number of taxpayers in the top brackets only. If successful for the higher-bracket taxpayer over some years of operation, it could be extended gradually to larger numbers of taxpayers, thus enlarging the scope of the expenditures tax and reducing the scope of the income tax. This gradual from-the-top-down approach was utilized in the spendings-tax experiment in India, which generally followed Kaldor's recommendations; but even this beginning was unsuccessful.

On the question of whether the spendings tax can be extended to the mass of income-tax payers, Professor William Vickrey of Columbia University has made observations that will give pause to those who might think in terms of a simple computation of spendings for the average taxpayer.[4] Vickrey has pointed out that in nearly all cases, even the roughest approximation of spendings requires the addition or subtraction of other items such as gifts, borrowings, lendings, bank balances, life insurance payments and premiums, and investment and

---

[3] Nicholas Kaldor, *An Expenditure Tax* (London: Allen and Unwin, 1955).

[4] William S. Vickrey, *Agenda for Progressive Taxation* (New York: Ronald Press Co., 1947) Chapter 12.

disinvestment of various kinds. On the other hand, he notes that an advantage of the spendings tax is that the tax base can be accurately computed for those with accruals of various kinds to account for; that is, it deals with such items as capital gains in terms of spendings.

In contrast, an advantage of the income tax is that in the case of the wage earner, it can be easily computed and checked. Vickery believes that changes in the income base would have to be made in order to provide a comprehensive income concept, including fuller taxation of capital gains for consistent deduction of capital losses and the use of a cumulative averaging method of assessment.

The spendings-tax approach, despite a long tradition of theoretical support, has never been adopted in the United States, Canada, or any other major industrial country. The only actual experience with such a tax to date has been in India (from 1957 to 1966) and Ceylon (from 1959 to 1963), where it apparently proved unsatisfactory and was repealed. The Indian and Ceylonese spendings taxes were limited in application to a relatively few wealthy taxpayers.[5] Thus, they represent practical administrative testing of a class-basis spendings-tax approach only. On the other hand, they reflect the experience with the more complicated capital transactions of upper-bracket taxpayers, an area in which the spendings tax could perform its unique functions more effectively than it could in the lower-income brackets, where other forms of consumption taxation would do about as well.

A recent analysis suggests that the discouraging experience in these two countries "may have added substantially to prevailing opinion that expenditure taxation is not a practical fiscal measure."[6] On the other hand, special conditions and limitations on administration in these countries may qualify the lessons of their experience as they apply to more advanced economies. One conclusion drawn from these episodes is that the special administrative regulations and procedures, additional auditing and investigatory techniques, and education of both government staff and the taxpaying public involve costs that call for sufficiently

---

[5] It is reported that only about 8,000 taxpayers were affected by the tax in India. See O. Prakesh, "An Indian View of the Expenditure Tax," *Manchester School of Economic and Social Studies* 26 (January 1958): 48–67, cited in John F. Due, *Government Finance,* 4th ed. (Homewood, Ill.: Irwin, 1968), p. 462.

[6] Patrick L. Kelley, "Is an Expenditure Tax Feasible?" *National Tax Journal* 23, no. 3 (September 1970): 248.

high rates and a sufficient tax base to justify the inevitable additions to administrative and compliance burdens.[7]

The discussion that follows is designed to touch at least briefly on the whole range of technical and administrative problems involved in the evaluation of the feasibility of a spendings tax and in the preliminary formulation of a spendings-tax plan.

The Expenditure Concept

One of the first conceptual matters bearing upon administrative problems is the expenditure concept itself. Individuals cannot be expected to report expenditures directly. Both compliance and audit are much easier if the measure of spending is derived indirectly from two concepts: funds available for expenditure during the taxable year from income, assets, and borrowing and nontaxable use of funds during the same period, including savings, certain direct taxes such as personal income tax, and certain "meritorious" or necessary forms of spending that are made deductible for equity, social, or administrative reasons.

The determination of the tax base is still some steps away because personal exemptions must be deducted and other adjustments such as averaging may possibly have to be made before the spendings-tax rates can be applied.

Mechanics of computing the spendings-tax base. This section outlines some of the chief compliance and administrative problems encountered in developing the simple listing that the taxpayer would have to make in computing a spendings-tax base. This listing would include not only taxable income and nontaxable receipts but also asset and liability items because changes in assets and liabilities would reflect spendings and savings entering more proximately into the expenditures concept.[8]

First of all, the taxpayer would list all cash receipts, regardless of source, and assets available for spending (or capital transactions).

---

[7] Ibid., p. 251.

[8] This discussion assumes that only changes in assets and liabilities relevant to the spendings computation would be reported. A more elaborate alternative, mentioned later, would require systematic reporting of all personal balance-sheet items and derivation of net worth as of the beginning and end of the taxable year.

From this total, he would subtract the sum of all outlays that for one reason or another are exempt from the spendings tax or are creditable as savings items. The difference is his taxable expenditures. This figure, of course, includes his spendings from many receipts not subject to income tax, such as tax-exempt interest, gifts, insurance benefits, conversion of capital assets into consumer goods, and new borrowing, including consumer credit, book account, installment-payment plans, conditional sales, and credit cards.

As this brief summary indicates, for many taxpayers the spendings-tax base bears only an approximate relation to the taxable-income base. This is important in appraising the compliance and administrative aspects of the tax. It is also significant in countering objections and misunderstandings to the effect that the spendings tax is merely an additional income tax in disguise.

The mechanics of bringing together the various sources of funds available for expenditure are not difficult. It is merely a matter of making sure that the listing is logically complete. Similarly, it is not difficult to take inventory of the various possible uses of funds that might be deductible for spendings-tax purposes. However, it is more difficult to establish agreement on what the appropriate deductions should be. There is considerable room for differences about whether particular items should be regarded as taxable expenditures, depending in part on the objectives and strategy of the spendings-tax plan. For the taxpayer, the whole procedure involves more complete periodic record keeping, especially for balance-sheet items, than the income tax calls for, although figures for the tax basis of assets are required for income-tax purposes.

What would an individual expenditures-tax return include? The first major item on the individual expenditures-tax return would be *funds available for expenditure.* A typical list of these items might include: (1) cash and bank balances on hand at the beginning of the year; (2) salaries and other compensation received for personal services; (3) dividends and interest received, including insurance policy dividends; (4) interest received on all government obligations; (5) rent and royalty receipts; (6) annuity receipts, pensions, and insurance benefits of all kinds; (7) withdrawals from businesses, professions, partnerships, and trusts; (8) cash gifts and bequests received; (9) receipts from the sale of capital assets; (10) receipts from debt repayment; (11) borrowings, including debt incurred on installment purchases, open book account, and credit cards; (12) all other receipts in cash or in the form of goods and services; and (13) a total of items 1 to 12.

The next group of reportable items would come under the heading of *deductions for nontaxable use of funds*. This list would include: (14) cash and bank balances on hand at the end of the year; (15) cash gifts and contributions; (16) interest paid, with the possible exception (which is controversial) of interest payments on a debt on owner-occupied homes, assuming rent is taxable and equivalent basic expenditures of the homeowner are similarly taxable; (17) taxes paid during the year, with the exception of consumer excises, other consumption-related taxes, and possibly taxes on owner-occupied homes; (18) fines and penalties (again, this may be a controversial item); (19) purchase of capital assets; (20) life insurance premiums, or at least the savings component thereof, and purchase payments for annuities or pensions, such as employee payroll contributions toward social security or other retirement plans; (21) debts repaid in cash, including payments on installment purchases and other forms of debt that are carried beyond a year; (22) loans made; (23) all other nontaxable payments; and (24) the sum of deduction items 14 to 23.

Item 25 in this array would then be *expenditures subject to tax,* representing the total shown in item 13 minus the total shown in item 24. From item 25, the taxpayer would be able to deduct the personal exemptions allowed under the spendings tax and other possible adjustments preceding the actual tax calculation. If the spendings-tax plan included an averaging rule applicable to spending, various adjustments might be called for after the annual taxable expenditures have been determined. Such a rule would permit expenditures in prior years to be taxed in the current year or would allow some carry-over in order to reduce the lumping of expenditures in the current year.

Administrative practicability and the rise of affluence. The analysis of the spendings-tax plan proposed during the World War II era, was preoccupied with a list of such technical and administrative problems as these: the definition of the tax base, including available funds, savings, and exempt items; treatment of consumer-durables purchases; housing and the homeowner-tenant equity problem; the taxpayer unit and the exemption structure; simplified returns; filing requirements;

anticipatory buying; hoarded cash; enforcement techniques, such as information returns; and business perquisites, such as cars, personal services, travel and entertainment, and recreational facilities.

The 1942 analysis reached the conclusion that a spendings tax was administratively practicable at least in relation to wartime conditions and stabilization needs. The administrative and compliance costs of such a tax were not considered excessive because a collection framework and nearly adequate personnel already existed in connection with the personal income tax. Furthermore, most of the information required from taxpayers was, in any case, needed by them in making out the personal-income-tax return.

This conclusion seems to have been based to a considerable extent on the judgment, admissible under wartime conditions in a tax aimed at mass consumption, that the balance-sheet adjustment portion of the spendings-tax computation is relatively unimportant.

It is less acceptable, however, in terms of the current period, in which so-called affluence has become widespread, more taxpayers have acquired a number of asset- and liability-account changes affecting the spendings computation, and there is necessarily a greater concern with possible spending by the affluent taxpayers from sources other than the taxable income routinely reported on income-tax returns.

Some Straightforward Administrative Problems

The formulation of a spendings tax involves facing up to a number of technical and administrative matters involving potential problems of hardship and tax avoidance or evasion.

The taxpayer unit. In general, the taxpayer unit would presumably be about the same as it is for the income tax. The family basis for spending would generally be followed. The present rule under the income tax which provides that minor dependents and certain other dependents who are full-time students file their own returns while being claimed as dependents by the parental unit would have to be reconsidered. Parental gifts to these minor dependents and students would ca. for special treatment both to avoid double taxation to the family unit and to prevent tax avoidance through splitting of family expenditures.

Simplified returns. Simplified returns have long been the great goal of simplification plans under the income tax. However, the so-called postcard return or its equivalent tends to go down the drain in practice. If a simplified return is difficult to achieve under the current income tax, it would be even more difficult to achieve with a spendings-tax appendage.

Proponents of simplified returns for income and spendings taxes usually resort to the presumptive-expenditure[9] route in order to achieve this kind of simplification. However, to the extent that the plan resorts to a presumptive-expenditure concept for a large number of lower-income individuals, the plan is in essence an increase in the income tax. In this form, it would be indistinguishable in the taxpayer's mind from an additional income tax, and the incentive effect on saving and spending would be almost entirely lost. The word *almost* is used here because the presumptive approach might permit the establishment of an actual savings figure as an option. Such an option, however, would both lose revenue and add still another complication.

Filing requirement. It would apparently be impossible to tie the filing requirement for the spendings tax entirely to the filing requirement for the income tax because there will be a number of people whose spendings from the depletion of capital will be substantial although they will have little or no taxable income.

This would suggest that the filing requirements for the income tax and the spendings tax might be consolidated and stated in the form of gross receipts from all sources, including gross income plus other available funds used to finance total expenditures during the taxable year. This approach would certainly introduce a considerable element of novelty and confusion to the whole income-tax filing picture in view of the long period of education that went into the gross-income filing requirements, which have recently been refined and increased under the Tax Reform Act of 1969 in order to eliminate the filing requirement for persons below the poverty level.

The protection of persons below the poverty level under a spendings tax would introduce some interesting questions. Some persons

---

[9] The "presumptive" approach merely assumes that the individual spends (or saves) a specified (possibly graduated) percentage of his income, just as the present standard deduction technique assumes that the individual has deductions equal to a specified percentage of income.

considered to be below the poverty level for income-tax purposes might conceivably be expected to pay a spendings tax because the various sources of spendable sums from income, welfare, food and rent subsidies, and so forth might well exceed a spendings level deemed taxable if maintained by an ordinary income-tax payer. One possibility, not necessarily desirable, and indeed undesirable from the standpoint of a broad-based spendings-tax system, would be to define an exempt level of spending that would be relatively high and would limit the application of the tax to middle-class taxpayers and the affluent.

Information returns. The enforcement of the spendings tax would probably call for a considerable extension of the reporting mechanisms and requirements in order to cover money receipts or payments and capital transactions that are not now included in the information-return system for the income tax.

Such information returns would have to cover the sale of securities, real estate, and personal property and the withdrawal of funds from bank deposits, accounts in savings banks, and shares accounts in savings and loan associations. It would also have to cover payments by insurance companies.

Since net savings are a key factor in measuring spending, the information needed on bank- and savings-account changes would be the net accruals, positive or negative, to the account in the nature of principal changes, with a separate figure for the net interest or dividend earned on the account.

The implication of a withdrawal of funds from a bank account would not be very great if the individual merely withdrew the money from one account or savings institution to deposit it in another. Nevertheless, to secure comprehensive and effective enforcement, all such transfers of funds or their net effect on year-end balances would have to be brought within the purview of the system as capital transactions per se or as part of a determination of changes in net worth.

It appears from this brief analysis that those individuals who wish to engage in fairly complicated financial maneuvering could leave quite a complex network of capital transactions that would be very difficult to trace. It is true that their spendings could be reflected in a comprehensive record of net withdrawals of funds, sales of assets, and the like versus net deposits, purchases of assets, and so forth. However, the best check on spending in these complicated cases would be a comprehensive inventory of assets and liabilities at the beginning and the end of the year in order to get at changes in net worth.

In light of these complications, it would seem that one main function of information returns on capital transactions would be to bring to the attention of the Internal Revenue Service all the various transactions that create a potential supply of funds for spending (or support a net-savings deduction). The question arises whether, in the interest of saving paper work for all concerned, fairly substantial amounts of transfers or sales would have to be exempted. Such an exemption in terms of dollar amounts per account could hide a relatively substantial amount of sales of assets or withdrawals from multiple bank accounts that would make it possible for the unscrupulous to get away with a considerable amount of spending within the tolerance of the information-return system.

Current payment and intrayear reporting procedures. The spendings tax would call for current collection by two methods: collection at source from income on a presumptive basis and tentative quarterly returns by persons subject to higher-bracket rates or with income not subject to collection at source. Graduated withholding techniques could reduce or eliminate the need for quarterly returns from persons, even in the higher brackets, who earn the great bulk of their income from withheld sources. Amounts collected during the year would be credited against the ultimate liability when the final return was filed. Any excess of spendings-tax payments over liabilities could be credited against unpaid income-tax liabilities, and any balance still remaining would be refunded to the taxpayer.[10]

If refunds resulted to high savers, these individuals would in effect be required to lend a fraction of their savings to the government for part of the year without interest. Collection at source would tend to hide the current inducement to saving because the effect of savings on the tax would not be immediately apparent to the taxpayer, showing up in his tax payments or refunds only in the following year unless tentative quarterly settlements were required. The inducement to saving would be especially important for those subject to the higher spendings-tax rates.

---

[10] It goes without saying that excess income-tax withholding could be applied against spendings tax; in simpler terms, combined withholding for income and spendings taxes could be applied against the combined tax liability.

For taxpayers whose tax was not fully withheld on a presumptive basis, the quarterly returns could therefore play a significant role in making the individual more keenly aware of his spending level and its tax consequences. The quarterly filing requirement would of course be geared to the annual filing and reporting rules. If the individual were not made periodically aware of his cumulative spending, the effect of a spendings tax in cutting down consumer spending would probably be muted.

The quarterly returns might involve an approximate estimate of savings rather than a detailed statement of income and savings, the actual calculation of expenditures being postponed until the year-end adjustment. The quarterly return would, however, permit the bulk of the tax to be paid or collected during the year and the inducement effect to be apparent at short intervals.

As these observations suggest, there would be considerable compliance and administrative burdens connected with any effort to make the savings-inducement effect psychologically discernible to the taxpayer through the current-payment system.

Treatment of Specific Items in Spendings Computation

The formulation of a spendings tax involves a number of controversial issues that may be resolved in alternative ways, with varying administrative consequences.

Housing: homeowner versus tenant. One of the difficult problems of designing a spendings tax is the imputed rent of owner-occupied homes. On grounds of equity, it could be argued that if imputed rent cannot be taxed in full, rent paid by renters ought not to be included fully in the spendings-tax base.

If mortgage interest and property taxes on owner-occupied homes were included in spendings,[11] a substantial portion of the typical homeowner's housing expenditures would be taxable. However, in the case of the individual who owns his home outright, with no mortgage debt, the inclusion of the local property tax only would still exclude from the

---

[11] Since these items are now deductible for income-tax purposes, their inclusion in a spendings-tax base relying on a taxable-income starting point would involve a special adjustment that added these to expenditures.

tax base the imputed income from the house itself. The crudities of this approximation of housing consumption are obvious.

Perfect uniformity of treatment would presumably require the inclusion in the spendings-tax base of the gross rental value of the owner-occupied home. Mortgage interest and property tax paid would be taxed either as components of the imputed rental value or as separate consumption items. This would tend to equalize homeowner and renter and, within the homeowner group, would tend to equalize the treatment of those with more or less mortgage indebtedness. However, the determination of imputed rental value would obviously give rise to serious problems.

One simplifying compromise sometimes suggested for the spendings tax in the housing area (as a companion to taxing rent as a consumption expenditure of the tenant) would be to treat the sum of residential-property tax and straight-line depreciation (say, over an estimated life of forty years for a new house) on the owner-occupied home as the homeowner's basic housing consumption. This would ignore imputed rental value (as under the income tax) but would in effect spread the purchase price of the depreciable part of the home over its approximate useful life, in a manner similar to that discussed (in the next section) in connection with consumer durables generally. It would also tax as spendings the homeowner's property tax subsumed under the tenant's rental payment. Presumably, also, mortgage interest would be treated in the same way as interest paid to finance purchase of consumer durables generally, as discussed in the next section.

Purchase of consumer durables. Considerations similar to those applicable to homeownership would arise in connection with the acquisition and use of various other types of consumer durables. These goods constitute various amounts of saving because they, too, release their utilities slowly over time. They also result in a certain amount of imputed income. They may be purchased outright or financed through various forms of installment payments or conditional sales contracts. In the past, most analysts have regarded the imputed income from durable consumer goods as troublesome but not sufficiently important to require the kind of specific adjustment for income-tax purposes that might be entertained more sympathetically in the case of a home. However, the difference between the two situations is essentially one of degree rather than kind.

Purchases of consumer durables would probably call for the allocation of the purchase amount over a period of years in order to prevent lumping of expenditures in a single year, which would result in a higher tax than if the same aggregate were spent over the useful life of the durable. This would introduce a considerable complication depending on how large a durable purchase was subject to the allocation procedure.

Because the purchases of consumer durables would represent taxable spending, provision would be necessary to prevent the retirement of consumer installment debt from being treated as a savings item (or the incurring of such debt as a source of funds), an adjustment that would mean additional compliance and administrative complications.

Interest payments. As noted in the section "Housing: homeowner versus tenant," interest payments on a mortgage on an owned home might be included in a spendings-tax base that involved the taxation of rent and other basic housing expenditures.

Interest paid on business debts would, of course, not be deductible again by the individual for spendings-tax purposes if previously deducted in the determination of proprietorship profits or partnership earnings that were allocated to the individual partner. The same would be true of interest paid on indebtedness involved in holding income-producing property.

Other interest payments, particularly for the financing of consumer-durables purchases, would be taxable as spendings (not deductible, as they are under the income tax) because they would represent a form of personal expenditure. If this treatment were not applied, there would be a discrimination against the leasing of durable goods because rental payments would represent expenditures. Interest on personal loans of various other types, including loans on life insurance policies, presents problems of specification.

Taxes. All state, local, and probably federal income taxes should be deducted from the base because they represent a form of compulsory spending not available for discretionary outlays. This exclusion would also be necessary to prevent confiscatory combined rates of spendings and income taxes. There is, however, some body of opinion to the effect that federal income tax should not be deductible for spendings-tax purposes because this would be counterprogressive.

Business taxes would, of course, not be deductible if they had already been deducted in the computation of business earnings included in sources of funds available for spending.

What about the various forms of sales and consumer excises? On net balance, it would appear that they should be treated as a form of consumption. If a deduction were allowed, there would be the problem of distinguishing between manufacturers' excises that entered into the purchase price and retail excises that were identifiable. The various excise and sales taxes are also discretionary to some extent. This raises a question: Would this treatment tend to encourage state and local governments to go over to direct forms of taxation that were deductible and away from sales- and excise-type taxes that were not deductible for purposes of the federal spendings tax?

Fines and penalties. There may be some disagreement on the treatment of fines and penalties. They resemble taxes in that they are not voluntary expenditures in the usual sense. On the other hand, it may be argued that it is contrary to sound public policy to allow this kind of exclusion for spendings-tax purposes. However, the actual burden of a substantial fine could become highly onerous if both income and spendings taxes were applied to this kind of payment at highly graduated rates.

Interpersonal gifts. Interpersonal gifts inside and outside the family give rise to problems of both specification and administration. It can be argued that gifts to individuals outside the family do not constitute a consumption expenditure by the donor. Rather, they should be taxed under a spendings tax to the donee unless he saves the receipts, in which case a compensating savings-deduction item arises. What about gifts between family members? Under a graduated spendings tax, for example, the head of the family, subject to higher-bracket rates, might wish to transfer the expenditure to one of his children.

Gifts between family members thus present some of the problems of income splitting under the income tax. Some of the difficulty here hinges on the definitions of *inside* and *outside* the family. In the example given in the preceding paragraph, the problem would depend upon whether the recipient child could establish himself as a separate taxable unit. If he was able to do so, then, of course, the possibilities of spendings splitting arise.

Problems of Avoidance and Evasion

The spendings-tax plan would force substantial record keeping. It is the rare taxpayer in the middle and lower brackets who knows his precise net worth as of any given date or who can ascertain his assets at original cost adjusted or his precise liabilities. It might be possible to get around this snapshot of beginning- and end-of-period assets and liabilities by simply reporting capital transactions (i.e., cash withdrawals and deposits, sales and purchases of capital assets, and the like). This is indeed the method (discussed earlier in this chapter) usually contemplated for applying a spendings tax. But the capital-transactions-reporting approach involves the danger that investment purchases would be recorded but not sales or transfers of cash and the like to finance purchases. In any event, errors and oversights would be numerous. The opportunity for errors that could not be fully detected would be exploited by some taxpayers. The cost of substantial policing of capital-assets transactions would probably be heavy. Perhaps complete balance-sheet reporting for higher-bracket taxpayers might be appropriate, with a supposedly simpler capital-transactions-only approach reserved for the lower brackets.

Anticipatory buying. As the treasury recognized in its wartime proposal for a spendings tax, it is essential that the effective date of the plan be set either retroactively or at the point of first public notice of the plan. This would be essential in order to prevent large-scale buying and hoarding of consumer goods in anticipation of the enactment of the spendings tax. In addition, unless the spendings tax became effective as of the date on which it was first announced or brought to public attention, individuals would be given an opportunity to convert their bank deposits, which are assets of record, into currency in the hope of thereby setting aside spendable funds upon which an adequate check could not be made.

Similar problems of anticipatory buying would occur in connection with rumors or public discussion of plans to increase spendings-tax rates. In this respect, the spendings tax would create the types of problems that arise in connection with proposals to increase excise-tax rates.

On the other hand, if the time should come when the spendings tax was to be repealed or significantly reduced, this prospect would tend to induce a disturbing slowdown (with later resumption and catch-up) of spending unless, again, a retrospective effective date was announced and was persuasive from the time the plan was first made public. Although such an announcement would prevent the program from artificially postponing spending, it would involve a considerable accumulated loss of revenue during the period in which the repeal or reduction plan was under discussion. There would be considerable public uncertainty in the meantime, and if the proposal for repeal or reduction was finally not adopted, taxpayers who might have been induced to spend on the strength of the proposals might feel some resentment.

Hoarded cash. One of the recognized weaknesses of the spendings tax during the transition would be the impossibility of knowing the exact extent of hoarded cash or other secret assets. Many people apparently hold substantial amounts of cash. Or they could begin hoarding cash as soon as the announcement of the spendings-tax proposal was made. It would be difficult to apply retrospective provisions that would deal with this problem effectively. It would be easier, however, to deal with hoarding that was induced by the tax plan through withdrawal of deposits because such hoarding would be reflected in the level of deposits for which information would be available. It would also be necessary to study what other possible hidden assets (other than hoarded cash) individuals could draw on for spending. Such assets would, of course, include secret bank accounts in foreign countries, which have been a problem under the income tax. Stronger information-reporting and enforcement procedures have recently been made possible under Public Law 91–508, which was approved on October 26, 1970, and became effective on May 1, 1971. Safeguards in this area are still far from perfect and are still under study and in the process of further development. It would be important to determine the extent to which preexisting secret accounts and various other manipulations of this type would not be reached by the anti-income-tax-evasion procedures.

Immigrants and foreign visitors. Individuals (such as immigrants and foreign visitors) entering the country for the first time would presumably be required to make a full declaration of their assets. In many cases, these assets would be held abroad and would be difficult to check. Unless an accurate inventory was made of the assets of entrants into the system, or subsequent transfers from these sources were fully reported, immigrants would be able to spend from such preexisting assets or count as current savings the acquisition of newly recorded assets drawn from such secret resources.

International movements of persons. Another consideration is related to the problem of immigrants: How would the spendings-tax system deal with a person who earned an income of, say, $10,000 in year 1 in the United States, reporting large savings from such income and thus incurring a relatively small spendings-tax base, and who then went to Canada for year 2 in order to spend the savings of year 1 while sojourning outside the United States. Such an individual might then reappear in the U.S. tax system in year 3 and repeat the process. It would be difficult to charge this individual for the reduction in his assets during his year of absence because this would, in effect, represent spending made in a year in which the individual was a bona fide resident abroad.

Casual labor. Even under the existing income tax, certain forms of casual labor are not subject to withholding or information returns. Such income may easily be treated by many individuals as tax-exempt income. Although this represents a form of illegal tax evasion, its presence has to be recognized. Under a spendings tax, the existing premium on casual labor would be enhanced because income derived from this source would be exempt from both the income tax and the spendings tax. Thus, an effective operation of a spendings tax would have to recognize that unless the casual-labor loophole was plugged satisfactorily, a substantial inequity and economic distortion would result, pushing labor supplies into various forms of casual activities not subject to withholding.

Production for home consumption. Under a spendings tax, home production of goods and services presents a problem of potential evasion or underreporting unless the tax plan deliberately exempts such income. Some tolerance in this area would be inevitable, but the resulting potential inequities are substantial.

Farmers would enjoy a tremendous advantage with respect to food production. However, the problem goes far beyond that. Home gardening generally would be given a considerable stimulus. So would various do-it-yourself projects such as home repair, painting, and decorating. It is evident that the spendings tax would encourage home barbering and hair styling, home beauty services, home dressmaking and tailoring, and so forth. In general, it would tend to discourage the supposedly more efficient exchange economy. From the administrative standpoint, this raises the question of whether an effort should be made to include in the tax base important forms of production for self-use in order to eliminate a loophole and possible distortions resulting in inefficiency and waste in the economy. Efforts at dealing with the home-production or self-delivery problem would clearly be difficult.

Business withdrawals versus profits. In the case of owners of unincorporated businesses, the entire amount of withdrawal from the business would count as a receipt for spending. Withdrawals might occur even though the business had a loss during the current year. Care would need to be taken to prevent evasive maneuvers such as a double deduction or exclusion for savings, for example, advances to the business for inventory accumulation in the business without a corresponding increase of business net income. A related problem would be unrecorded home consumption from business inventories, a form of evasion under the income tax that would be given further impetus under a spendings tax.

Consumer goods and services: exchanges and income in kind. Various forms of income in kind would have to be reported in order to prevent direct exchanges of goods and services for purposes of expenditures-tax evasion or avoidance. In World War II, the problem arose under the income tax in connection with the tax escape efforts of high bracket professionals. A commonly used illustration was the swapping of legal and surgical services between high-priced lawyers and surgeons in order to avoid income tax. Another example was the covert settlement of a substantial charge for professional services with a gift such as a case of liquor. A related problem in this connection would be the matter of perquisites and allowances in kind (such as automobiles, meals, travel, lodging, and recreational facilities) to business employees, particularly corporate executives.

Interpersonal loans. An interpersonal loan theoretically should be regarded as a deduction for the lender and a receipt for the recipient, very much in the manner of any other form of loan. However, it is apparent, that there are problems of evasion, avoidance, or at least deferment involved in interpersonal loans, particularly where there are family or other close relationships involved between lender and borrower. The high-bracket lender, for example, might well deduct what is ostensibly an interpersonal loan, the proceeds of which are used for the purchase of goods and services by the lower-bracket borrower more or less on behalf of the lender.

Distinction between consumption and investment purchases. Many consumption expenditures might be clothed as investment or business acquisitions. For example, a man buys a farm or ranch, hunting lands, a beach home. He claims these are business or investment acquisitions. He may even have a complaisant tenant who gives him liberal access to the property. How should the acquisition and the carrying costs of such property be treated? How can administrative procedures ferret out abuses? Even with liberal treatment of the homeowner, it would be questionable to exempt or substantially exclude (either by specific legal provision or de facto by administrative inadequacy) various other forms of affluent spending on second and third homes, other real estate, and so forth, used for at least semipersonal or recreational purposes. (In a sense, two separate issues are posed here: Should a second or third home be treated as liberally as the primary residence? How can the administrative machinery cope with disguised second and third homes and similar purchases?)

Capital-asset manipulations. Capital-asset transfers accomplished prior to the beginning date of the spendings tax (e.g., to family members or dummies not subject to much spendings tax) would represent another loophole. The amounts thus transferred could later be brought back for unreported spending or for window dressing on the end-of-year balance sheet. This problem is a variant of secret cash hoards accumulated prior to the effective date of the spendings tax. Secret borrowing to bolster the end-of-year cash holdings could accomplish the same evasion.

Exempt Items and Deductions

A spendings-tax plan will necessarily confront various needs and claims for exemption or deduction of certain forms of expenditure. Such exemptions, which would complicate the spendings tax in concept and in implementation, would fall into several categories. Some of these would be: socially important forms of expenditure such as tuition and other educational and training expenses; unavoidable expenditures such as medical expenses, taxation of which would result in putting the individual in a severe tax bind and financial hardship (the spendings tax might have to follow the income tax in excluding large medical costs); charitable contributions; professional and other service expenses such as those for legal advice, which, in addition to containing a business or investment element, are involuntary or may represent hardship or personal-crisis situations; and goods and services that exist in abundant supply or in industries where overcapacity exists and potential output threatens to go to waste as a result of the tax (or failure to secure exemption).

Tuition. For social reasons, there would be considerable pressure for the exemption of tuition and possibly other educational expenses. Apart from the social aspects, it might be essential from the standpoint of relief for parents who have expanded personal budgets because of heavy college, university, and other educational costs. There has already been considerable pressure for a credit for educational expenses under the income tax. The application of a spendings tax—which would be equivalent to an income tax and would hit not only income but the expenditure beyond income that is characteristic of a family supporting children in colleges, universities, and private preparatory schools—would certainly lead to strong pressure for such relief.

Medical, dental, nursing, and hospital services and medicines. Social and equity considerations would lead to a strong case for the exemption of most or all kinds of medical expenses. Since unusual medical expenses are already deductible for income-tax purposes, a similar deduction or exclusion for the spendings tax would not involve a large step from the administrative standpoint.

One impelling reason for exemption of medical costs is the fact that recipients of free medical care are in effect receiving very sizable incomes in kind that, if converted into taxable cash income, would most certainly exceed any exemption proposed under the spendings tax. To exempt such welfare or charity recipients from a spendings tax while requiring the payment of tax on an equivalent amount financed by provident or middle-class persons would lead to an intolerable inequity.

With an exemption for medical expense, the spendings tax would place even more severe pressure than now exists under the income tax on the definition of medical expenditure. There would be a stronger stimulus to luxurious trips to treatment centers and so forth.

Domestic service. Some would argue that domestic-service expenditures should be deductible in order to achieve greater equity between families with and without a working wife or between a widowed breadwinner with dependent children and more normal families, to cite just two examples. In short, the spendings tax would aggravate similar problems that have given rise to babysitter deductions for income-tax purposes.

Charitable contributions. The question of deductibility of charitable contributions for purposes of the spendings tax would require specific attention. Since these items are deductible under the income tax, the presumption would be that they should also be deductible under a spendings tax. Perhaps a case could be made for a more liberal ceiling limitation or no limitation under the spendings tax. Another specific issue would relate to the treatment of those using the standard deduction, rather than itemizing charitable and other deductions, for income-tax purposes. Gifts of appreciated property would presumably not be treated as liberally under the spendings tax as they are under the income tax, and adjustments to correct this would involve another complication.

Public services paid for by fees, licenses, and so forth. It may be argued that such charges should be exempt because they are a public-revenue source similar in nature to user charges or taxes. Unless they were exempted, local governments would be under pressure to finance them with a type of tax that would be deductible for spendings-tax purposes. Fees are, however, payments for services, and they do involve the use of factors of production. The exemption of specific items of this type would, of course, complicate compliance, auditing, and enforcement.

Service charges. Some have even argued that certain kinds of semibusiness expenditures (e.g., legal services, accounting services, investment advice, and other financial services) should be exempt as nonconsumption items. In many cases, they are income-tax deductions of a business or income-producing character; in these situations, they would be excluded from the spendings-tax base anyway unless a specific adjustment was made to the taxable-income concept to reverse the income-tax deduction. In other situations, they represent nondiscretionary or, sometimes, personal-emergency expenditures. A further consideration is that some of these services, such as legal assistance, are provided free for low-income people, who would thus enjoy a further advantage over the taxpayers who paid their own expenses plus income or spendings tax thereon. Whatever the conceptual merits of the case one way or the other, this appears to be an area of potential complexity, particularly if more than the income-tax-deductible amounts are excluded from spendings.

Memberships in organizations. Professional association and union dues are now a trade or employment expense deductible for income-tax purposes. In the absence of a reversal of the income-tax treatment, these amounts would thus be exempt for purposes of a spendings tax. Other membership dues for social, educational, or cultural organizations, which are not eligible for income-tax deductions as employment or professional expenses, might be considered for special deduction or exclusion for spendings-tax purposes. The various possibilities for handling these items would complicate both the formulation and the implementation of a spendings tax.

Exempt income and special income-tax deductions. The construction of a comprehensive concept of income alone (exclusive of other nonincome receipts from capital sources) would involve a thorough canvass of the income-tax structure and, if the comprehensive income goal was to be adhered to in the implementation of the spendings tax, an elaborate set of instructions to the taxpayer to avoid omission of potential spendings sources. The list of exempt-income items is more formidable than might be initially suspected. Interest on state and local securities, social security and railroad retirement benefits, and the portion of other pensions and annuities representing return of principal are only some of the items that would have to be considered. An array of subsistence items immediately comes to mind. A few of these include items allowed members of the armed forces; veterans' benefits; combat pay; Peace Corps allowances; clergymen's housing, rental, and related allowances; sick and disability pay; and insurance benefits of various kinds.

The whole array of special (and regular) income-tax deductions or exclusions would also need to be reviewed in order to determine whether these are to be retained or reversed for spendings-tax purposes. Moving expenses, travel undertaken as education for employment, work clothing, and so forth represent areas in which it would be difficult to reverse the income-tax exemption, yet hazardous to leave an avenue to freedom from the combined burden of income and spendings taxes. In any event, instruction and education of taxpayers on these aspects of the spendings-tax concept would involve considerable tasks.

Life insurance premiums: savings portion versus pure insurance. What about life insurance premiums? The portion involving payment for current protection might be considered a spendings item. The portion going for savings would be deductible in accordance with the exemption of savings. This would introduce a new compliance complication. Policy dividends would have to be broken down, which would complicate the determination. For these reasons, the deduction of all the life insurance premiums might be desirable.

Balance-Sheet Reporting by Taxpayers

Many proponents of a spendings-tax scheme think of it as being practicable only on a rather limited scale that involves basically the reporting of income and the deduction of savings. Anything that requires comprehensive and accurate reporting by the mass of taxpayers of either capital transactions or a complete balance-sheet picture with net-worth changes they regard as a nearly decisive argument against a spendings tax. If this judgment is correct, it means that really full-scale application of the spendings-tax principle might have to be confined to the taxpayers in the middle or upper parts of the income and wealth scale, as was the case in India and Ceylon. But even this restriction would not eliminate the possibilities of excessive compliance and administrative burdens and the basic failure of the tax, as apparently happened in those two countries. A taxation-of-the-elite-only approach would make the plan a net addition to the progressive elements in the income tax.[12]

Avoiding net-savings calculation through limited-savings-deduction approaches. In the World War II period, spendings-tax planning covered *inter alia* plans to permit the deduction only of savings- or defense-bond purchases in arriving at taxable spending. The objection to this, of course, was that it disregarded savings invested in other directions and also disregarded transfers of savings from other assets into the eligible bond purchases. Of course, this crude defense-oriented form of the spendings tax need not prejudice future efforts toward a more fully developed plan. However, it does throw light on the formidableness of the comprehensive balance-sheet or capital-transactions approach that apparently tended to discourage some experts scouting the matter in the 1940s.

Balance-sheet versus capital-transactions approach. Some observers urge full balance-sheet reporting rather than a listing of capital transactions only (i.e., changes in balance-sheet items affecting net worth and therefore the spendings-savings determination). The balance-sheet computation involved in determining the individual's net saving or dissaving would require a snapshot, so to speak, of his bank balance and other accounts and assets at the beginning and the end of the year. It is easy to talk about taxpayers submitting beginning- and end-of-year balance sheets on a cost basis, rather than merely listing all transactions in capital assets and all changes in the holding of cash and bank balances. It is technically feasible and should be no more than a vigorous and even salutary compliance exercise for taxpayers who have reasonably good data on their assets and liabilities. It can also be pointed out, for instance, that an adjusted-cost basis

---

12 This would be open to objections on nonadministrative grounds. These could be met by balancing the top-bracket spendings tax with a value-added tax or similar broad-based consumption levy (just as a value-added-tax initiative could be balanced with a progressive spendings tax). But the character and economic thrust of the plan would be basically altered in this truncated version inspired by practical administrative limitations.

should be available for all capital assets in order to put the taxpayer in position to comply with the capital-gain and -loss provisions of the income tax.

However, the reality probably is that many taxpayers do not keep full, systematic, and easily usable records of their assets and liabilities but, instead, scramble to assemble the needed data only when required to do so in connection with a capital-gain or -loss transaction. Requiring taxpayers to produce a full balance sheet at the beginning and end of each year would involve quite an initial wrench as well as continuing record keeping and assembling, which taxpayers now tend to shirk. In light of this, as well as taxpayer resistance to full balance-sheet and net-worth disclosure, it seems that the line of least resistance from the administrative standpoint would be to limit the spendings-tax requirements to the reporting of only capital (asset-and-liability change) transactions that reflect funds available for spending or saving.

Checking-account lag and float. An illustration of the technical compliance problems in either the complete balance-sheet or the capital-transactions approach to the spendings-tax computation is the handling of the important bank-account item. The individual often does not really know what his bank account, at least his active checking account, is as of the end of a year. His checkbook balance may be sloppy. Service charges may not be known exactly. The bank's balance will not reflect outstanding checks. The bank may thus not be able to furnish him with a picture of his balance as of December 31. Only an approximation can be arrived at on a particular date.

Thus, it would be necessary to decide how the individual's check flow should be treated, that is, outstanding checks representing expenditures that he had made but that had not yet been charged to his account. If the individual were not charged for this float, he would, at least in the first year, be able to secure a substantial advantage by writing a lot of checks toward the end of the year; these would still be outstanding at the time of his spendings-tax report. The following year, of course, such outstanding checks would have been cashed and would be reflected in his expenditures. However, the process could be repeated at the end of the year, possibly on a larger scale, in order to offset the recapture of the previous year's spendings deferments. The tax advantages involved might induce a special end-of-year seasonal in spending.

Charge accounts. Problems similar to those involved in reporting bank balances would arise in connection with charge accounts. Individuals may not have good up-to-the-minute records of their charges on regular book accounts or credit cards. Late-in-the-year spending might not be reflected in any readily available records. The use of credit could thus be employed to secure initial-year and continuing tax deferment.

Voucher-accounting system to support deductions for investment under the spendings tax. One approach sometimes proposed to simplify the justification, record keeping, and auditing of deduction claims for investment under a spendings tax is a voucher system. Such a plan might be either compulsory and universal or optional. Under this plan, an individual making an investment would purchase a voucher and transfer the voucher to the seller of the investment, who in turn would receive cash for it.

Although this approach would provide a ready method of checking reported investment, it does not meet the real problem: checking on the source of the funds used to make the investment. That is, although the taxpayer would present vouchers for credits reducing his tax base, he would not always have to hand over vouchers certifying the amount of debits or additions to the base.

Where the will to evade exists, the check of reported investments would seem to add little to the effectiveness of the compliance measures unless it is coupled with further measures to check on capital transfer. If the provision is made for certification of purchases in order to obtain deductions on a routine basis without also providing adequate information on sales or withdrawals, capital transfer might in some cases actually be encouraged for tax-escape purposes.

With a compulsory and universal plan, the seller of the asset would go through the voucher-cashing procedure, thus establishing a record of his sale. However, a cross-check of sellers' and buyers' reports would seem to be a massive task, even with the use of electronic data processing methods. Under such a method of reporting capital transfers, a purchase voucher would include information identifying the seller. The voucher would then constitute both a receipt and an information return. However, this would have to be supplemented by information returns from banks, insurance companies, and so forth for complete coverage of capital transfer and withdrawal. The task of assimilating millions of information returns and plugging them into a computer system for retrieval and use of the data would be very substantial, particularly since individuals have many more bank accounts and many more capital transactions than they have employers or income receipts. This is true at least of many situations in the middle-income brackets in which the capital-balance-sheet aspects of the spendings tax would be important.

What can be said in summary about a voucher-plan approach? It would be an additional piece of red tape that would absorb resources. Vouchers certifying investments or sales of investments would undoubtedly be helpful to the Internal Revenue Service, but additional paper work and accounting would be involved for the investment firm, the IRS, and the operation of the voucher mechanism itself. This would mean additional transfer costs for buyers and sellers of capital assets unless the government underwrote the whole plan. It would, however, reduce the amount of investigative work involved in auditing. It would provide an automatic check on sources of funds used insofar as the voucher system gave information on the sale as well as the purchase of assets.

Capital-asset acquisitions. Consistent with the principle of deducting savings in computing the spendings tax, expenditures for the acquisition of capital assets by an unincorporated business would be deductible. Depreciation allowances would then not be deductible for purposes of a spendings tax, and the flow of tax-free money under the income tax from capital recovery would represent a receipt or dissavings item for purposes of the spendings tax. Transactions such as reinvestment of the return of capital funds in machinery and equipment or retention as liquid savings would, of course, prevent a spendings-tax burden on this money. However, it is immediately clear that there is considerable potential for inconsistency between the income- and spendings-tax bases with respect to depreciable assets, depletable assets, and a number of other forms of property, including intangibles, that are subject to some form of amortization or capital-recovery allowance. Inventory and inventory changes may not be entirely innocent in this respect. This may be regarded as essentially a routine technical or conceptual matter. However, it is apparently a source of probable compliance difficulty.

Spendings-Tax Audit as a By-Product of Other Audits

One of the major arguments in favor of the spendings tax from the administrative standpoint is that a large part of the compliance time spent by the taxpayer in filling out an expenditures-tax return would be essentially the same as or a by-product of filling out the income-tax return already required. Audit and check of expenditures-tax returns would also be largely by-products of income-tax administration as far as income receipts and, to some extent, asset-sales proceeds are concerned.

To state the point more explicitly, many items of information needed for the spendings tax—including income receipts, sale of assets, substantial gifts, and even loans or borrowings (on which the interest paid is deductible to the borrower and taxable to the lender)—are already required in filing reports for income- or gift-tax purposes. Bank balances that are not ordinarily reported for income-tax purposes would theoretically offer little difficulty (except for fraudulent concealment practices).

Some additional auditing personnel might be required because the additional weight would be placed in effect on adequate reporting of income, since both spendings- and income-tax liabilities would be involved. The spendings-tax return would also be formidable even if the items of information could be derived in large part from income-tax returns. The ratio of the added compliance and administrative costs to the yield from such a tax would depend, of course, on the spendings-tax rate.

Some spendings-tax proponents have argued that the spendings tax is simpler than the income tax because it avoids such income-tax difficulties as those connected with differential treatment of capital gains, personal tax advantages for retained corporate earnings, and deferment of tax on unrealized appreciation. However, the argument is weak, if not irrelevant, in practicality because a major role is retained for the income tax. Moreover, it is in the nature of the spendings tax to exempt savings, including retained earnings and unrealized appreciation (except insofar as they are reflected in higher personal expenditures from available cash and credit sources); in other words, this tax accepts as part of its concept and rationale the nontaxation of income in the form of accretion to capital. Its advantage in this respect over the income tax is the result of a shift in objectives and a restructuring that treats all savings (not merely those in the form of unrealized capital accretion) favorably.

Certain observers, generally those seeking a strong, interlocking, progressive tax system, see advantages, administrative and otherwise, in the interplay of income, wealth, and spendings taxes. For example, understatement of wealth accumulation for wealth-tax purposes would penalize the taxpayer for spendings-tax purposes.[13] However, this range of ideas is merely noted here as background; it is not relevant to the feasibility of the expenditures tax.

Although some comfort may be drawn from looking at the overlap of income- and spendings-tax information items, the fact remains that the personal-expenditures tax imposes technical, compliance, and administrative burdens because it is a form of tax that looks at all the receipts and financial transactions of an individual and the changes in his net worth as they relate to his personal expenditures· and requires some precautions for distinguishing effectively between personal and business expenditures that may have a consumption aspect. The double reporting, the readjustments necessary to get to a comprehensive income concept, the use of liability items, the proof of net savings, and other aspects all add up to a still-novel form of taxation with a new compliance dimension that would impose a more severe test of the capacity of Americans for self-assessment than the income tax has imposed.

On the basic question of whether a spendings tax is practicable, this chapter reaches the qualified conclusion that it probably is practicable within a relatively restricted scope of high-income, substantial-wealth taxpayers. The risks of excessive cost, substantial breakdown, and even an administrative debacle would probably increase if the tax were applied on a broad scale approaching that of the personal income tax.

The expenditures tax is, it is true, simpler to apply for low-income than for high-income taxpayers. However, in the present age of relative affluence among taxpayers of only modest income, the number of capital transactions that would enter a true determination of net savings and spendings would probably be surprisingly high. The practicability issue in a sense boils down to the question how far down in the income and wealth scale it is feasible to go before the tasks of compliance and record keeping become disproportionate to the sophis-

---

13 See, for example, Kelley, "Is an Expenditure Tax Feasible?" pp. 237–253.

tication and resources of the taxpayer on the one hand and the revenue yield and desired economic effects attained on the other.

The personal-expenditure-tax approach is probably not needed anyway to tax consumption in the low- and middle-income ranges because the use of credits against income tax could be developed in order to render a value-added tax, with its various other advantages, sufficiently nonregressive and sensitive to the family and dependency status of the taxpayer.

The implication of these observations seems to be that a comprehensive, progressive approach to taxation of consumption involves either a combination of value-added tax and spendings tax or the acceptance of mass problems of paper work, information returns, electronic data processing, and a new range of complications in tax reporting under an essentially fragile self-assessment system for taxpayers whose desire for simplification has been almost continually disappointed and frustrated since World War II.

A partial approach involving a progressive expenditures tax for higher incomes only along the lines of the Kaldor model would sidestep major risks of nonfeasibility but would fail to fulfill all the needs of a consumption-directed tax program. It would involve the group of taxpayers for whom the spendings-tax computations are most complex. However, since their numbers are smaller and their capacity to handle complex tax matters is presumably greater than that of the average taxpayer, the administrative risks of a spendings-tax experiment in the upper brackets are less than under a mass spendings-tax approach. Even on this basis, there are unpleasant possibilities of intolerable complexity and taxpayer resistance.

Substantial complexity, laxity, and morale-destroying avoidance and evasion under a spendings tax now, whether on a mass or a class basis, could weaken the whole tax structure and in particular the income tax, with which the spendings tax would probably be linked.

APPENDIX
Administrative Problems of an Emergency Spendings-Tax Plan: The 1942 Treasury Proposal

The evaluation of the spendings tax undertaken during the World War II period indicated that it involved certain unusually difficult compliance and administrative problems that demanded careful consideration in making a final judgment on its desirability. The two main difficulties were then recognized as the computation of spending that would serve as the tax base and the current collection of the tax. For both taxpayer and government, the computation of spending involved difficulties not present in any other tax then in use. Nevertheless, the Treasury then considered the tax possible to administer, at least under wartime conditions and for wartime purposes of inflation control.

Rationale of the 1942 Treasury Plan

The Treasury's 1942 proposal for a spendings tax was apparently made after consultation and discussion with other government agencies and departments concerning the most feasible approach to reducing consumption, increasing savings, producing important incidental revenues, and thus combating inflation.

The resulting restriction on spendings was considered elastic rather than rigid because there would be no prohibition on spendings; instead, there would be a tax that increased in rate as spendings increased. This elasticity, it was believed, would make unnecessary many administrative determinations of special justifications for selective types of spending for one purpose or another, which expenditure rationing, for example, would involve.

Other administrative advantages of the spendings tax were seen at that time. It was believed that existing tax-collection machinery could be used in administering the spendings-tax collection at source and that the return forms could be handled in conjunction with those of the income tax. Furthermore, personal exemptions for the spendings tax could be aligned with those of the income tax so that virtually the same persons would be involved in collecting the two taxes.

Complex Nature of the 1942 Proposal

It is a remarkable fact that in recommending the spendings tax for war finance in 1942, the Treasury chose to advance the proposal in the complex form of two taxes. One was a flat-rate (10 per cent) refundable tax on total spendings with exempt levels of $500 for a single person, $1,000 for a married couple, and $250 per dependent, the tax on the total spendings not to exceed the amount of spendings in excess of the exempt level. The other was a progressive surtax (ranging from 10 to 75 per cent) on spendings in excess of conventional exemptions of $1,000 for a single person, $2,000 for a married couple, and $500 for a dependent.

The proposal thus combined all the special problems of determining spendings with a compulsory lending or refund feature, a dual-tax and dual-exemption structure, and a notch provision. In this form, it is not surprising that the plan was quickly rejected by the Senate Finance Committee.[14]

The Proposed Spendings-Tax Schedule

The Treasury proposal of 1942 apparently contemplated a simpler schedule for persons not subject to the spendings surtax. Those subject to the surtax would have filled out a form covering twenty-one items or lines. Of these, eleven were to be devoted to the detailing and totaling of funds at the disposal of the individual (including cash and bank balances at the beginning of the year); nine to the detailing and totaling of nontaxable uses of funds (including cash and bank balances at the end of the year); and one line was to show taxable expenditures reflecting the difference between available funds and nontaxable uses. The illustrative surtax schedule accompanying the Treasury proposal of 1942 did not include spaces for the reporting of exemptions or the computation of tax (or dual tax), credit for current payment, and the assortment of other adjustments and reconcilations that are inevitably involved in such a procedure.

It is significant to note that the proposal apparently did not contemplate reporting of beginning- and end-of-year balance sheets of individuals even under the more complex spendings-surtax schedule for more affluent individuals not eligible to use a simplified adaptation of the income-tax return. Rather, it merely relied on the reporting of cash made available or disposed of in connection with capital transactions.

---

14 For further details, see U.S. Treasury Department, *Annual Report of the Secretary of the Treasury* (1943), pp. 93–94; and "Exhibit 82," pp. 411–413, and 415.

Compliance

At the outset, it was clear that very few taxpayers know how to, or can easily, compile a record of their spendings over a year or any substantial period of time. Plans for a spendings tax therefore had to provide for an indirect computation of spending following the pattern of the Irving Fisher formula, in which the amount of spending would be the amount of income and other receipts minus net increases in savings or plus net decreases in savings, as the case may be. The various forms of savings included cash, bank accounts, life insurance, real estate, securities, and other forms of investment.

It was recognized that there is nothing impossible about this computation; it can be made by almost anyone. However, it is a kind of balance-sheet reckoning that taxpayers had not previously been called upon to make and that millions of them would undoubtedly have substantial difficulties with, especially in the early years.

Administrative Difficulties

It was recognized that administrative checks would have to be made of a considerable sample of spendings computations in order to enforce the tax. Types of information that would have to be checked included cash on hand, bank accounts, insurance premiums, loans on insurance, security holdings, and other forms of investment. Sources of information would be available in most cases, but not readily; and they would be expensive to utilize.

Another administrative consideration was that deductions follow a more or less uniform pattern for income-tax purposes and only returns showing deductions deviating substantially from that pattern would indicate the necessity for a thorough check. The savings pattern, however, might not have this uniformity; or at least considerable experience and study might be required before it could be relied on.

It was felt that cash on hand would be an important item, virtually impossible to check as of the beginning of the first year and presenting a substantial loophole to persons hoarding and not reporting such cash in their computation of spending.

Current-Payment Methods

As early as 1942, it was recognized that current-payment methods would involve collection at source and current declarations of estimated income, just as they do under the income tax. Successful collection at source requires a fairly fixed exemption for a taxpayer over a considerable period of time. A flat-rate spendings tax could be collected at source in one of two ways. One way would be to allow current credits for saving, having the taxpayer declare his intention to save a certain amount during the year. Such a declaration, however, would inevitably be in some error and subject to deliberate overstatement, resulting in the necessity for large lump-sum payment at the end of the year. The difficulties of withholding would be substantially increased by an exemption that varied from person to person. If some adjustment for high savers was not made, there would, of course, be a hardship problem with refunds. The other approach would be to withhold without regard to anticipated savings and then allow refunds at the end of the year when the return was filed. This would result in overcollection for high savers, some alleged hardship, some actual serious hardship, and considerable public resentment.

A progressive spendings tax would be harder to withhold than a flat-rate tax or, for that matter, a progressive income tax. Quarterly declarations for the spendings tax might be necessary on a wide scale both to bring the tax to the current attention of the taxpayer and make him aware of it and to assure current payment to make up for the various deficiencies in withholding.

Needless to say, it was felt that the spendings tax would not be consistent with a strong drive toward tax simplification. In this light, it was justified, if at all, only by the exigencies of war finance and stabilization efforts.

Evaluation of Administrative and Compliance Problems

The Treasury's public analysis of the 1942 spendings-tax plan concluded with this overall evaluation of the administrative aspects:

> Like any new tax, and perhaps more than some taxes, a spendings tax necessarily involves administrative and compliance problems. These problems are reduced by the fact that a spendings tax can be

administered in conjunction with the individual income tax. As a consequence, the refundable tax will require no additional returns, and the collection of the refundable tax at source will impose no additional burden on either withholding agents or the Bureau of Internal Revenue. Nevertheless, the spendings tax will create an administrative problem in checking on information not now required on income tax returns, in familiarizing the public with a new type of tax, and in helping the public to fill out the forms that they will be required to submit. Compared with other measures of like importance in meeting the inflation and revenue problems, the administrative difficulties should not prove disproportionately large. In time of war, administrative difficulties cannot be allowed to stand in the way of measures vital to the Nation's welfare.[15]

A contemporary observer concluded that the Treasury's 1942 spendings-tax plan would present substantial problems in the first year or so of operation but that after this initial period, it would not result in administrative difficulties substantially greater than those of the income tax.[16]

---

[15] Ibid., pp. 414–415.

[16] Kenyon E. Poole, "Problems of Administration and Equity Under a Spendings Tax," *American Economic Review* 33 (1943): 63, cited in Kelley, "Is an Expenditure Tax Feasible?" p. 253.

Part Three: Revenue Sources for Stabilization

William H. Branson

THE USE OF VARIABLE TAX RATES FOR STABILIZATION PURPOSES

THE INCOME-TAX SURCHARGE in 1968 did not sufficiently slow the growth of aggregate demand. Whatever the reason, this fact has led to renewed questioning of the usefulness of variable, or flexible, income-tax changes for stabilization purposes. It has also led to a search for, or at least some thinking about, alternative variable taxes that might prove more effective as stabilization measures. As a contribution to that search, this chapter considers several alternatives within the context of a fairly standard consumption-multiplier view of how tax changes affect the levels of demand, output, and employment. It is my conclusion that a variable sales tax on some subset of total durable goods, particularly those with longer-than-average product lives, may be the best place to begin a system of flexible taxes for use in achieving stabilization.

The first section of this chapter develops the view that tax-rate changes, as well as government purchases and monetary-policy changes, affect the level of demand through a direct policy-induced change in expenditure blown up by a multiplier effect. The direct effect of the tax change can be differentiated according to its income and price effects. The income effect is the impact of the tax change on expenditure through a change in disposable income; the price, or substitution, effect is the impact through a change in relative prices. Different taxes have

AUTHOR'S NOTE: I wish to thank my colleagues Charles Berry and Alan Blinder and the editor of this volume, Richard Musgrave, for valuable comments on drafts of this paper. Remaining errors are my own responsibility.

267

different price effects. In particular, a predictably variable tax on post-ponable expenditures (i.e., on durable-goods purchases) will have an *intertemporal* price effect; that is, consumers and businesses will vary the timing of durables purchases in order to take advantage of inter-temporal relative price changes. This intertemporal price effect is the main focus of this chapter.

The second section of the chapter examines the differing income and price effects of changes in income taxes as compared with the effects of changes in taxes on expenditures. Permanent taxes on income or expenditures have similar income effects on demand, with the income tax having a recognized bias toward present rather than future consumption through its price effect. However, the situation concerning variable, or flexible, taxes is much different. Here, the permanent-income view of consumption and investment demand and the recent experience with the income-tax surcharge suggest that the income effects of variable taxes on income or expenditures are small and uncertain. But the variable tax on expenditures would have, in addition, the intertemporal price effects just described. Thus, the tax on expenditures dominates the income tax as a flexible fiscal instrument. This assumes, however, that the variations of the expenditures tax from the normal level are certain and fairly short, so that purchasers can take advantage of them.

The third and fourth sections of the chapter discuss the coverage and form of a variable tax on expenditures. It is noted that the inter-temporal price effects can be obtained by taxing durables, that is, post-ponable purchases of business plant and equipment or of consumer goods. It is further suggested that the longer the life of the asset, the more sensitive the timing of its purchase will be to a predictably tempo-rary price variation. Moreover, if the goal is substantial price variation without potentially disturbing revenue effects, a tax base that is narrower than the total business fixed-investment or consumer durables might be called for. These considerations suggest the desirability of a variable expenditure tax on a subset of longer-lived producer and consumer durables.

Limiting the tax to durables, which account for only 15 per cent of either consumption or national income as a base, argues in favor of imposing a sales tax rather than a value-added tax. If the tax is not to be based broadly on total consumption or investment, then it will be much easier to tax particular transactions under the sales-tax approach rather than to separate value added by type of output or purchaser.

The Stabilization Impact of Tax-Rate Changes

The stabilization aspect of fiscal policy is basically concerned with regulating the level of total demand in the economy. If demand falls short of potential output or supply, as it did in the early 1960s, an unacceptably high level of unemployment will result. If demand substantially exceeds supply, as it did in the late 1960s, prices will rise faster than their average rate of 2 or 3 per cent per year. Fiscal policy acts to regulate demand either directly, through changes in the federal government's purchases (i.e., the amount of goods and services the government buys), or indirectly, through changes in tax rates or transfer payments. For example, an increase in personal-income-tax rates directly reduces disposable income and presumably brings a direct policy-induced reduction in consumer demand. The elimination of the investment-tax credit (ITC) raised the net price to business of capital goods, causing a direct policy-induced decrease in investment demand. Each of these tax actions had a stabilization impact to the extent that it did, in fact, generate this initial direct policy-induced change in private demand.

Policy-induced demand effects and the multiplier. The final effect of a fiscal-policy change on the level of aggregate demand will be the initial direct policy-induced change in demand augmented by a multiplier effect. For example, if the elimination of the investment-tax credit directly reduced investment demand by $3 billion at the 1969 level of the gross national product (GNP), this $3-billion drop in incomes of the factors producing equipment might have caused a further drop of $2.5 billion in consumer spending, and so on. Eventually, total demand (annual rate) would fall by perhaps two or three times the initial policy-induced drop in demand.[1] This full annual rate is largely reached

---

[1] See Arthur M. Okun, "Measuring the Impact of the 1964 Tax Reduction," in *Perspectives on Economic Growth,* ed. W. W. Heller (New York: Random House, 1968), for an example of this kind of calculation for a permanent tax reduction.

within perhaps two years. This is the way in which the macroeconomic impact of the elimination of the investment-tax credit was calculated by the Council of Economic Advisers in 1969.

Once the initial policy-induced expenditure change resulting from any fiscal action is determined, its multiplier effect is not likely to depend much on exactly what kind of fiscal action is taken. For example, an ITC change that directly reduces investment by $3 billion should have about the same effect on total demand as a personal-tax increase that directly reduces consumer spending by $3 billion. Thus, it is useful to analyze the relative stabilization effect of different types of fiscal measures by focusing on the direct policy-induced demand changes they generate. From that point on, they all work through more or less the same multiplier. (This holds true for monetary policy as well. In order to calculate the effect on total demand of a given change in the money supply, the effect on consumer and business spending at the initial level of income must be determined, and that change in demand must then be run through the multiplier.)

Income and price effects of tax changes. In general, the demand change directly induced by a change in tax rates can be divided into an income effect and a price, or substitution, effect. A tax increase will reduce income, and this income reduction will generally reduce demand. The income effect is closely related to the initial effect of a tax change on government revenue; the revenue increase *is* the decrease in private-sector income; thus, the income effect is a propensity to spend multiplied by the initial revenue increase. Therefore, in general, alternative tax changes with the same revenue effect will have about the same income effect.[2] This is particularly true of income, expenditures, final-sales, and value-added taxes, all of which have roughly the same tax base: national income. (Changes in corporate-profits tax rates, on the other hand, may have much different effects. For this reason, the corporate-profits tax does not fit well into a general discussion of income or expenditures taxation.)

In addition to their income effects, tax changes will generally

---

[2] The usefulness of the full-employment surplus or of changes in it as a measure of fiscal stimulus depends on this equivalence of income effects. To the extent that income effects are not equivalent, a given full-employment surplus would have different fiscal impacts depending on the composition of tax revenue within the given surplus.

have price effects on demand. Any partial sales tax on goods that can be substituted easily will tend to reduce the sales of the taxed goods in favor of the untaxed goods. In this case, the net price effect on total demand may be negligible, although there will be an income effect proportional to the revenue raised by the tax.

By taxing interest income, the U.S. income tax reduces the reward for saving and thus creates an incentive for consumption expenditures in the current period, as opposed to the future. By shifting consumption from the future to the present, the price effect of an income-tax increase works against the income effect. (The income tax also reduces the net wage; thus, its price effect tends to reduce labor supply. This works against the income effect on the supply side of the economy.)

The investment-tax credit is a good example of a tax meant to operate largely through its price effect. The credit effectively reduces the price of capital goods, thus increasing total sales and output.

If tax changes for stabilization operate largely through price effects rather than through income effects, the usefulness of the full-employment surplus as a measure of fiscal stimulus is further diminished. Two taxes with equal revenue and income effects may have very different price effects and thus different stabilization impacts. In the case of stabilization taxes that operate mainly through price effects, the relevant measure is the impact of the government budget on combined total of private and government saving, rather than on the government surplus only.

Significance of temporary price changes. The variable investment-tax credit involves the concept of an intertemporal price effect that may be particularly powerful in the case of temporary variations in taxes on expenditures. A temporary, or reversible, tax change can generate price effects over time by changing current prices relative to future prices. For example, imposition of a 10 per cent tax on automobile sales to consumers at the beginning of 1969, with the assurance that the tax would be lifted at the end of 1969, would have created a strong incentive for consumers to postpone auto purchases for a year. In general, these intertemporal price effects can make temporary variations in taxes on postponable expenditures a more powerful stabilization tool than temporary variations in income taxes. For example, a tax change causing a 10 per cent price increase for a year would provide a purchaser with a 9 per cent return for waiting, that is, for saving. If the tax were imposed for only six months, this rate of return would rise to 19 per cent. Thus, temporary variations in taxes on expenditures can provide variations in effective interest rates that are far greater than those obtained by monetary policy.

Permanent Versus Temporary Taxes on Income and Expenditures

The usual comparison of taxes on income versus taxes on expenditures is made in terms of permanent taxes. Clearly, tax rates on expenditures can be set at levels that give the same income effects as the income taxes. In particular, if Y is income and cY is the amount of income that is spent, then the ratio of expenditures-tax rate (t_c) to income-tax rate (t_y) that gives equal income effects is just $1/c$.[3] If the marginal propensity to consume (c) is 0.8, then a 12.5 per cent tax rate on expenditures is equivalent to a 10 per cent income tax.

However, as already noted, an income tax that is applied to interest income reduces the reward for saving and thereby gives an incentive for present rather than future consumption. On the other hand, a permanent tax on expenditures is neutral concerning present and future expenditures, taxing both at the same rate. A temporary tax on expenditures is biased in the other direction, encouraging the postponement of expenditures until the tax is lifted.

If the effects of short-run variations in tax rates as opposed to the effects of permanent taxes are taken into account, the comparison between taxes on income and taxes on expenditures changes considerably. Again, both kinds of taxes would still have more or less the same income effects, although the experience with a temporary income-tax change in 1968 suggests that the size of these effects may be small. But variations in the tax on expenditures may well have powerful intertemporal price effects that make it superior to the income tax as a short-run stabilization measure.

---

[3] The policy-induced income effect on spending generated by an income tax is $c \cdot t_y \cdot Y$, where t_y is the income tax rate. The income effect of an expenditures tax is $c \cdot t_c \cdot cY$, where t_c is the expenditures-tax rate. For income effects to be equal $c \cdot t_y \cdot Y = c \cdot t_c \cdot cY$ and $t_c/t_y - 1/c$.

Income effects. The equivalence of the income effects of permanent changes in income-tax rates and in expenditures taxes also holds true for temporary tax changes. To the extent that temporary variations in income-tax rates cause changes in consumer demand, there is some variation in tax rates on expenditures that would exert the same effect through its effect on real disposable income.

However, the more interesting question is: How large are these income effects expected to be? With the exceptions of the monetarist school and, more recently, Robert Eisner, economists interested in stabilization policy have generally assumed that the income effect of temporary variations in income-tax rates would be about as large as the effects of permanent changes or, in any case, that the income effect would be substantial.[4] In 1969, the Council of Economic Advisers proposed that the president be allowed to vary income-tax rates proportionately within specified limits, subject to congressional veto, for stabilization purposes. The Committee for Economic Development has proposed that the president be allowed to vary rates up to 10 per cent, and Herbert Stein, now chairman of the Council of Economic Advisers, in a report prepared for President-elect Nixon late in 1968, suggested that the president should be able to set a variable income-tax surcharge annually in his budget message. This widespread support for the use of flexible income-tax rates for stabilization purposes suggests a fairly broad consensus within the stabilization-policy branch of economists that the income effects of temporary tax changes are similar to those of permanent tax changes.

Doubts about temporary tax changes. This consensus coexists with the fact that the two major economic theories concerning consumer behavior—the permanent-income theory of Milton Friedman and the life-cycle hypothesis of Albert Ando and Franco Modigliani—both suggest that temporary and short-run variations in income-tax rates should have little effect on consumer expenditures. The implication of both views is that if, for example, the consumer sees that his income-tax rate varies randomly by 10 per cent of his long-run average marginal tax rate of 20 per cent (i.e., his marginal tax rate randomly fluctuates

---

[4] See Robert Eisner, "Fiscal and Monetary Policy Reconsidered," *American Economic Review* (December 1969); and "What Went Wrong?" *Journal of Political Economy* (May-June 1971), for more discussion of this issue.

between 18 and 22 per cent), he will adjust his consumption pattern to an average rate of 20 per cent and balance the tax changes by altering his saving rate. In their study of the effects of the 1964 tax reduction, Albert Ando and E. Cary Brown found that that action, which was a permanent tax cut, substantially increased consumer expenditures as expected. They qualified their results by noting that "strictly speaking, our results are applicable only to situations in which a permanent tax reduction takes place." In the case of temporary income-tax changes, they noted that "indeed, as consumers become used to the manipulation of rates, they may begin to ignore the short-run variations completely and base their consumption decisions on the longer-run average rate around which variation was being made."[5]

The 1968 experience. Further doubts about the income effect of temporary variations in income-tax rates have been raised as a result of the experience with the income-tax surcharge that was applied at a 10 per cent rate from the third quarter of 1968 to the fourth quarter of 1969, at a 5 per cent rate in the first and second quarters of 1970, and expired in July 1970. Table 1 shows the ratios of personal outlays, saving, and tax and nontax payments to personal income for the years 1967 to 1970. The quarters during which the surtax applied generally had low ratios of saving to personal income. In the six quarters from the first quarter of 1967 to the second quarter of 1968, personal tax and nontax payments averaged 13.3 per cent of personal income. In the six quarters of the full surcharge, from the third quarter of 1968 to the fourth quarter of 1969, this tax ratio rose to 15.3 per cent, an increase of 2.0 per cent of personal income.

Theoretically, if the temporary tax change affected consumer expenditure in the same way as a permanent tax change, this 2.0 per cent of additional taxes would be expected to come mainly out of personal outlays, causing the ratio of personal outlays to personal income to fall by a bit less than 2.0 per cent. This outcome would show the saving ratio remaining constant or falling only slightly. On the other hand, if the surtax was regarded as purely temporary, the

---

5 Albert Ando and E. Cary Brown, "Personal Income Taxes and Consumption Following the 1964 Tax Reduction," in *Studies in Economic Stabilization,* ed. Albert Ando, E. Cary Brown, and A. F. Friedlaender (Washington, D.C.: Brookings, 1968), pp. 136–137.

ratio of personal outlays to personal income would fall only slightly, with nearly 2.0 per cent of personal income coming out of saving.

In fact, the ratio of personal saving to personal income fell from an average of 6.4 per cent in the period from the first quarter of 1967 to the second quarter of 1968 to 5.1 per cent in the period from the third quarter of 1968 to the fourth quarter of 1969, a drop of 1.3 per cent. During the same periods, the ratio of personal outlays to personal income fell from 80.3 per cent to 79.6 per cent. Thus, the 2.0 per cent increase in the tax ratio resulting from the surcharge seems to have reduced the saving ratio by about 1.3 per cent and the personal-outlay ratio by about 0.7 per cent. This suggests that about 35 per cent

Table 1. Per Cent of Total Personal Income Distributed Among Personal Outlays, Personal Saving, and Personal Tax and Nontax Payments, 1967-1970

Quarter	Personal Outlays	Personal Saving	Personal Tax and Nontax Payment
1967			
First	80.4	6.5	13.1
Second	81.2	5.9	12.9
Third	80.4	6.4	13.2
Fourth	80.0	6.7	13.3
1968			
First	80.5	6.2	13.3
Second	80.0	6.5	13.6
Third	80.0	5.3	14.6
Fourth	79.3	5.8	14.9
1969			
First	79.6	4.7	15.7
Second	79.6	4.5	15.7
Third	79.0	5.5	15.5
Fourth	79.1	5.3	15.6
1970			
First	79.3	5.7	15.0
Second	78.9	6.4	14.7
Third	79.3	6.5	14.2
Fourth	79.4	6.3	14.3

Source: U.S. Department of Commerce, *Survey of Current Business* (July 1971).

of the surtax was paid out of personal outlays and 65 per cent came out of saving.

This estimate is roughly the same as that made by Arthur Okun in a recently published paper on the effect of the surcharge.[6] Using four econometric models, Okun calculates the expected path of consumer spending under two assumptions: that the surcharge has zero effect and that it has full effect on consumption. The models already adopt the permanent-income view of consumer expenditure to the extent that "during the entire interval [of the surcharge], a little more than half the surcharge's drain on disposable income was expected to be reflected in consumer outlays, with a prolonged small effect continuing after the expiration of the surcharge."[7]

Turning to the actual results, Okun finds that the surcharge was from 63 to 88 per cent effective; that is, it reduced consumer spending by those fractions of the amounts the models anticipated. Since the models anticipated an impact of only a little more than 50 per cent, these results suggest that, in fact, the drop in consumer spending directly induced by the surcharge amounted to 30 to 50 per cent of the tax's drain on disposable income.[8]

These estimates indicate that under an income-tax surcharge imposed for two years or so, less than half of the effect on disposable

[6] Arthur M. Okun, *The Personal Tax Surcharge and Consumer Demand, 1968–70*, Brookings Papers on Economic Activity, no. 1 (Washington, D.C.: Brookings, 1971).

[7] Okun, *The Personal Tax Surcharge and Consumer Demand, 1968–70*, p. 194. It should be noted that he is speaking of the expected values generated by the models, not those promulgated by advocates of the surcharge in 1968.

[8] Okun's preferred estimates are given in *The Personal Tax Surcharge and Consumer Demand, 1968–70*, Table 3, p. 190. In making those estimates, Okun arbitrarily altered the disaggregated results that he considered unreasonable. The first three rows of the table show that only two of his twelve categories (three consumption equations in each of the four models) give results that are between the zero- and full-effect views, that is, are between 0 and 1 in the table. The other ten estimates indicate that the surcharge either stimulated spending or reduced it by more than the reduction in disposable income. Okun resolved this difficulty by setting each of these estimates to its extreme plausible value: 0 or 1. The resulting estimate of the effectiveness of the surcharge is clearly sensitive to how expenditures have been disaggregated. If estimates must be obtained by simulating these models, I would prefer the estimates that are without the constraint. On the other hand, the fact that only two out of twelve estimates fit a range that Okun considered theoretically acceptable suggests to me that this whole approach to estimating the effect of the surcharge is not very useful and that the estimates are fairly unreliable.

income (and perhaps as little as a quarter) shows up as an effect on consumer spending. Furthermore, the effect on spending is still building up after the surcharge period has ended, presumably after the end of the period of desired fiscal restraint. Thus, in addition to having a small effect during the period in which it is in force, the surcharge may be destabilizing in the sense that the effect continues and grows after the surcharge is taken off. The combination of the degree of uncertainty attached to estimates of the effectiveness of temporary income-tax changes and their modest effect on consumer spending even on the best available estimates suggests that expectations of the effectiveness, through income effects, of these tax changes should be revised downward and that the range of uncertainty applied to these estimates should be widened.

There are two central points here. First, whatever the income effects of temporary income-tax-rate changes, there is some variation in tax rates on expenditures that will give the same income effects. Second, these equivalent income effects may be both small and uncertain, making the income tax an inappropriate fiscal instrument for short-run stabilization policy. On the other hand, a variable tax on postponable purchases may have price effects that make these small or uncertain income effects irrelevant.

Price effects. In the case of permanent taxes on income or expenditures, the expenditures tax is neutral concerning present and future consumption; whereas the income tax may have a bias toward present consumption that is perverse from the stabilization point of view. Consideration of the price effects of temporary tax changes leads to the opposite results. Whereas the income tax still has a small bias toward current rather than future consumption, the expenditures tax should have a strong price effect that is desirable from the stabilization-policy point of view.

The intertemporal price effects of variations in a tax on durable-goods purchases would come from the postponability of such purchases. Although a business or a consumer wants a steady stream of services from durable goods, the purchase of these goods can be timed to take advantage of predictable price changes. This effect was quite evident in the huge increase in machine-tool orders just before the investment-tax credit was abolished in April 1969. Thus, a temporary increase in an expenditures tax on a durable good would provide a strong incentive to postpone purchases, moving demand from the present to the future; and a reduction in the tax would move demand from the future to the present. The effect of a temporary tax or subsidy on expenditures would depend largely on the length of time the tax is to be in effect and on how certain consumers and businesses are that the tax will, in fact, revert to its normal level (perhaps zero) at the appointed time.

The length of the tax period. The more temporary the tax rate (i.e., the shorter the period during which the tax is not at its normal value), the greater the effect on purchases. For example, if the tax is in effect for longer than the average useful life of the durable good, it takes on many of the characteristics of a permanent tax. Another way of viewing this point (as described in "Significance of temporary price changes") is that a tax change causing a 10 per cent price increase and remaining in effect for one year provides the purchaser with a 9 per cent return for waiting (saving). If the same tax were imposed for only half a year, the annual rate of return for waiting would rise to 19 per cent. Table 2 shows the effective rates of return for waiting for tax changes of various sizes.

Table 2. Rate of Return for Expenditures-Tax Changes of Six-Month and One-Year Durations (per cent)

Increase in Price Due to Tax Change	*Effective Return From Waiting*	
	6 months	*1 year*
5	10	5
10	19	9
15	32	13
20	44	17

Certainty of tax period. In order for this crucial factor of temporariness to work effectively to promote stabilization, purchasers must be certain that the tax will revert to its normal level at the appointed time, so that they can make suitable revisions in their purchasing plans. This means that the government must be able to predict fairly accurately the length of the incipient slump or boom that it is trying to level off and then be willing to allow the tax to be removed on schedule, even if the prediction turns out to be at least partially incorrect. If the government fails in several instances to remove such a tax, purchasers will be uncertain about the duration of the tax when it *is* imposed, and the equivalent rates of return for waiting will decrease as the expectation of the duration of the tax period lengthens.

This requirement—that the duration of the tax be certain—raises the need for good information concerning both future economic conditions and the effects of the variable tax itself. The government must be able to predict both fairly well if it is to guarantee the duration of the tax. This suggests that a fairly thorough and careful study of whatever evidence is available concerning this type of intertemporal price elasticity of demand for durable goods is required if a variable tax on purchases of such goods is to be considered seriously as a tool for stabilization.

In summary, it appears a priori that a variable, or flexible, tax on durable-goods expenditures would be a much more effective stabilization-policy tool than the widely recommended flexible income tax. One important question raised by this conclusion concerns the coverage of a variable expenditure tax: What items should be taxed? Another question is: What form should the tax take? Should it be levied on personal or business expenditures, on sales, or on value added?

What Expenditures Should Be Taxed?

In order to be most effective as a stabilizing measure, a variable expenditures tax should be placed on postponable expenditures. The three obvious candidates are nonresidential structures (which accounted for $38.2 billion of GNP in 1971), producer durables such as equipment (on which $73.6 billion was spent in 1971), and consumer durables (which accounted for $100.5 billion in 1971). The business-fixed-investment categories add up to $111.8 billion, so that business fixed-investment and consumer durables as tax bases would be roughly equivalent fractions of GNP.

Residential structures are left off the list because it is generally felt that this sector is already highly sensitive cyclically as a result of its response to monetary policy. This is one reason for considering a new and more powerful fiscal-stabilization tool that will shift the mix of stabilization responsibility from monetary toward fiscal policy; the housing sector should do less of the stabilizing, not more.

Which of these sectors or their subsectors should be subject to the variable expenditures tax depends on many factors, not all economic. The following paragraphs offer some of the more obvious factors for consideration; no a priori conclusion about the best sectors to subject to the variable tax can be reached without much more detailed study.

Allocation and stabilization. The first consideration that should be noted is basically a nonconsideration. This chapter focuses on taxes that vary for stabilization purposes around some long-run average level chosen to secure an efficient allocation of resources to various uses. For example, if it is decided that, on the average, a 10 per cent investment-tax credit is needed in order to allocate more resources to business investment in equipment, this conclusion would be reached in terms of some long-run objective that involves the stream of output from those machines.[9] In a discussion of stabilization, then, the focus is on variations in the credit around the 10 per cent level in order to influence the timing of investment purchases without substantially altering the long-run stream of output from the capital stock. Thus, the stabilization and allocation arguments should not be confused; the focus here is taxes varying around an average level that is presumed to be correct from the allocation point of view.

It might be useful to note here that a pure stabilization tax could well have a normal, or average, level of zero. It would then function positively (as a tax) when restraint is needed and negatively (as a subsidy) when a stimulus is needed. In this case, the tax would generate zero revenue at its normal zero level. When it is positive, sales of the taxed good would fall, but revenue would rise; when it is negative, the reverse would occur. In general, this kind of tax might be a revenue loser because symmetrical variation in the rates would yield greater subsidies on the down side than revenues on the up side.

Similarly, if the tax varies symmetrically around some positive level, it is possible that the variation feature would lose revenue both ways. If the intertemporal price elasticity is high, an increase in the

---

[9] This is not to suggest that the author thinks a permanent investment-tax credit would be a good thing. This example is offered purely as an illustration.

tax might reduce sales so much that, on balance, total revenue from the tax falls; whereas on the down side, a decrease in the tax might not stimulate a rise in sales sufficient to prevent a revenue loss.

The point is that if a part of the permanent revenue system depends on the level of output of the taxed goods (which it must through the income multiplier and the income tax), then if the intertemporal price elasticity of the taxed good is sufficiently high, net revenue losses may result from the variation of the expenditures tax in either direction.

A tax on investment or consumption. It seems likely that businesses would show a greater and more certain response to variations in an expenditures tax than consumers would. Consumers are presumed by economists to be maximizing something rather vague called *utility;* some observers suggest that their behavior is dominated by sentiment or mood or even that it is random. Thus we think that the reactions of consumers to systematic variations in the price of consumer durables should be in the right direction, but it may well be quite variable, since the objective function of their behavior is often specified only implicitly.

Businesses, however, have a more concrete objective (profits) and a more precise set of tools by which to measure how well they are doing (balance sheets and income statements) than consumers do. Thus, it is reasonable to expect corporate treasurers to calculate the effects of a variable tax on their incomes and net worths with a sharper pencil than consumers would and to react accordingly. This suggests that larger and more certain expenditure responses should be expected from an expenditures tax on business fixed-investment than from a tax on consumer durables.

Furthermore, there is some experience, albeit meager, with variations in an expenditures tax on producers' durable equipment in the form of the investment-tax credit. This experience should be studied in some detail within the framework of explicitly temporary variations in the tax. If such research narrows the degree of uncertainty concerning investment reactions to a variable expenditures tax, it might be best to initiate the tax in that area. The government might then be more confident in the use of the tool, and the public would get less of a feeling that fiscal policy is more or less flying blind. At the same time, experimentation and research on the consumer-durables side could continue with the goal of expanding the options for variable expenditures taxation to that area.

A tax on a broad or narrow base? Two considerations should affect any decision about whether the variable tax should be placed upon the broad categories of business fixed-investment or consumer durables or upon some subset of these goods. The first has to do with the length of life of the good; the second, with uncertainty concerning the income effects of the tax.

Length of life of the taxed good. The longer-lived the taxed good, the easier it will be to postpone the purchase of a new item, thus extending the life of the currently owned item for a given length of time. This has two implications. First, longer-lived goods will presumably have greater intertemporal price elasticities of demand; thus, taxing longer-lived rather than shorter-lived goods would raise the effectiveness of the variable expenditures tax. Second, the very reason that this difference in effectiveness exists is that the purchasers suffer smaller losses in profits or utility from the postponement of the purchases of longer-lived goods. Thus, concentration of the tax on such goods might be superior from both the fiscal-effectiveness and the social-cost points of view.[10]

This line of argument suggests that the tax might be concentrated on longer-lived assets within business fixed-investment and consumer durables. This conclusion is buttressed by the consideration of uncertainties concerning the income effects of the tax.

Price elasticity and income effects. If the variable tax on expenditures is to be effective, it must induce price variations that are large enough to be noticed by purchasers and to induce the purchasers to act. This argues for placing the tax on a reasonably narrow base of durable goods with high intertemporal price elasticities. If the tax were on a broader base (such as total consumption) that included a large propor-

---

10 Note that this argues for putting the variable tax on residential construction instead of consumer durables. The reason for making fiscal policy assume more of the stabilization responsibility is not that monetary policy has imposed large cyclical variations in housing starts; by the previous argument, that is a good thing. But monetary policy seems to be relied upon more in the restrictive than in the expansionary phases of the cycle, so that reliance on monetary policy has reduced the long-run average level of housing starts as well as increased its variability; and that is what is bad. If the only way to reduce the long-run effect of monetary policy is to increase the variable effects of fiscal policy on nonhousing items, thus easing the variation in housing activity as well as raising its average level, then housing should be omitted as a candidate for a variable expenditures tax.

tion of goods with low intertemporal price elasticities (such as services and nondurable goods), the tax variations needed to ensure variation in purchases of the price-elastic goods within the base could yield huge revenue effects. For example, a 10 per cent change in a tax on total consumption, which might be required to reduce purchases of consumer durables substantially, would yield $60 to $70 billion in revenue at the 1971 consumption level of $662 billion. A tax on durables only, or even some subset of durables, could yield a substantial effect in terms of postponement of expenditures with much smaller or even negative revenue effects. Initial consideration of a variable tax on expenditures might focus on a subset of longer-lived goods such as producers' structures ($38.2 billion in 1971) or consumer purchases of automobiles ($35.3 billion in 1971). The tax would thus be limited to longer-lived goods with high intertemporal price elasticities, avoiding the large revenue effects of variable tax changes on price-inelastic goods.

In What Form Should the Tax Be Imposed?

A tax on expenditures can be imposed in any of three ways on the same base. If the desired base is consumer expenditure, the tax could be a personalized expenditures tax of the sort proposed by Nicholas Kaldor, a retail-sales tax, or a value-added tax of the consumption variety (VAT-C). If the desired base is extended to business fixed-investment, the expenditures tax could include a tax on investment spending by business in the form of an investment-tax debit, a total final sales tax, or a value-added tax of the income variety (VAT-I). Unless the investment-tax debit is graduated, it is essentially the same as the investment component of the final sales tax. The expenditures tax could be made progressive on both cases; whereas the regressivity of the sales tax could be alleviated by introducing a sliding exemption into the personal income tax that would vary with the fraction of income normally spent on the taxed items as a function of the level of income. The value-added taxes would presumably be proportional.

The administrative feasibility of a Kaldor-type expenditures tax is questionable, even on total consumer expenditures.[11] This matter is dis-

---

[11] See also Patrick L. Kelley, "Is an Expenditure Tax Feasible," *National Tax Journal* (September 1970), for the view that a total expenditures tax is indeed feasible, especially if coupled with a wealth tax.

cussed in detail in the chapter by Richard E. Slitor. If, as the arguments in the previous section suggest, the tax should be placed on a subset of consumer expenditures (durables or even a subset of durables), the Kaldor-type expenditures tax is out of the question. Thus, the focus here is on a comparison of the value-added and sales-tax routes of taxing the desired base. If that tax base is consumer expenditure, the comparison is between a retail-sales tax and a consumption-type value-added tax. If it is investment expenditure, the discussion applies to a retail-sales tax plus an investment-tax debit (a final sales tax) versus an income-type value-added tax.

Broad-based taxes. If the flexible, or variable, tax is to be broadly based either on total consumer expenditures or on income, then the choice between a sales tax and a value-added tax depends mainly on administrative considerations. The chapters by Carl S. Shoup (favoring the value-added tax) and John F. Due (favoring the retail-sales tax) review these administrative considerations in detail.

The base for these taxes would be total consumer expenditure or national income. Only about 15 per cent of each of these bases is in durable-goods production or purchases. Thus, a variable VAT on these broad bases would yield a price effect on only a small fraction of the base and an income effect on the entire base. This means that variations in a broad-based value-added tax or sales tax would not differ much from variations in an income tax in their stabilization effect. The additional fiscal-policy advantage that comes from temporary variations in expenditures-tax rates results from the intertemporal price effects; this suggests the advisability of focussing on taxation of durables, which are only 15 per cent of consumption or of the net national product (NNP), in order to increase the effectiveness of tax policy for stabilization.

Taxes on durables only. If, instead of taxation of total consumption or NNP, a tax on a much smaller subset of that total (expenditure on durables) is considered, the sales tax is distinctly superior to the value-added tax. First, if firms produce both durables and nondurables or services, it will be difficult to separate value added by type of product. If a further distinction between producer and consumer durables is made, the problem of separating value added by buyer is introduced. If the base is narrowed further, to longer-lived assets, for example, the problem becomes virtually insolvable.

Thus, if the arguments presented in this chapter—that a variable tax should be placed on purchases of durables (i.e., postponable purchases) and that perhaps subsets of these purchases might be taxed, at least initially—are convincing, the best choice appears to be a variable sales tax on the desired base. The base can be fairly easily identified by transactions but not by value added or by personalized expenditure.

In most cases, the sales tax could be set annually in the budget message at a stated normal rate (perhaps zero), but occasionally, it could be set at a rate above or below that, depending on stabilization needs. If it becomes clear that more frequent adjustments or shorter periods of nonnormal tax levels are needed, the midyear budget review could provide another opportunity for changing the rate.[12]

In summary, a flexible value-added tax on a broad base would have essentially the same stabilization characteristics as a flexible income tax. A flexible sales tax on some subset of durables purchases, with temporary but certain changes in rates, would add an intertemporal price effect and increase the usefulness of a flexible tax policy for stabilization above the level achieved by current policy.

---

[12] The British "regulator" tax allows the government to vary all indirect taxes by up to 10 per cent of the normal rate. This tool was used only twice between 1960 and 1967, mainly because the government generally changes normal rates each year. Thus, an annual opportunity to set the variable sales-tax rate may be sufficient.

MEMORANDUM OF COMMENT, RESERVATION, OR DISSENT

IN MY VIEW the chapter by Nancy Teeters does not adequately discuss some very complex issues involving the integrity of the social-security system. The basic difficulty in this analysis arises from an attempt to discuss the payroll tax and social-security financing wholly apart from the entire benefit structure and the fundamental concept of assuring beneficiaries a statutory "right" to benefits without converting social security unintentionally into a "welfare" program.

While it is appropriate to consider the incidence of the federal income tax apart from the various expenditures it makes possible, it is not appropriate or desirable to review the social-security program without considering the income and benefits together.

Social security is not primarily a tax system; it is a *tax-benefit* system which exists only if both aspects are considered together. The present benefit structure would not exist were it not primarily financed by payroll taxes; nor would the payroll taxes exist in their present form apart from the existing benefits. The two persist because they are married together.

I happen to agree that the social-security system should be financed in part from general revenues. I have held that position since 1934. I also favor several of the author's specific recommendations. I particularly favor a refund of part of the social-security contributions made by low-income persons. But I am conscious of the fact that not all employers, blue-collar workers, or members of Congress share my views. I believe we must be very careful to be absolutely sure that changes in the financing of the social-security program do not cause some future President and Congress to impair the eligibility of individuals to benefits by watering down the contributory earnings-related

286

right to benefit. Changes in financing could result in changes in benefit rights.

The Teeters' analysis, in my view, completely overlooks the sensitive psychology involved in various provisions of existing public social policy, the incentives for work and savings that are reinforced, and the political insulation that the present contributory social-security program has so far assured.

If increased federal income taxes are desirable for the social-security program, they are equally or even more necessary and desirable to help finance many other needed programs. The author overlooks the fact that already over $13 billion a year is expended out of federal general revenues for all the programs in the social-security act. In my opinion we need more general tax income to finance social programs in education, health, welfare reform, and the environment. The author, however, gives no attention to the increased difficulties involved in increasing federal income taxes. I question the political wisdom of making all the basic changes proposed in this chapter without being sure that the increased tax yield is actually in hand; that succeeding Administrations will honor all the liabilities incurred; and that federal income taxes will not be reduced—as has occurred in recent years to the detriment of public social programs and the advantage of private affluence.

It is very easy to criticize the present social-security taxes, but I am reasonably certain there will also be criticism against increasing income taxes. If we are going to increase general revenues in our social programs, I suggest that we first finance part of national health insurance and all of welfare reform from this source, and then proceed to introduce general revenue financing into the social-security program in a much different way than the author suggests.

My priorities and legislative strategy differ from the author's because I see social security as only part of the totality of public social programs that need general revenue financing. By contrast, the Teeters chapter focuses largely on the public-finance aspects of the program. It does not discuss, for instance, how much employers, employees, and the general public might lose by premature, piecemeal surgery on a program that has worked much better than other programs financed from general revenues or considered as general welfare.

The author focuses primarily on the retirement benefits in the program. They are very important. But she does not give attention to the other important benefits to the disabled under age sixty-five, to widows and young children, and to the Medicare benefits. One could argue that whatever changes are made in the financing of their benefits, the political strength of the aged could preserve their rights to benefits. But is this conclusion equally applicable to widows, children, and the disabled?

The withholding of appropriations and the cutbacks proposed in 1973 in federal programs financed from general revenues, while the contributory social-security benefits are continuing to be paid according to law, is ample evidence to me that even the changes both Nancy Teeters and I support should be staffed out much more carefully than she indicates. Man does not live by macroeconomics alone. I suggest a more comprehensive review is warranted and desirable before far-reaching decisions are made.

WILBUR J. COHEN

THE CONTRIBUTORS

WILLIAM H. BRANSON is associate professor of economics and public affairs at Princeton University and consultant in international economics to the Council of Economic Advisers, the Federal Reserve Board, and the Organization of Economic Cooperation and Development. He received his Ph.D. from Massachusetts Institute of Technology (1967) and served as a senior staff economist for the CEA. He is the author of *Macroeconomic Theory and Policy* (1971) and other books and papers.

HARVEY E. BRAZER has directed tax studies for the state of Michigan, served as deputy assistant secretary of the U. S. Department of the Treasury, and been a consultant to the Council of Economic Advisers and other bodies. Among his voluminous writings is *Income and Welfare in the United States* with J. N. Morgan, M. H. David, and W. J. Cohen (1962). He has held academic appointments at several universities and is professor of economics at the University of Michigan.

JOHN F. DUE, professor of economics at the University of Illinois since 1948, has been a consultant for both the U.S. Department of the Treasury and for several state governments. He has also directed tax study projects for Zambia, Chile, and other developing countries. The fifth edition of his *Government Finance* appeared in 1973.

CHARLES J. GOETZ teaches, writes, and consults in the fields of public finance and nonmarket decision making, price and welfare theory, and urban and regional economics. He received his Ph.D. from the University of Virginia (1965), was a NATO postdoctoral fellow at the University of Pavia, and is now professor of economics at Virginia Polytechnic Institute and State University.

C. HARRY KAHN, whose untimely death occurred on April 28, 1972, was a distinguished authority in the field of taxation. Born in Frankfurt, Germany, he received his Ph.D. from the University of Wisconsin (1957) and held a number of academic and other posts. He served on the research staff of the National Bureau of Economic Research and as a consultant to the Brookings Institution. He was author of *Employee Compensation Under the Income Tax* (1968) as well as many other books and studies. At his death, he was professor of economics at Rutgers University.

HELEN F. LADD has been a lecturer in the department of economics at Dartmouth College and at Wellesley College. After graduating from Wellesley, she received an M.Sc. degree at the London School of Economics in 1968, and is now working on her doctoral dissertation at Harvard University on the property tax.

CHARLES E. McLURE, JR., associate professor of economics, has served on the Rice University faculty since he received his Ph.D. in public finance at Princeton University in 1966. He has been a senior staff economist for the Council of Economic Advisers, a consultant to the U.S. Department of the Treasury, and an advisor to the governments of Malaysia, Colombia, and Panama.

RICHARD A. MUSGRAVE, professor of economics at Harvard University, has gained international renown in the field of public finance. He has been a research economist for the Federal Reserve Board, chief of the ECA Fiscal Mission to Germany (1951), and a consultant to the Commission on Money and Credit, among many similar assignments. He received his undergraduate degree at the University of Heidelberg (1933) and his Ph.D. at Harvard University (1936), and has taught at universities here and abroad. His most recent books are *The Theory of Public Finance* (1959) and *Fiscal Systems* (1969).

CARL S. SHOUP has been a member of the Columbia University faculty since 1928. He has been director of the Twentieth Century Fund Survey of Taxation in the United States, a staff member of the Council of Economic Advisers, and a member of the Fiscal and Financial Committee of the European Economic Community, to name some of his many posts here and abroad. Among the most recent of his many books are *Federal Estate and Gift Taxes* (1966) and *Public Finance* (1969).

RICHARD E. SLITOR retired in 1972 as economist in the Office of Tax Analysis after thirty years with the U.S. Department of the Treasury. He has also served as federal executive fellow at the Brookings Institution, a member of Treasury Department missions to various foreign countries, and professor of economics at the University of Massachusetts. He is the author of many papers and studies on taxation and public finance.

NANCY H. TEETERS has been a staff economist for the Federal Reserve Board, the Council of Economic Advisers, the U.S. Bureau of the Budget, and the Brookings Institution, where she is now a senior fellow. She has also taught at the University of Michigan and the University of Maryland. Her papers have appeared in scholarly and government publications, and she is an author of *Setting National Priorities: The 1973 Budget,* with Charles L. Schultze, Edward R. Fried, and Alice M. Rivlin.

INDEX

The text of this book was set entirely in Linotype Times Roman, and the tables in
IBM's Press Roman. Composition, book and cover designs supplied by Cambridge
Editorial and Production Service. Carl Rieser of the Committee for Economic
Development supervised and coordinated all editorial and production functions.

Library of Congress Cataloging in Publication Data

Musgrave, Richard Abel, 1910–
Broad-based taxes: old and new options.

1. Taxation—United States—Addresses, essays, lectures.   2. Revenue—
United States—Addresses, essays, lectures.   I. Title.
HJ2381.M88   336.2'00973   72-12361
ISBN 0-8018-1489-8
ISBN 0-8018-1490-1 (pbk)